# Clark Kerr's
## University of California

# Clark Kerr's
## University of California

Leadership, Diversity, and
Planning in Higher Education

## Cristina González

**Transaction Publishers**
**New Brunswick (U.S.A.) and London (U.K.)**

Library of Congress Catalog Number: 2010017603
ISBN: 978-1-4128-1458-4
Printed in the United States of America

Library of Congress Cataloging-in-Publication Data

Gonzalez, Cristina, 1951-
    Clark Kerr's University of California : leadership, diversity, and planning in higher education / Cristina Gonzalez.
        p. cm.
    Includes bibliographical references and index.
    ISBN 978-1-4128-1458-4
    1. Kerr, Clark, 1911-2003. 2. University of California (System)--History. 3. University of California, Berkeley. 4. Education, Higher--California--History. 5. Education, Higher--United States--History. 6. Education, Higher--Aims and objectives--California. 7. Education, Higher--Aims and objectives--United States. 8. University of California, Berkeley--Presidents--Biography. I. Title.

LD755.K47G66 2010
378.794--dc22

2010017603

For my son, University of California alumn John G. Cohen,
this reflection about his alma mater

# Contents

# Prologue

*And, though the warrior's sun has set,*
*Its light shall linger round us yet,*
*Bright, radiant, blest.*
——Jorge Manrique's "Elegy on his Father," 15th Century,
translated from the Spanish by Henry Wadsworth Longfellow,
*The Complete Poetical Works of Longfellow*, 592.

Clark Kerr was one of the fathers of American higher education, and in particular of the University of California, and we in the academic community owe him a great deal. Although his sun has set, its light does indeed linger with us. It certainly lingers with my students, for whom Kerr's visionary leadership is a model. He himself thought that the kind of leader he was had gone out of style, a belief with which I never agreed. If he had lived a few more years, he would have marveled at the country's strong desire for visionary leadership. Perhaps then he would have revised his theories about the demise of vision. He was not afraid to say that he was wrong, because he was right in all things that really mattered, chiefly in his love of fairness and in his devotion to education. Kerr was intensely interested in ideas—the building blocks of vision—and it was a delight to see his eyes light up in a youthful, almost innocent, gaze when he heard things that made him think. He was a true scholar, whose perpetual search for meaning has been a great source of inspiration for me, and I would like to express my deep appreciation and gratitude for him. He is remembered fondly and greatly missed.

My first interactions with Kerr date from the late 1990s, when I was Dean of Graduate Studies at UC Davis. Kerr was very interested in the Spanish philosopher José Ortega y Gasset, who had a great influence on his thinking. He was particularly influenced by Ortega's 1930 book *Mission of the University*, and he had written an introduction to an English translation of it. Coming from Spain, I knew Ortega's works well. In fact, I had studied with Ortega's main disciple and commentator, Julián

Marías, who taught for many years at Indiana University and helped me go there as a graduate student in 1976. So Kerr and I had some common philosophical interests. But the main thing we had in common was our interest in the nature of leadership.

Kerr asked for my opinion on an article that he had recently written, titled "The 'City of Intellect' in a Century for the Foxes?" which later became chapter 9 of the 2001 edition of *The Uses of the University*. This piece discussed many issues affecting the university and concluded with a very interesting comment about two different types of leaders: hedge-hogs, who are visionary, and foxes, who are shrewd. Kerr saw himself as one of the last hedgehogs and thought that contemporary universities were facing such complex conditions that they needed foxes to lead them instead. I took issue with that. In my mind, complex conditions called for vision, as much as, or more than, shrewdness, and I told him so. He said that he found my reaction interesting and that a group of young UC faculty members with whom he had recently met had expressed similar feelings. Nevertheless, he thought that the era of hedgehogs was over and did not change his mind about that. Neither did he substantially alter the content of his article, which became the gloomy last chapter of the last edition of *The Uses of the University*, in which he conceded to the foxes. I continued to argue that we needed academic vision much more than corporate shrewdness.

In fact, this friendly disagreement inspired me to create a couple of courses on higher education with a focus on academic leadership. First, I taught a freshman seminar in the fall of 2002. I told Kerr about this in a November 18, 2002, letter, in which I said that the more I thought about the university, the more I believed that it was time for hedgehogs to return to leadership positions. One year later, in the fall of 2003, when Kerr was already very ill, I taught a graduate seminar on higher educa-tion and academic leadership, which was an expansion of the freshman seminar I had offered previously. I thought that he might want to know, so on October 27, 2003, I sent him a letter telling him that my students believed that he was too pessimistic and concluded that we really needed more hedgehogs like him.

This letter was to be my last, for his health was deteriorating, and he was no longer able to communicate. My seminar ended on December 1. That evening, I took my students out to dinner at a local restaurant, and we spoke about Kerr. They all felt inspired by him and ventured some predictions of their own, emulating his fondness for forecasting. It was a cheerful evening. We did not know that he had died earlier that day. When I got home and checked my e-mail after many hours away from my computer, I found a message with the bad news. It was hard to believe that his crystal ball had gone dark forever and that his pen would never write another word.

Kerr was famous for his minuscule handwriting, which Eric Ashby (Levine, 1987) once described as "tiny fluctuations such as one might get on a seismograph recording a slight volcanic eruption ten thousand miles away" (16). Indeed, according to Arthur Levine (1987), Kerr "could write the Bible on an index card" (16). His letters, written in this diminutive script, usually with green ink, came with an attached transcription typed by his assistant, Maureen Kawaoka. They were very brief, normally consisting of one or two lines. Kerr was very proud of his minimalist style. In a brief evocation I was privileged to be able to contribute to his memorial service program, I mentioned this aspect of his writing:

> Whenever I wrote an article on a higher education issue, I would send it to Dr. Kerr, and he would reply in his endearing telegraphic manner. It didn't take me long to decipher the code. "Thank you for your article" meant he was not excited about it. "I read your article with interest and approval" meant he really liked it. I came to look forward to his funny little notes. I never quite knew which article was going to catch his fancy. For example, he did not show any emotion about an essay on the diversity debate, which I believed was well-reasoned, but he sounded enthusiastic about a less-theoretical piece on Latino identity, which I thought might be a bit too personal. On an article about women administrators, he actually wrote three lines: "Thanks for your interesting paper. I think women have an advantage as administrators as they are more likely to think horizontally as well as vertically." (University of California, Berkeley, 2004:10)

These comments show that, until the very end, Kerr continued to think about leadership and about diversity. The connection between leadership and diversity is of great interest to me and has informed my teaching of higher education courses, which continued after Kerr's death and eventually led to writing this book. My study is a personal reflection on higher education in the United States, with a particular focus on the University of California, which is both a totally unique and a quintessentially American institution.

This book draws on disciplines that are not often put together—history of higher education, history of the University of California, leadership studies, and diversity theory—as well as on my personal experiences as a faculty member and an academic administrator at various American research universities over the past twenty-nine years, the last thirteen at UC Davis. It also draws heavily on my teaching and is greatly inspired by the lively interactions I have had with my students. A considerable number of these are women and minorities who aspire to enter academic administration and are eager to gain practical insights into that world. In addition to experts in the areas of higher education, leadership, and diversity, the book's intended audience includes other students like mine; past, present, and prospective academic administrators; government officials and other decision-makers; and interested members of the public. Thus, this work has two emphases: on one level, it is an interpretation of the history and evolution of the University of California, while on another, it is a study of leadership and diversity that presents that history as a cautionary tale in which various presidencies, particularly those of Kerr and David P. Gardner, serve as examples of the inner workings of power at institutions of higher learning.

After comparing two different kinds of leaders, Kerr—a visionary hedgehog—and Gardner—a shrewd fox—(chapters 1-2), the study focuses on Kerr's intellectual history, showing how he crafted a new vision out of ideas articulated separately by others. He was a collector of concepts, because concepts are the building blocks of vision. He took ideas that were floating in the air and made them his by naming them—a typical hedgehog's modus operandi (chapters 3-6). In addition to showing how the mind of the hedgehog works, this exploration of Kerr's thinking points out that hedgehogs have blind spots, and Kerr's was diversity, which never fully entered his field of vision. Although he had a strong intellectual commitment to the idea of equality of opportunity, and he never stopped thinking about diversity issues, he had trouble putting himself in the shoes of women and minorities. Like many of his contemporaries, he never fully appreciated the challenges and opportunities facing the university and the country in this respect.

The book then provides a brief history of higher education from its inception to the present. This section highlights the fact that advancements in education oftentimes hurt educational opportunities for women and/or minorities, as in medieval Europe and colonial Latin America, when the establishment of universities further marginalized women, in the first instance, and Indians in the second (chapters 7-8). This is the backdrop against which the history of the University of California is narrated, following the ups and downs of women and minorities there and showing that advances for the university often have resulted in further marginalization of these groups (chapters 9-11). This was true of the California Master Plan for Higher Education, which resulted in increased social stratification, as access to the highest level of learning—that offered by the University of California—was reduced from the top 15 percent to the top 12.5 percent of the state's high school classes. This made it more difficult for students from underrepresented groups to enter the university, a problem that has worsened over time and has now come to a head with the restrictions caused by the budget crisis.

Building upon the hedgehog/fox dichotomy, the work studies the triumphs and tribulations of the various presidents of the University of California, most particularly of Kerr himself, who was a quintessential hedgehog, and of Gardner, an archetypical fox. Central to the book's argument is its explanation of the rise of the University of California as due to the articulation and implementation of the "hedgehog concept" of systemic excellence codified in the Master Plan. The book further contends that the university's recent problems flow from a national phenomenon, a "fox culture," characterized by a free-for-all approach to the pursuit of resources, which started to unfold in the 1980s, when the gap between rich and poor grew. This has included a progressive reduction of support for public higher education, forcing universities to engage in privatization and to become key participants in "fox culture." Thus, academia's gradual increase in corporate behavior, including high executive compensation, which mirrored what was happening in the business world.

The study suggests a path to leadership renewal that takes advantage of the talents of a diverse pool of potential leaders and maximizes the university's, and the nation's, inherent competitive advantages in a diverse global society. Along these lines, it explores recent events in which women and minority leaders have born the brunt of attacks on fox culture. These are exemplified by the media storm of Fall 2005, in which public anger became focused on the compensation received by three woman executives: M.R.C. Greenwood, openly-gay Denice Denton and African-American Celeste Rose. The denigration of university leadership has primarily focused on women and minorities, and it continues, as attacks on recently appointed administrators demonstrate (chapters 12-13).

The work argues that the collapse of fox culture, at both the institutional and national levels, has brought the University of California to the brink of the greatest crisis in its history, a crisis in which the hedgehog concept of systemic excellence has, for the first time, been placed in serious jeopardy. It calls for updating the University of California's hedgehog concept, as well as for a new vision for public higher education in general. In particular, it advocates re-funding and re-democratizing public higher education and renewing its leadership through thoughtful succession planning, with a special emphasis on diversity (chapters 14-16).

I contend that what is needed now is a diverse group of hedgehogs to articulate this new vision, as well as a diverse group of foxes to help to implement it. Fox culture is destructive, but foxes who serve a hedgehog concept can be very helpful. In my view, what is most urgently required now is for a critical mass of hedgehogs to be put in place and allowed to lead. We need new Clark Kerrs to overcome fox culture and articulate a new hedgehog concept. Change has to start at the top. There are many external factors affecting the fate of a public university like the University of California, and the power of its leaders is limited. But leadership does matter. This book attempts to show why.

# Acknowledgments

I would like to thank Jud King and John Douglass for inviting me to speak on my work at the UC Berkeley Center for Studies in Higher Education (CSHE) on February 14, 2006. The lecture I gave there contained the initial iteration of some of the thoughts discussed in this book. An expanded version of that paper was published by the CSHE in 2007. I am grateful to the CSHE for allowing me to use that text in this book, which is a further elaboration of the same ideas, with some additional materials. I would like to thank Irving Louis Horowitz, Chairman of the Board and Editorial Director of Transaction Publishers for his enthusiastic support for this project. Mary E. Curtis, President of Transaction Publishers was very helpful, as was Jennifer A. Nippins, Associate Editor, who provided excellent suggestions and revised the text with great care.

I am very grateful to Marian Gade, Kerr's longtime research associate and co-author, for her immensely helpful comments on various stages of the manuscript. Steve Chapman, John Douglass, Jud King, Anne MacLachlan, Karen Merritt, Douglas L. Minnis, Debbie Niemeier, Patricia Pelfrey, Sheldon Rothblatt, Neil Smelser, Daryl Smith, Linda Morris Williams, and Ila Phillip Young, also have offered valuable perspectives about the project at various phases of its development. The manuscript has benefitted additionally from valuable suggestions by Hanna Gray, who kindly shared the text of her 2009 Clark Kerr lectures on the role of higher education in society, as well as her thoughts on my book, with me, and James Duderstadt, who has been a great source of information and encouragement. Without meaning to imply that they necessarily share my views, I am indebted to all of these generous colleagues. In addition, I am very grateful to all my wonderful colleagues at UC Davis, who have been so good to me over the years. I very much appreciate their support. I also would like to express special thanks to David P. Gardner, who not only has been exceedingly gracious about my conscripting him as Kerr's fox counterpart in the fox-hedgehog metaphor, but kindly reviewed the manuscript and made many insightful comments. My teaching has been a crucial source of inspiration for this book, which could be described as an attempt to create a bridge between my students' views and Kerr's vision. Thus, I owe my students as much as I owe Kerr. Finally, I would like to acknowledge the advice and assistance provided by my friend and mentor Samuel F. Conti, as well as the invaluable editorial comments of my husband, Richard A. Cohen. Now, as always, his clear thinking and strong values have helped me focus on the things that matter.

# Introduction: Reading Clark Kerr

Referring to the need for elite universities to engage in serious reflection about the future, David Breneman (2008) states that "we need a set of leaders in the spirit of the former presidents Howard R. Bowen of the University of Iowa, Ernest L. Boyer of the Carnegie Foundation for the Advancement of Teaching, and Clark Kerr of the University of California, who can go beyond the narrow focus on a single institution to speak to the enterprise as a whole" (A40). Indeed, we need visionary leaders like Clark Kerr. Harold T. Shapiro (2005), for whom Kerr "must have been doing something right," because he "was denounced enthusiastically by both the political left and the political right" (ix), emphasizes that this leader never lost sight of the university's goals:

> Like all truly great educators within a liberal society, Kerr considered the future to be a carrier of even greater possibilities and, therefore, to be of ethical significance. As a leader he took risks both to safeguard an institution and to provide for its future. His experience reminds us all of the need to defend the intellectual independence of the university. Leadership requires fighting many battles, even those battles where one expects a momentary defeat. (Shapiro, 2005: x)

Shapiro (2005) adds that Kerr's "voice of reason and logic was also a voice of conviction and passion" that has provoked many academics "to sustain the intellectual energy and moral direction to do better things," noting that there is "a virtual army of persons who continue to be fascinated by his experience as president of the University of California" (xi). Yet no comprehensive biographical study or systematic analysis of his work has been published to date. This book does not pretend to fill that void, which will have to be addressed by scholars with higher levels of expertise than mine. Rather, it is a personal reflection on leadership and diversity that takes Kerr's life and writings as a point of departure.

Kerr died on December 1, 2003, at his home in El Cerrito, California, leaving his wife, Catherine, two sons, Clark Kerr and Alexander Kerr, a daughter, Caroline Gage, seven grandchildren, one great-grandchild, and the legions of friends, colleagues, disciples and admirers he had made in a long and productive life that spanned most of the twentieth century and took a peek at the twenty-first. During that period, American higher education went from elite to universal access, and Kerr played an important role in refashioning colleges and universities to reflect that transformation. Who was this man and why did he have such an impact?

Kerr was born on May 17, 1911, on a small farm in Stony Creek, Pennsylvania, and was raised there until age ten, when his family bought a bigger farm in Oley Valley, also in Pennsylvania. His parents ran the farm but were no ordinary farmers. His father, a school teacher, came from an educated family and had a bachelor's degree from Franklin and Marshall College and a master's from the University of Berlin. His mother was a milliner with only an elementary education, but her brother was a lawyer, and she refused to get married until she had saved enough money to put any children she might have through college. Thus, both of Kerr's parents' families greatly valued schooling and were familiar with the higher educational system. While his sisters attended Oberlin, Kerr chose to go to Swarthmore, which turned out to be a life-changing experience. He took "honors work" under the famous Frank Aydelotte plan and, although his grades were low at first, he graduated with high honors. In addition, he served as president of the student body and captain of the debate team, an early indication of his leadership qualities.

In college, Kerr joined the Quakers, which helped him hone his oratorical skills, as well as affording him the opportunity to travel widely as a "Peace Caravaner" during the Great Depression (Stuart, 1980; Padilla, 2005). His volunteer work exposed him to the desperate conditions of the poor. This had an impact on Kerr's choice of career, for he abandoned his plan to attend Columbia Law School to study for a Ph.D. in Economics at Berkeley under Paul Taylor, an expert on farm labor. The idea of becoming a small town lawyer in Pennsylvania did not attract him anymore. When the San Joaquin Valley cotton pickers' strike of 1933 started, Kerr found himself in the middle of things:

> Taylor sent me out into the field to talk with farmers, sheriffs, strikers. Here was life in the raw as I had never seen it. There had been vigilante massacres in Pixley and Arvin at the southern end of the great valley. Strikers were living on the banks of irrigation ditches that were both sources of water and receptacles of sewage. There was hunger. There was violence as strikers entered the fields with sticks and stones to drive out nonstrikers. There was hatred, not only between strikers and farmers but among the strikers: between the "Okies," led by their politically conservative lay preachers, and the "Mexicans," led by Communist Party officials. It was a long way from the peaceful Oley Valley in eastern Pennsylvania where I had been raised on a family farm. (Kerr, 2001b: 4-5)

This experience had a great impact on Kerr and resulted in his special-izing in labor disputes. During this time, Kerr met his wife, Catherine Spaulding, whom he married shortly afterwards. He never went back to Pennsylvania. He finished his dissertation and became a professor at the University of Washington, where he started to do arbitration. He had become the leading arbitrator in the Seattle region when Berkeley cre-ated the Institute of Industrial Relations. Kerr was invited to be its first director. This was the beginning of a distinguished career that culminated in his appointment, first, as chancellor of the Berkeley campus and then as president of the University of California system.

During much of his career, Kerr continued to work as an arbitrator, becoming one of the best in the country. His ability to make people agree on difficult issues became legendary. As Alan Pifer indicates, "somehow or other, by some magical process, he always got his way" (Levine, 1987: 17). Levine explains his magic tricks in more detail:

> Clark Kerr is a magician. I don't know how many times I've seen seen him perform my favorite trick—sitting around a table at which the members of a group offer every opinion under the sun—black, yellow, white, red, and orange. Clark asks the group if they mean turquoise. Every head around the table nods in unison. (Levine, 1987: 17)

Kerr did this by being courteous, patient, and persistent, "a marvelous recipe for successful leadership," according to Daniel J. Evans (Levine, 1987: 17).

Kerr was indeed a very successful leader. His tenure as first chancellor of Berkeley (1952-1958), however, was not easy because the president, Robert Gordon Sproul, was not interested in sharing power with him or anyone else. Sproul, in fact, was against the creation of the chancellor position, which was forced upon him by the regents. Kerr wondered why Sproul picked him for the position. Kerr had become known for his reasonable positions during the loyalty oath controversy, when as a member of the committee on privilege and tenure, he was an advo-cate for the faculty who refused to sign the loyalty oath, although he was himself a signer. He was well-liked, but lacked administrative experience. He had never been provost or dean. Kerr suspected that Sproul saw him as "the least potential threat in an unwanted position" (2001b: 34).

Due to these circumstances, Kerr had to struggle to define his sphere of action as chancellor and establish an agenda for his office. He wisely decided that his approach should be "one of accepting past administrative practices, with a few essential changes, and of developing areas of past neglect into a solid and distinguished force for progress" (2001b: 37). In other words, because Sproul was a micromanager who did not allow him to make the myriad small decisions that administrators are responsible for every day, Kerr focused on long-range planning. This activity, which Sproul probably considered quite harmless, turned out to be extremely important. Kerr engaged in academic planning first, followed by physical planning and finally budget planning. He conducted enrollment planning, setting a specific cap on the number of students Berkeley should take, a novelty for a public university in those days. He improved facilities for student life and recruited very competent and ambitious department chairs, who, in turn, hired top-of-the-line faculty members. Sproul's micromanagement turned out to be a blessing, for it allowed Kerr to develop and implement a vision for the campus, which in 1964 was rated as the "best balanced distinguished university," ahead of Harvard, Princeton, and Yale, which were numbers two, three and four, respectively (2001b: 58).

When Kerr became president of the UC system in September of 1958, he simply expanded the long-range planning in which he had engaged as chancellor of the Berkeley campus to the entire UC system and, in fact, to the entire state through the California Master Plan for Higher Education. The UC system was growing, with the expansion of some campuses and the creation of others. Kerr decentralized power, giving the campuses a great deal of autonomy. At the same time, he put in place coordination mechanisms to insure common standards of quality. It was during this period that the University of California system as we know it today was established. This was largely accomplished through the Master Plan, which by assigning specific functions to each segment of public higher education—the community colleges, the California State University and the University of California—delineated the identity of the University of California system, with its single student recruitment and faculty promotion standards.

The Master Plan was Kerr's biggest magic trick. With the three segments of public higher education competing for resources and status, he managed to find a solution that was acceptable to all. This was not easy, particularly because California State University did not want to give up its aspiration to offer Ph.D. degrees, but Kerr, working closely with his friend and associate Dean McHenry, found a solution at the last minute. As Charles Young, then a staff member at the president's office, explains:

Working through Dean, he managed the proceedings from beginning to end, ultimately developing a consensus where none had seemed possible among a group composed of representatives of the public-university systems and a member chosen by the private universities, and chaired by Arthur G. Coons, then president of Occidental College...At the 11th hour, however, all seemed lost. Then we met with Clark late at night in his seldom-used office to hear the compromise he had devised (it involved establishing a joint doctoral program to be offered by the university- and state-college systems). It saved the day. (Young, 2003: B10-B11)

Kerr worked very hard at developing a consensus. He put Coons, a respected academic from the private sector whom he knew he could trust, in charge of the process, which diffused the tensions among the three systems, and followed the negotiations very closely, stepping in as needed. In his memoirs, he says that he got the idea for the joint doctoral programs from Herman Wells, president of Indiana University, who had established a similar arrangement with Ball State University. This was the "sweetener" that would make the deal palatable for the California State University. Like the "turquoise" color of the Levine anecdote, this was not one of the options on the table, but rather a new, different alternative that was minimally acceptable to all concerned. But that was all that was needed, and Kerr became the most famous academic administrator in the country.

Kerr's approach to academic administration was to take it as a temporary assignment. Consequently, when he was chancellor, he did not change his faculty lifestyle and he kept his salary low out of deference to his fellow professors. Then, when he became president, he insisted on keeping his salary under that of the governor when the regents tried to increase it to a higher level. As he reveals in his memoirs:

I did not want to become too attached to any perquisites of the office. I never wanted to feel compelled to conform against my will. I wanted to feel independent, to be able to say "no" as well as "yes." I wanted to be willing to mow my own lawn and enjoy it, to be able to teach my classes, to write my articles, to preside over industrial relations arbitrations—which I continued to do albeit on a very reduced basis. I did not want to build prison walls around myself. Being aware of the perils of the position, I took precautions to anticipate possible eventualities and looked upon myself as a faculty member otherwise engaged for an uncertain period of time. (Kerr, 2001b: 33-34)

John Kenneth Galbraith (1990) notes that fear of loss is the great disciplinary force of the establishment, but Kerr was not afraid to lose: "He lost big because he won big" (53). Kerr was indeed prepared to lose, as well as to win, which is why he never stopped acting like a "faculty member otherwise engaged." This helped him deal with the trauma of losing the presidency, which occurred when Ronald Reagan won the election for state governor on a conservative platform that, according to Kerr, focused on three issues selected by a consulting firm: "welfare queens," "mental health malingerers" and the "student revolt at Berkeley" (2001b: 288). In particular, Reagan pounded on "cleaning up the mess in Berkeley," which brought images of "demonstrations, drugs, sex, long hair, and rock music" (Levine, 1987: 25).

Immediately after entering office, Reagan reduced the UC system budget by 10 percent. Kerr responded by freezing admissions. The die was cast. Kerr, who due to his liberal thinking and in particular his handling of the student revolt at Berkeley had been under attack for some time, was asked to resign. Young (2003) underscores the role played by the FBI and J. Edgar Hoover in laying the groundwork for Kerr's removal with constant insidious attacks during the previous twenty years. Indeed, Reagan's was just the last act of a tragedy that started much earlier, but it was a drastic denouement. Reagan basically treated the presidency of the UC system as a political position reporting to him and, therefore, to be occupied by someone loyal, or at least not suspected of being disloyal.

Kerr had to choose between leaving quietly and fighting. He chose the latter as a matter of principle, because as he said in the remarks made upon his dismissal, he did not believe in the tenet that "because there is a new governor there needs to be a new president of the university" (2003: 324). The regents, under pressure from Reagan, dismissed him by a vote of 14 to 8. Kerr defended the autonomy of the university, and consequently, as he later quipped, he was "fired with enthusiasm" (2003: 309). Although he was capable of talking about this event with humor, it was very painful, and he never truly recovered from it. In a way, he spent the rest of his life trying to prove that he was right and Reagan was wrong. He succeeded, for Reagan has gone down in history as the villain of this drama. A contemporary cartoon depicts Kerr stabbed in the back and lying on the floor in the background, while Reagan, his hands dripping with blood, declares that Kerr's dismissal came as a complete surprise to him. This shows how this event came to be represented in popular imagination from that moment onward (Kerr, 2003: photograph 17).

Kerr did not have to make a great effort to become a hero. In fact, all he had to do was to be himself. While most people are smaller than the positions of power they occupy, and lose their prominence once they leave those posts, Kerr was larger than any office he ever held. This became clear when he stepped down from the presidency to find himself one of the most influential intellectuals in the country. The Carnegie Commission on Higher Education and the Carnegie Council on Policy Studies in Higher Education, which he chaired from the moment he left the UC presidency in January of 1967 until his retirement in 1980—the year Reagan was elected President of the United States—were built around him. Kerr published many works, gave many lectures, and received numerous awards, including honorary degrees, from universities around the world. He was a powerhouse in higher education, but his influence was not bestowed upon him by any institution. Rather, it emanated from his vision, his integrity, and his independence.

Ironically, his dismissal was a major source of his power, for he refused to resign on principle and that is precisely what made him a hero. The regents' decision to fire him brought about massive demonstrations all over the UC system and caused outrage around the country. After this traumatic episode, Kerr underwent a process of "canonization" and turned into an academic saint of sorts. Shapiro (2005) notes that the role of the university as society's critic, as well as society's servant, created tensions between the university and its sponsors, which affected Kerr. Kerr stood for the autonomy of the university and, in doing so, became a martyr of American democracy, which according to Sheldon Rothblatt was "his first love" (University of California, Berkeley, 2004:16). Thus, his life was dedicated to finding ways to allow systems of higher education to provide equality of opportunity.

With American democracy at a crossroads, Kerr's life and writings are of greater import than ever before. My students, both graduate and undergraduate, find them very inspiring. That is why what began for me as a couple of isolated seminars taught on a volunteer basis has turned into a steady string of regular courses. Young people are hungry for vision, integrity, and independence and are eager to make a contribution. Many of the students I teach are women and/or minorities, and many aspire to become academic administrators. They know that education is the "organ of fine adjustment between real life and the growing knowledge of life" (DuBois, 1903a: 84). Therefore, they are not shy about sharing their views on the past, the present, and the future and do not regard Kerr or anyone else they might admire uncritically. By far, their favorite readings are the Kerr memoirs, together with those of another very successful president of the UC system, David P. Gardner, a very different kind of leader, which afford an interesting contrast.

While Kerr was a Quaker from rural Pennsylvania, Gardner was a Mormon born and raised in Berkeley who spent his childhood summers working on the family farm in Utah. Both leaders lost their mothers at an early age and were raised by step-mothers. Both had very supportive wives who helped them with their careers, and both were devoted to the University of California. Whereas Kerr had a typical faculty career, Gardner started as a staff member in the California Alumni Association. He was never a full-time faculty member or even a full-time Ph.D. student, having completed a doctoral degree in higher education and joined the faculty on a part-time basis while working as a full-time administrator. His efforts to improve himself eventually resulted in his being appointed vice president for public service of the University of California system, a position from which he was recruited to be president of the University of Utah. After a decade in the Beehive State, Gardner was appointed president of the University of California system in 1983, a position he held until 1992. Gardner was one of the most successful UC presidents in terms of his ability to obtain funding and to use it to advance academic quality. During his tenure, the University of California's prestige reached new heights. Thus, his memoirs are an interesting counterpart to Kerr's. If Kerr articulated the UC system with his insightful perspective, Gardner strengthened it with his practical abilities.

My students say that the memoirs of these two UC presidents provide more information about the inner workings of the university and the nature of academic leadership than all of their other readings combined. It is very interesting to see how, when they are a few chapters into the two memoirs, the students begin to identify with these two leaders. They try to understand them as individuals and to imagine what they might have done in their respective places. The fact that most of my students are not white males, however, complicates the process of identification and invites reflection about the relationship between leadership and diversity.

# Part I

# Exploring Clark Kerr's Thinking

# 1

# Hedgehogs and Foxes

Chapter 9 of the 2001 edition of Kerr's classic work *The Uses of the University*, titled "The 'City of Intellect' in a Century for the Foxes?" concludes with a very interesting comment about leadership. Using an ancient animal metaphor, Kerr defines two types of leaders: the fox and the hedgehog. The seventh century B.C. Greek poet Archilochus wrote: "The fox knows many things, but the hedgehog knows one big thing" (2001a: 207). In his famous work *The Hedgehog and the Fox*, Isaiah Berlin (1953) used this metaphor to distinguish between writers such as Plato, Dante, Pascal, and Dostoevsky, who "relate everything to a single central vision," and those who "pursue many ends, often unrelated and even contradictory," including Aristotle, Shakespeare, Montaigne, and Pushkin (1). According to Kerr, hedgehogs are centripetal and foxes are centrifugal:

> The hedgehog tends to "preach"—"passionate, almost obsessive;" while the fox is "cunning"—clever, even sly. Order versus chaos; unity versus multiplicity; the big vision versus adjusting to miscellaneous unanticipated events; certainty versus uncertainty. (Kerr, 2001a: 208)

While Berlin used this concept to shed light on Tolstoy, whom he saw as a fox trying to be a hedgehog, Kerr employed it to distinguish between two different kinds of leaders: the shrewd fox and the visionary hedgehog. Each deals with multiplicity in a different way: the fox, following his instinct, picks one option and runs with it, whereas the hedgehog uses his intellect to create a holistic model out of many fragments.

Kerr had previously discussed other terminologies, such as Hutchins' (1956) "troublemaker" and "officeholder," Harold W. Dodds' (1962) "educator" and "caretaker," Frederick Rudolph's (1962) "creator" and "inheritor," Henry M. Wriston's (1959) "wielder of power" and "persuader," and Eric Ashby's (1962) "pump" and "bottleneck," as well as James L. Morrill's (1960) "initiator" and John D. Millet's (1962) "consensus-seeker" (2001a: 23-24). In recent times, other terms have been used to express the same distinction. For example, Warren G. Bennis and Burt Nanus (1985), Joyce Bennett Justus, Sandria B. Freitag and L. Leann Parker (1987), and John W. Gardner (1990) distinguish between "leaders" and "managers," and James McGregor Burns (1978) writes about "transformational leaders" and "transactional leaders," a very successful terminology that has been explained and expanded by Bernard M. Bass (1985), who points out that the best leaders are both transformational and transactional, and the worst are neither.

The hedgehog/fox terminology has been used by a number of scholars in the last decade to describe the same dichotomy. Hedgehogs are transformational leaders, while foxes are transactional ones. There are writers who do not favor one type over the other. For example, Stephen Jay Gould (2003) discusses two equally good kinds of scholars: foxes, who explore many different fields, and hedgehogs, who work on a single, big project. Philip E. Tetlock (2005) studies two types of forecasters: foxes, who are right more often on short-term predictions, and hedgehogs, who when proven right about long-term forecasts, are very right. Hedgehogs' big successes cancel their equally big mistakes, while foxes blend perspectives and "do intuitively what averaging does statistically" (179). Some scholars favor the fox. For instance, Claudio Véliz (1994) used this terminology to distinguish between the Spanish and British Empires in the Americas, attributing the ultimate success of the latter to its fox-like innovative shrewdness, which prevailed over the old-fashioned hedgehog vision of the former. Other thinkers prefer the hedgehog. Jim Collins (2001, 2004 [1994], 2005, 2009), for example, theorizes that only companies with a "hedgehog concept" achieve true distinction. Finally, there are scholars, such as Abraham Zaleznik (2008), who believe that foxes are good for normal times and hedgehogs are needed in times of crisis, while emphasizing that when hedgehogs are wrong, they are very wrong and can cause a great deal of damage.

Kerr saw himself as one of the last academic hedgehogs but thought that modern universities were facing such complex conditions that they needed foxes to lead them. This book's thesis is that conditions at present are such that they require hedgehogs at the helm again. This is a time of crisis, which calls for vision more than for shrewdness. It is important to clarify, however, that both hedgehogs and foxes are necessary, and universities should have a combination of both in their leadership teams. Hedgehogs bring a sense of history needed to craft new visions connecting the past with the future, while foxes provide an understanding of geography, of present conditions in the terrain they inhabit, which is necessary to obtain resources and avoid trouble. This book's premise is not that hedgehogs are good and foxes are bad. Both types of leaders have strengths and weaknesses and can be good or bad. Hedgehogs who create helpful visions are good, while those who come up with harmful ones are bad. Foxes who place their shrewdness at the service of a productive vision are good, while those who use it to advance a pernicious one, or who do not follow any vision at all, are bad. Foxes do their best work when they have a good vision or "hedgehog concept" to guide them, but fox qualities do not lend themselves to the articulation of visions. That is the task of hedgehogs. Some moments in history require a preponderance of foxes, while others call for hedgehogs to take the lead. I think that the current crisis falls into the latter category. What I find worrisome at the moment is the almost total elimination of hedgehogs from leadership teams, which are now almost exclusively populated by foxes. I also am very concerned about the spread of "fox culture," a free-for-all system, in which foxes pursue goals at random: shrewdness for the sake of shrewdness rather than in the service of a vision. At present, this culture permeates the entire country, which is experiencing what I call "fox fatigue" (González, 2007: 35).

This became evident during the 2008 presidential election, which, in my opinion, showed that the country was calling for the return of the hedgehogs. Interestingly, some journalists used the fox/hedgehog metaphor to describe the various candidates. But there was some confusion about who fit which description and which type of leader was needed more. Thomas P.M. Barnett (2007), who saw George W. Bush as a hedgehog and was unhappy with his performance, concluded that the country needed a fox. For Barnett, the nation needed another leader like Franklin Delano Roosevelt, whom he saw as a fox. Other analysts, however, seemed to favor a hedgehog, even though they thought Bush fit into this category. For example, Arianna Huffington, who in 2004 defined Bush as a hedgehog and Kerry as a fox, stated in 2008 that what the country needed was a hedgehog. If, as Tetlock (2005) indicates, when hedgehogs are right they are very right, and when they are wrong they are very wrong, perhaps Bush was just a hedgehog who was very wrong, and the public was looking for another hedgehog who would set things right. In any case, they clearly favored the hedgehogs (Obama and McCain) over the foxes (Romney and Clinton), and they gave the presidency to the candidate who most resembled Roosevelt.

Why were people so tired of foxes and why was that feeling of exhaustion linked to Bush, who, with his "big" idea of democratizing the Middle East by invading Iraq, seemed to fit the profile of a hedgehog? I think that, whatever Bush was personally, he presided over the declining phase of a fox culture that had developed over the previous few decades. The irony is that this culture, whose internal contradictions brought it to a breaking point during Bush's tenure, had started to unfold under Ronald Reagan, a confirmed hedgehog, who had enchanted many people with the simple notion that the country could be great again if only it returned to traditional values like self-reliance, which he argued could best be achieved by reducing taxes and regulations, as well as government benefits and services.

Reagan's vision was a reversal of the one embodied in Roosevelt's New Deal, which was based on a hedgehog concept of fairness. Reagan's vision of self-reliance by its very nature fostered, as well as reflected, a fox culture characterized by a lack of solidarity. Individuals were left to their own devices, with the economic elite having very few restrictions on their ability to accumulate wealth and working people having very limited protections from exploitation, leading to their losing ground dramatically. This culture, aided and abetted by members of both political parties, eventually resulted in the current crisis, as deregulatory zeal led, first, to enormous stock and real estate bubbles and then to an equally large financial collapse.

Obama inherited a crisis parallel to the one that Roosevelt faced, and he appears to be attempting to address it in a similar way: by enunciating a new hedgehog concept of fairness to remedy the excesses of the recent past. Obama resembles Roosevelt in many ways, including their combining transformational and transactional characteristics that are the hallmark of successful leaders. Indeed, both demonstrate an interesting combination of fox and hedgehog traits. Roosevelt became president in the midst of the Great Depression. As now, the United States faced a crisis of confidence, and there was a feeling of despair. Roosevelt brought hope to the American people with his New Deal policies, which facilitated a recovery from the crisis. His leadership during World War II helped the country enter its period of greatest splendor. According to Michael R. Beschloss (1981), Roosevelt was a fox who understood the power of ideas, "a leader in search of a cause" who "could horsetrade with the best of transactional leaders" but for whom the presidency "was a platform for transforming leadership" (272-273). Perhaps this is why he surrounded himself with intelligent counselors, including his wife Eleanor, a quintessential hedgehog, whose influence on his political career cannot be overestimated. She was a key member of what has been called his "brain trust" of advisors. I believe that Roosevelt's love for ideas of all kinds was a hedgehog feature. He may have looked for ideas with randomness, but he articulated them with hedgehog logic in the service of a public purpose.

James MacGregor Burns (1956) uses a different animal metaphor to describe Roosevelt's leadership style. Instead of the fox and the hedgehog, he refers to the fox and the lion, highlighting the contrast between shrewdness and courage. This metaphor comes from Niccolò Machiavelli (1995 [1513]), who said that rulers had to be both foxes and lions, since the lion "is defenceless against traps" and the fox "is defenceless against wolves" (55). For Burns, Roosevelt was a fox who became a lion when there was a crisis, thus his skilled performance during the Depression and the war. Burns (2003) also describes Roosevelt in terms of being a "transactional" leader who became a "transforming" one, "just as Lincoln had midway through the Civil War" (23). The fox-lion metaphor fails to address the issue of vision, however, which is why I prefer the fox-hedgehog analogy. I believe that Roosevelt's political trajectory shows a man who was a fox in tactics and a hedgehog in strategy. His biggest accomplishment, and the main reason he is considered a great leader today, was the New Deal, the hedgehog concept of fairness that he articulated and implemented in order to lift the country out of the economic hole into which it had fallen. This achievement made him one of the most memorable hedgehogs in American history.

Like Roosevelt, Obama has been perceived both as a fox and a hedgehog. For example, Huffington (2008) presents him as a hedgehog, but Stephen Clark (2009) believes that he is a fox. Like Roosevelt and other successful leaders, he seems to share traits of both, with his fox side informing his tactics and his hedgehog qualities guiding his strategy. What George Lakoff (2009) calls "the Obama code" is a narrative of fairness that pervades his various policy proposals. All of his initiatives have been connected to this central vision or frame, which according to Manuel Castells (2009), is more than "just words," because words matter, showing the importance of "communication power" (384).

Curiously enough, during his first year in office, Obama seemed to lose some of this "communication power," failing to keep what Thomas L. Friedman (2009) calls "the poetry of his campaign" and making some people fear that he was not going to follow Roosevelt's example after all (Mills, 2010). In large part, this may have been due to his desire not to rock the financial boat excessively, which led to anger by considerable segments of the public. People were furious about perceived financial giveaways to the banking and automobile industries and mistrusted fox maneuvers by members of Obama's financial team. I believe that the public was angry because, at least with respect to the economy, they did not see a break with fox culture. On the contrary, it appeared that the same players were running the show. The health care debate also contributed to the perception that Obama was losing his focus, as much fox-like maneuvering was employed to pass the legislation, and opposition to it was furious. In the end, however, the health care bill passed and was "the most sweeping piece of federal legislation since Medicare was passed in 1965" (Leonhardt, 2010), firmly establishing Obama's credentials as a hedgehog.

Albert Einstein (Oakley & Krug, 1991) is credited with having stated that "the significant problems we face today cannot be solved at the same level of thinking we were at when we created them" (13). If the United States is to overcome the fox culture of the last few decades and articulate a new hedgehog concept in this period of transition, more hedgehogs will have to be appointed to top political positions so that they can develop a new level of thinking. The same thing can be said about American universities, which would be well-advised to start looking for administrative teams including critical numbers of hedgehogs charged with crafting a new vision for a country at the crossroads of history. In the knowledge-based global economy, this new vision must include a dramatic increase in access to quality higher education for every segment of the population. The nation needs a master plan for higher education, and it needs optimistic and altruistic Clark Kerrs to make this happen. But where will the Kerrs of the future come from? What will they look like? Just as Roosevelt's heir apparent does not look like Roosevelt, the Kerrs of the future might not resemble Kerr either. Thus, American universities must cast their nets widely when they look for visionary leaders who can bring about real reform, because now, as always, academia's role is to serve society, and society is desperately calling for the return of the hedgehogs.

# 2

# Leadership Styles

Kerr's memoirs provide a great deal of information about his leadership style. A comparison with Gardner's memoirs is instructive. Kerr was clearly a hedgehog. Gardner, on the other hand, can easily be described as a fox, although Kerr does not use this term to refer to him. Indeed, Kerr does not give any examples of foxes at all, perhaps because being a fox seems less elegant than being a hedgehog. His description of Gardner's deeds, however, points to positive fox qualities:

> Under President David Gardner (1983-92), a wonderful combination of circumstances literally saved the University from academic decline. The economy of the state improved substantially, creating enhanced state resources. The new governor, George Deukmejian (1983-91), had campaigned for office on a program of support for education. Gardner saw the possibilities of the situation, took the risk of proposing, and then securing, the passage of an almost one-third increase in state funds for the university in a single year. His triumph equalized faculty salaries (they had fallen 18.5 percent below those of comparable institutions, see Table 27) and made possible many other gains. That convergence of circumstances and Gardner's efforts led to the academic rankings of 1993. (Kerr, 2001b: 414)

Gardner recognized the potential for gain and acted swiftly and decisively, a typical fox maneuver. Gardner discusses this and other similar episodes at length in his memoirs, giving us a fascinating insight into the mind of the fox and providing the perfect counterpart to Kerr's reflections, which show the thinking of a hedgehog. Although Kerr and Gardner were presidents of the same institution, knew each other quite well, and shared many values, they were strikingly different types of people. Kerr's focus was primarily intellectual, while Gardner's was intuitive.

This is not to say, of course, that Kerr did not have feelings or that Gardner lacked ideas. On the contrary, both were complex and sophisti-

17

cated human beings: Kerr had many fox qualities, and Gardner had considerable hedgehog attributes, which is why they were both so successful. Great leaders combine hedgehog and fox traits, with one of them being dominant. Some, like Kerr, are primarily hedgehogs and, thus, more intellectual in outlook. Others, such as Gardner, are essentially foxes and therefore more apt to seek solutions through human interactions. Expanding on the work of such scholars as Lee Bolman and Terrence Deal (1984), and Robert Birnbaum (1988), which distinguish among four cognitive frames for leaders, namely bureaucratic, collegial, political, and symbolic, Estela M. Bensimon (1989) studied the leadership styles of thirty-two university presidents. She found that some presidents had only one style while others combined two, three, or even four. I believe that Kerr and Gardner combined all four traits, with Kerr stronger on the symbolic (articulation of vision) and bureaucratic (codification of vision) and Gardner more attentive to the collegial (human understanding) and political (human negotiation).

It is important to note that although hedgehogs are visionary, foxes are not blind. On the contrary, they can see everything that happens around them very well. They just see different things. Hedgehogs have tunnel vision, a long-range view connecting the past and the future. Imagination is about memory. Visions are built by projecting the past onto the future. Tunnel vision, by definition, has blind spots, and hedgehogs can miss things that are happening in their immediate surroundings. Foxes, on the other hand, have a short-range, circular, view. They cannot see very far ahead. They also are less aware of what came before. What they have is an exceptional awareness of the terrain they inhabit, together with shrewdness to navigate it safely. If hedgehogs are good at history and prophecy, foxes excel at geography and survival. Accordingly, Kerr was very proud of his ability to make accurate predictions about the future, which he usually connected with the past in meaningful ways, while Gardner prided himself on his ability to read present events. Kerr was a collector of concepts, while Gardner was a collector of people.

Kerr, by his own admission, was more intellectual than sociable. He says that he did not like to play golf. In other words, he was not one of the boys. Sometimes, he was not well-attuned to people's feelings. For example, he confesses that he failed to understand that student activists in the 1960s were moved by passion instead of being guided by a rational cost-benefit analysis. It was a romantic movement, not one seeking compromise, or, as Alain Touraine (1997) says, it was "more expressive than instrumental" (206), but Kerr did not understand that at the time:

I was too accustomed to rational thought within the academic community and the field of industrial relations: verifying facts, clarifying issues, calculating costs and benefits, trying to apply good sense and consider all aspects and consequences of actions. I was not accustomed to a more irrational world of emotions, of spontaneity, of sole adherence to some political faith. (Kerr, 2003: 238)

In part, this was due to his personality:

A second burden was that I was not easy-going enough and accessible enough to get along smoothly with some regents and legislators and students. I was all agendas and concerns and not given to easy conversation, not affable enough; by nature too shy, too reserved. (Kerr, 2003: 238)

According to Arthur Padilla (2005), Kerr's management style reflected his personality. He generally saw people in his office only one or two days a week, working from home most of the time. His assistant brought the mail to his house in the afternoon and picked up the materials he had gone over in the morning. His interactions with the members of his administrative team were largely in writing. In addition to minimal face-to-face exchanges, Kerr ran tightly-structured meetings, where most of the material had been written down in advance and was presented for discussion and approval. This technique worked well with the regents, who always gave him unanimous votes, of which he was very proud. But Padilla believes that his distant and aloof management style was a major factor in his problems during the Free Speech Movement, as he failed to appreciate the gravity of the situation.

This is also the opinion of Franklin D. Murphy (1976), who in his oral history, complained about Kerr's constant absences from the office, as well as his indirect way of communicating with the chancellors, often through his underlings, something that the chancellors resented. Murphy, who was chancellor of UCLA, is not the most impartial witness, as he had a strained relationship with Kerr, with whom he had an on-going competition during his entire tenure—it appears that Murphy coveted the presidency in spite of his declarations to the contrary. He was considered for it twice, unsuccessfully: first when Kerr got it and again when he lost it. His comments about Kerr's management style, however, echo those of other Kerr associates. Kerr was definitely not a people person, and he did travel around the country and abroad often, as he was in great demand. In fact, Kerr was in Asia when the trouble with the students began, and he had a hard time catching up with events when he came back. As Murphy suggests, he probably did not realize to what degree people were unhappy with him, an unhappiness that I believe was caused, at least in part, by his status as a hedgehog. It seems that the qualities and conditions that allowed him to articulate and communicate his vision—ability to collect concepts and use them as building blocks; rationality; time to read, write, and think; and opportunities for public speaking—weakened his political position, as people did not feel personally connected to him.

Gardner, on the other hand, did not have that problem. People found him very personable. He was certainly one of the boys. In his memoirs, he constantly discusses the people he knew. Whenever he introduces a new character into the narrative, he explains when and how they had met—and he seemed to have met many of the players previously. He was very good at collecting people, constantly enlarging his network of useful contacts. As Nancy N. Diamond (2006) indicates, Gardner emphasized teamwork. Accordingly, he was very focused on emotions, including his own, which he mentions often, noting the impact of his mood on events:

> I was in an ambivalent and uncommonly pensive move on September 15 as the first day's meeting began: still shocked by the proximate death of my parents, exhausted from the events of the previous several months and of our family's move and the disruption to our family in making this move, wondering how the reorganization and several other items on the agenda would go. I decided that I was not very happy about it all when I should have been excited and anticipatory. I was in a sour mood, not usual for me. (Gardner, 2003: 172)

Conversely, he often notes the impact of events on his mood:

> But as I left our July meeting, I really did wonder if our vaunted constitutional protections meant as much as I had always supposed (it was just as well that I left for our Montana cabin for a needed several weeks' rest immediately after the meeting, when I was in a negative and sour mood; I was in an upbeat and positive one on my return). (Gardner, 2003: 290)

As one might expect, the two leaders' achievements reflect this fundamental difference in attitude. Kerr's principal accomplishments—the California Master Plan for Higher Education, which combined access with selectivity, and the building of the UC system as an elite public research university in which all campuses were expected to reach the highest levels of excellence—were the result of his tunnel vision. Gardner's main contribution was his ability to convince the legislature and members of the public to provide generous funding for the institutions he represented. His most spectacular success—obtaining a 32 percent budget increase for the UC system during his first year as president—flowed from his short-range, circular view, as well as from his shrewdness.

Kerr could see the big picture where everyone else was stuck on details. He "had a singular ability to look at mountains of information and discern patterns and trends where others saw only a jumble of unrelated facts and statistics" (Pelfrey, 2004: 39). Eric Ashby describes Kerr's modus operandi as follows:

> With the impassivity of a computer (I mean this in admiration, not criticism!), he would (let me imitate his style): a) set out the facts; b) arrange and classify them (I never met a man who could so swiftly tidy up a mass of information); c) consider what deductions can be made from the facts; and d) make recommendations based on these deductions. To watch this was to witness the "Minute Particulars" (as Blake called them) falling into a pattern, and the pattern evolving into policy. (Levine, 1987: 18)

Kerr was able to connect the pieces into a workable whole, or "a story that made sense to the variety of constituents" (Howard Gardner, 1995: 129). All the elements of the Master Plan were in place: the three systems of higher education—UC, CSU, and the community colleges—each with its distinct mission. He did not create them. What Kerr accomplished was to transform confusing and unstable political arrangements into clear and solid policy. Over and over again in his memoirs, we see how he seeks to impose order on chaos by establishing policy.

Gardner, on the other hand, was more focused on politics than on policy. He had a sixth sense that told him when to jump and what to grab. Out of a multiplicity of options, he knew which to choose and when to choose it. At a time when his UC advisors would have been happy to accept an incremental increase to the budget, he sensed that a much more ambitious request might be granted and he audaciously pursued it. In Gardner's memoirs, there are many examples of his extraordinary ability to obtain funding for the university by picking the right moment to ask for it.

If these two university presidents' successes were different, so were their problems. Kerr's painful dismissal was caused by a change in state government, in which his vision came into conflict with that of a different kind of hedgehog, Governor Ronald Reagan. In contrast, Gardner's troubles arose from a perception that he was applying his legendary shrewdness to benefit himself, instead of the university, when it became known that he was going to receive a generous pension upon his retirement.

Both leaders made great contributions to the university: Kerr used his hedgehog's vision to shape the UC system into an institution of the highest caliber, and Gardner relied upon the shrewdness of a fox to consolidate those advances and transform the UC system into an academic superpower. A comparison of their memoirs is a useful exercise. Gardner's book, which is focused on his life before, during, and after his work at UC, is relatively short. Kerr's two volumes are a lengthy history of the University of California during his years as chancellor and president and are full of background information. Their different literary styles probably reflect distinct personal goals. Kerr appears to be trying to offer a well-documented narrative to prove his case, while Gardner seems intent on providing a pleasant narrative and causing a good impression. One example of this difference is how each of these leaders reacted when attacked about his beliefs.

Kerr, whom Padilla (2005) calls "the Berkeley Quaker" (79), was an independent thinker, which did not go over well in the McCarthy era. He was subject to investigation and harassed, as can be seen in the following episode:

> After I became chancellor of Berkeley, I was interviewed by a whole line of investigators, of whom most were well informed and courteous though some were not. One in the latter category came to my office one day and sat down at my table, opened his note book, and asked me a question: "Are you a 100 percent American?" I replied that I could not answer his question unless he defined what he meant by "a 100 percent American." He looked at me and said, "Anyone who does not know what is a 100 percent American is obviously un-American." He slammed shut his notebook, put away his pen, got up, and walked out of my office. That must have resulted in a black mark on my record. (Kerr, 2003: 49)

Indeed, as he says later, his independent attitude resulted in many more black marks and a thick FBI file with a note saying "Kerr is no good," initialed by none other than J. Edgar Hoover. With characteristic humor, Kerr declares that he looks at this document "as the equivalent of an honorary degree" (Kerr, 2003: 69).

While Kerr did not compromise and suffered the consequences, Gardner was a master in the art of avoiding conflict and staying cool, as Neil J. Smelser (2005) points out. This can be seen in his job interview with the UC presidential search committee, when one of the regents asked him if he was a Mormon and another followed up with a question about his position on the Equal Rights Amendment:

> I wondered how best to respond and finally said something along the following lines: "These two questions are, in the first instance, legally impermissible and, in the second, wholly inappropriate unless it's your intention to apply a religious and/or a political test to the appointment of the university's next president contrary to the

express provisions of the state constitution charging the regents to keep the university free of political and sectarian influence in the administration of its internal affairs. I will, therefore, not respond to your second question, nor elaborate on your first."

I let my words sink in for a moment, turned to the questioner, and said, "Why don't you rephrase your question? Ask me about my views of the educational and employment opportunities women should expect to find or would hope to find at UC. Phrased that way, I will be happy to answer." She said, "All right, what are your views?"

With some brief mention of my having four daughters and being keenly aware of the implications attending her interest, I said that "women should have the same freedom over their lives as men do, including, and not by way of limitation, their personal and professional lives, and that neither the law nor university policies and practices should impede or otherwise interfere with the exercise of that discretion." (Gardner, 2005: 145)

This answer, which was very deliberate, both in conception and execution, was calculated to produce a triple effect. First, it showed that he was tough, knew his rights, and was capable of defending them. Second, it demonstrated that he was a team player who could help a group move past a difficult moment. Finally, it addressed the committee's concern about his being too conservative by saying what its members wanted to hear.

In these two episodes, both Kerr and Gardner teased their critics, but Kerr did not give them an opportunity to save face, while Gardner did. Kerr's goal was to prove his case and follow his principles, even if that did not please people. Gardner's intent was to cause a good impression and please people without compromising his principles. Both narrate their adventures with great pride and relish.

These two academic leaders share many anecdotes about the attacks they had to endure and spend a lot of time analyzing their respective problems. Both were attacked, in spite of their accomplishments or, perhaps, because of them. Their detailed narratives concerning the troubles afflicting them at the end of their presidential tenures illustrate the contingent nature of power. Both narratives provide important lessons for administrators, showing that, whether hedgehogs or foxes, it would be wise for them to contemplate administrative positions as a marathon in which the incumbents have to accomplish as much as possible before running out of power.

In terms of the current needs of the University of California, I believe that these are twofold: the university needs a great increase in resources, but it also must have a new vision of inclusiveness. In my view, a strong and diverse team of hedgehogs and foxes is required. Given the need to break away from fox culture and to articulate a new hedgehog concept,

I will argue that this is a moment in which hedgehogs should take the lead. That is the essence of my friendly disagreement with Kerr. It is clear that the last few decades have been a fox-dominated period, but will this continue? Is the current displeasure with the ways of academic leaders not an expression of fox fatigue? Is the public not calling for the return of the hedgehogs?

Kerr did not anticipate such a call. In chapter 9 of *The Uses of the University*, he envisioned a future of foxes "looking around every bush, avoiding every trap, eating everything that happens to come along that can't eat them. No great visions to lure them on, only the needs of survival for themselves and their institutions" (2001a: 209).

In this chapter, which is the last chapter of the last version of this famous book, and therefore can be read as his political testament, he concedes to the foxes and simply says that he hopes they will have a few hedgehogs around them to remind them to protect academic values. He also offers them some advice—the things that he would do if he were a fox—including having an in-depth discussion about the ethical systems of the future university. The book ends with the following words:

> To the hedgehogs of the 1960s of which I was one: rest in peace; to the foxes of the twenty-first century: great expectations for success in your attempted escapes from the maze! (Kerr, 2001a: 229)

This is a depressing ending, a vision of a future without vision, but can there really be a future without vision?

# 3

# The Ingredients of
# *The Uses of the University*

James L. Fisher (1984) comments on the importance of academic leaders being conversant with the literature on higher education, a thought echoed by Steve B. Sample (2002), who states that academic leaders are what they read. Kerr certainly was conversant with the literature on higher education and was very much what he read. His famous 1963 vision of the university did not develop in a vacuum but rather evolved from his readings. Of all the authors he quotes in *The Uses of the University*, there were seven who, in my opinion, had a particularly strong influence on his thinking: Thorstein Veblen, Upton Sinclair, Abraham Flexner, José Ortega y Gasset, Sir Walter Moberly, Karl Jaspers, and Robert Maynard Hutchins.

Without their works, it would have been difficult for Kerr to make sense of the things that he was witnessing and experiencing as an academic administrator. I believe that these thinkers, most particularly Flexner and Ortega, provided the bulk of the inspiration for Kerr's 1963 vision of the university. Not coincidentally, Kerr later wrote introductions to Flexner's and Ortega's books about the university. These are the pillars on which he built his idea of the "multiversity."

## The Flour: Thorstein Veblen, Upton Sinclair, and Abraham Flexner

The basic ingredients of Kerr's thinking—the flour as it were—came from three American intellectuals of great prominence in their day who had a great impact on his conceptualization of the "multiversity": Veblen, Sinclair, and Flexner.

## Thorstein Veblen

Thorstein Veblen, one of the founders of the American school of institutional economics, was a very original thinker who looked at economic systems from an evolutionary point of view. His approach was like that of an anthropologist describing a culture very different from his own, with methods borrowed from sociology and psychology. His most famous book, *The Theory of the Leisure Class*, published in 1899, won him considerable acclaim at the time and is still read today. His convoluted style, although difficult to understand at times, had many felicitous moments. For example, he coined such terms as "conspicuous consumption" and "pecuniary emulation." Of the many books he wrote, *The Higher Learning in America*, which came out in 1918, is of particular interest to academics because it is a devastating critique of the university, which he believed had become part of the business enterprise. The first draft of this book dated from 1904 and was heavily focused on the University of Chicago. Veblen later realized that his observations about that institution applied to all American universities and changed the book accordingly.

Veblen points out that while the old American colleges had been led by men of the cloth, American universities of his time were controlled by businessmen, or "captains of industry." These businessmen not only constituted their boards of trustees but selected their presidents, or "captains of erudition," in their own image. The modern American university acts "as a business house dealing in merchantable knowledge, placed under the governing hand of a captain of erudition, whose office it is to turn the means in hand to account in the largest feasible output" (1918: 85). The new commerce schools mirror the old divinity schools, and money has become sacred. Thus, businessmen are considered wise because of their wealth, just as men of the cloth were seen as knowledgeable because of their calling. Accordingly, universities are controlled by lay governing boards composed of rich men and led by university presidents who act not as clerics and faculty colleagues, but as businessmen and employers.

The president has an opulent lifestyle, since he has to get donations from the rich and "transactions begin and end within the circle of pecuniary respectability" (1918: 156). Accordingly, he is very well-compensated, since, like a politician, he has to be "all things to all audiences" (1918: 256). As is the case with politicians, "the incumbents are chosen from among a self-selected body of candidates, each of whom has, in the common run of cases, been resolutely in pursuit of such an office for some appreciable time, and has spent much time and endeavor on fitting himself for its duties" (1918: 244). Once chosen, the president has a great deal of power, which he needs to advance the business of the university:

> He must be a strong man; that is to say, a capable man of affairs, tenacious and re-sourceful in turning the means at hand to account for this purpose, and easily content to let the end justify the means. He must be a man of scrupulous integrity, so far as may conduce to his success, but with a shrewd eye to the limits within which honesty is the best policy, for the purpose in hand. (Veblen, 1918: 90)

A minimum of scholarship is required for the job. What matters is business acumen, in order to keep the working force so "standardized that its rate of speed and the volume of its current output can be exhibited to full statistical effect as it runs" (1918: 87-88).

Veblen takes an evolutionary approach, pointing out the medieval origins of the university as an institution dedicated to train professionals, that is, as a vocational school. The human trait of "idle curiosity" and the "instinct of workmanship," however, made the university part of the quest for knowledge, thus transforming its endeavors (1918: 5). Philosophy, originally considered the "handmaid of theology," provided the basis for scientific inquiry (1918: 38). After that, "technology of handicraft" gave way to modern science (1918: 33). Thus, in recent times, the higher learning became an end in itself. Veblen states that it would be unwise to go back and make the university a vocational school again, or turn it into a "department store," as the business community demands.

Veblen, whose ideas seem closer to the German university model than to any other, believes that only graduate education deserves to be part of the university and should not be mixed with undergraduate education. The problem is that American universities grew out of undergraduate colleges and inherited their methods, which permeated the newly created graduate schools. So not only are graduate students and undergraduate students together, but they are treated according to the same principles, as "the undergraduate scheme of credits, detailed accountancy, and mechanical segmentation of the work, is carried over into the university work proper" (1918: 108).

According to Veblen, American universities' business culture manifests itself most clearly in their obsession with competition and prestige. Each institution wants to have the highest rankings, thus engaging in aggressive advertising, in addition to acquisition of beautiful grounds and buildings ("decorative real estate"), organization of solemn celebrations ("spectacular pageantry"), and hiring of well-known faculty members. Fortunately, the business model, which makes universities "competitors for the traffic in merchantable instruction, in much the same fashion as rival establishments in the retail trade compete for custom" (1918: 89), results in a strong need for good scholars, who inevitably reintroduce "idle curiosity" and the "instinct of workmanship" into the system, so "the principles of competitive publicity carry with them a partial neutralization of their own tendency" (1918: 177). In fact, there is an upward drift in American schools that makes institutions established to offer practical training gravitate towards non-utilitarian endeavors and eventually join the ranks of the seminaries of higher learning. Although universities are engaged in a quest for knowledge, "the course enjoined by the principles of competitive business sets toward the suppression or elimination of all such scholarly or scientific work from the university as does not contribute immediately to its prestige" (1918: 172).

For Veblen, the only way to fix the problems of the modern university would be to abolish the governing boards, eliminate the presidency, which gives "a deceptive appearance of a massive engine working to some common end" (1918: 281), and make each unit independent, which would allow the graduate school to act as "a shelter where the surviving remnant of scholars and scientists might pursue their several lines of adventure, in teaching and in inquiry, without disturbances to or from the worldly-wise who clamour for the greater glory" (1918: 286). The abolition of the presidency would destroy the university organization:

> The several constituent schools would fall apart, since nothing holds them together except the strong hand of the present central government. This would, of course, seem a monstrous and painful outrage to all those persons who are infatuated with a veneration of big things; to whom a "great"—that is to say voluminous—university is an object of pride and loyal affection. This class of persons is a very large one, and they are commonly not given to reflection on the merits of their preconceived ideals of "greatness." So that the dissolution of this "trust"-like university coalition would bitterly hurt their feelings. So intolerable would be the shock to this popular sentiment presumably be, indeed, that no project of the kind can have any reasonable chance of a hearing. (Veblen, 1918: 280)

Veblen knew that his proposal was not realistic, so his book ends with a statement to the effect that his argument had "little else than speculative value" (1918: 286).

*Upton Sinclair*

Veblen's abstract and cryptic analysis was turned into a detailed and gossipy narrative by the well-known and prolific socialist writer and outstanding investigative journalist Upton Sinclair in his 1923 book *The Goose-step: A Study of American Education*. This was part of his "Dead Hand" series—half a dozen books on various American institutions, including religion, journalism, art, literature, schools, and universities. Sinclair, who was famous for his 1906 novel *The Jungle*, which examined conditions in the meat packing industry, offered an aggressive critique of American universities and their German-educated leaders, who, he believed, had acquired authoritarian tendencies along with their imperial German schooling. His theory was that universities were controlled by plutocrats, who were trying to keep students in the dark about what was really happening in the world. This was accomplished by keeping faculty members under control through lack of job security and academic freedom. Based on many interviews conducted at universities around the country, as well as on published sources, this book provided a wealth of information and stories about events at institutions of higher learning. Clearly inspired by Veblen's views about the university, its stated goal was to encourage faculty members to unionize in order to secure such fundamental rights as tenure and the opportunity to be judged by their peers.

After reviewing his own education, which he finds very deficient, Sinclair discusses Nicholas Murray Butler, who was a philosophy professor at Columbia before his elevation to the presidency. Shortly after taking a course with Butler, Sinclair learned that he had joined the Episcopal Church in order to be able to aspire to the Columbia presidency. This shocked Sinclair, because he knew that Butler was not religious, since he had demonstrated in class "the impossibility of any valid knowledge concerning immortality, free will or a First Cause" (1923: 12).

Borrowing an expression from the 1913 Pujo Committee of the House of Representatives report about the "interlocking directorates" (1923: 19), a device by which three New York banks and two trust companies under them controlled one hundred twelve corporations in America, Sinclair calls Butler the "interlocking president" of "the University of the House of Morgan" (1923: 29). For him, Columbia, which at the time was the largest and richest university in the country, was an "education factory" (1923: 42) and an "academic department store" (1923: 54). His review of Harvard, Pennsylvania, Princeton, and Yale produced similar findings, as did his visit to the University of California, which he called "the university of the black hand" (1923: 126). After describing the members of the Board of Regents in unflattering terms, Sinclair refers to the Better America Federation as "a kind of 'black hand' society of the rich" (1923: 129). This society investigates faculty and students and blacklists people who are not "one hundred per cent capitalist" (1923: 130).

Sinclair concludes that at UC, like at other universities, there is no academic freedom, and professors are marginalized or fired when their views offend the powers that be. Although its president, Benjamin Ide Wheeler, is treated somewhat better than Butler and other academic leaders, Sinclair is critical of him because he called himself a liberal but made sure never to offend his chief benefactor, Phoebe Apperson Hearst, wife of wealthy businessman and U.S. Senator George Hearst and mother of newspaper magnate William Randolph Hearst. As for the spirit of the university, Sinclair found fault with the ferocity of its academic and athletic competition with Stanford, calling the students "future world conquerors" who "are pleased to portray themselves under the terrifying symbol of the Golden Bear" (1923: 142).

Sinclair's descriptions of other universities are equally unflattering, although he has some kind words for the early history of Johns Hopkins, which started as an institution focused on learning rather than business. Its facilities were very modest, but the intellectual caliber of its faculty was exceptionally high. In particular, he is quite positive about Johns Hopkins' first president, Daniel Coit Gilman, who retired to start the Carnegie Institution of Washington at the age of seventy. His daughter, Elizabeth Gilman, who was a socialist, was quite critical of the way her father's beloved university was being degraded by business interests, as she stated in a letter to Sinclair:

> The university has been to me more like a sister than an institution. I gloried in what she stood for and in what she accomplished. During the last few years it seems to me that she has lost much of her intellectual leadership in America, at the very time when academic freedom and democratic principles need brave champions. The fine new buildings and campus have not to my mind compensated for a considerable lowering of intellectual ideals and accomplishments. Money getting is horribly dangerous to institutions as well as to individuals, and the Johns Hopkins University has been out to get money. It is true that this money has been given for education and not for profit, and yet even so, there may be the insidious temptation of adopting purely business standards. We need in Baltimore, as well as throughout the country, courageous, untrammelled leadership, as expressed in the motto of the Johns Hopkins University, "The truth shall make you free." (Sinclair, 1923: 305)

The academic ideals that Gilman had brought to Johns Hopkins and, before that, to UC, were being overtaken by the realities of the emergent "multiversity" at both institutions and at other institutions of higher learning around the country. These realities included an increasing number of professional degrees, which Sinclair mocks by quoting course titles from college catalogues, where he found that at the University of Illinois, the University of Nebraska, and the University of Southern California they were teaching "millinery," while at Boston University they were teaching "how to collect tips at summer hotels" (1923: 320). Sinclair is equally unimpressed by the work being done in more traditional fields, quoting titles of dissertations such as "a Columbia thesis, composed by a man who is now a professor at Princeton: 'Metaphors Concerned with Nature in the Prose of Aelfric;' or a Columbia thesis, by a professor who is now at Charleston: 'The Dialect Contamination in the Old English Gospels'" (1923: 398). Sinclair declares that the educational system has become an obstacle to the development of intelligence and that "colleges are growing like those prehistoric monsters, the size of a freight car, with brains that fit inside a walnut-shell. And as they grow, there is more and more 'administration'" (1923: 398).

Indeed, Sinclair pays much attention to the administration, particularly the figure of the college president, whom he discusses in chapter LXXVI, titled "Prexy." For him, the college president tends not to tell the truth because he is a "reconciler of irrenconcilabilities":

> He is a chemist who mixes oil and water, the high priest who makes peace between God and Mammon, the circus-rider who stands on two horses going in opposite directions; and all these things not by choice, but ex-officio and of inescapable necessity. The college president is a man who procures money from the rich, and uses it for the spreading of knowledge; in fulfilling which two functions he places himself, not merely in the line of fire of the warring forces of the class struggle, but between the incompatible elements of human nature itself—between greed and service, between hate and love, between body and spirit. (Sinclair, 1923: 382-383)

The only way to succeed is by telling all constituencies what they want to hear. This "faker" and "prevaricator" has the salary and prestige of a plutocrat, living "on terms of equality with business emperors and financial dukes," to whom he gives honorary degrees. It is a "new aristocracy" with "a new set of titles of nobility" (1923: 388).

There are many traces of Veblen's and Sinclair's ideas in Kerr's thinking, beginning with his acute awareness of the existence of an upward drift in universities, which made him insist on preventing California State University from becoming a research university, a role that was reserved for the University of California in the California Master Plan for Higher Education. Kerr was also very aware of the university's connection to business and of the important role of the governing board, about which he later wrote a book titled *The Guardians* with Marian L. Gade (1989). In this study, which was published by the Association of Governing Boards of Universities and Colleges, Kerr takes a much more benevolent approach than Veblen or Sinclair, whose comments he characterizes as "vitriolic attacks" (1989: 23). Nevertheless, he followed their lead and engaged in an evaluation of this institution, offering recommendations for improvement.

Veblen and Sinclair had a great impact on Kerr's thinking and were instrumental in making him understand the university's newly developed "massive engine." He tried to make sense of it and of his own uncomfortable role as a "captain of erudition" or rather as "a captain of bureaucracy who is sometimes a galley slave on his own ship" (2001a: 25). He realized that the university was a central part of the economy, if not a "department store" or a "factory," at least "a knowledge industry," engaged in "knowledge production," which, as he noted, was becoming a very important part of the gross national product and "growing at twice the rate of the rest of the economy" (2001a: 66).

*Abraham Flexner*

Kerr's vision of the university combines Veblen's and Sinclair's views with the ideas of Abraham Flexner. Indeed, Kerr's book draws most heavily on Flexner's 1930 work *Universities: American, English, German*, which he edited with an introduction in 1994. While Veblen's brilliant analysis was abstract and cryptic, and Sinclair's juicy critique lacked scholarly rigor, Flexner, a respected academic who in 1910 had authored the famous report *Medical Education in the United States and Canada*, provided many concrete and well-documented examples about the increasing complexity of the university. Unlike Veblen and Sinclair, who limited their comments to the United States, Flexner's book is a comparative study of universities in three countries, which provides a broader perspective on the issues. His conclusions, however, are very similar. Like Veblen and Sinclair, he dislikes the changes taking place in academia, stating that universities should provide "not what society wants, but what it needs" (1994 [1930]: 5). Noting that "Chemistry made no progress as long as men were concerned immediately to convert base metal into gold" (1994 [1930]: 14), Flexner takes the position that most utilitarian activities have no place at the university, which should be dedicated to research and teaching at the highest levels. He then proceeds to examine how well American, English, and German universities follow this ideal, finding that the German university, although not lacking in problems, comes "nearest to giving higher education its due position" (1994 [1930]: 305). Among its virtues are intellectual focus, quality curriculum, and strong faculty. Among its weaknesses, he counts inelasticity, overloading, and class-consciousness, as well as a lack of resources. In spite of these problems, he believes that the German university will survive and thrive because academics and politicians understand and value education, while the United States, with its abundant resources, "neither regards higher education at its proper value, nor knows what it is" (1994 [1930]: 360).

Flexner's view of English universities is not quite as positive. For example, he states that he is "unable to understand in what sense the University of London is a university at all" (1994 [1930]: 231). It is a conglomerate of heterogeneous institutions that, in addition to "internal" academic activities, engages in numerous "external" service activities. The provincial universities follow the lead of the University of London, offering courses in such areas as "Brewing" (Birmingham) and "Photographic Technology" (Manchester) (1994 [1930]: 255). Flexner is more positive about Oxford and Cambridge, which are quite free of trivial activities and whose tutorial system offers undergraduates a true research experience, while graduate students enjoy a great deal of freedom to pursue their interests. Like the German universities, the English universities have powerful faculties, which he considers very positive.

As for American universities, he finds them to be "secondary schools and colleges for boys and girls; graduate and professional schools for advanced students; 'service' stations for the general public" (1994 [1930]: 45). Quoting the Spanish thinker Salvador de Madariaga (1928a), who discusses the influence of business on the life of America, Flexner highlights the identification of the university and the economy. Giving many examples of the aggressive methods universities such as Columbia and Chicago developed to recruit students, including opening branches in various locations, Flexner states that they introduced the "chain-store" concept in the field of higher education in the United States (1994 [1930]: 59). Expressing nostalgia for the Johns Hopkins of the Gilman era, Flexner laments the commercialization affecting all universities, including such venerable ones as Harvard, whose seal, he says, "might some day contain the words-'Veritas et Ars Venditoria!'" (1994 [1930]: 168). He believes that, instead of engaging in the art of selling their services to a large number of people, universities should focus on educating the elite, in other words, "instead of doing all they can, they should be doing as little as they can" (1994: 149).

Noting that "no nation responds to exacting leadership more readily than the United States" (1994 [1930]: 152), Flexner discusses the importance of the presidency in the American system of higher education, which was shaped by such luminaries as Gilman of Johns Hopkins, Harvard University's president, Charles William Eliot, and the University of Chicago's President, William Rainey Harper. Flexner thought that the job of the president, as it had been reconfigured, was too complex:

> The duties of the president are various and exacting: he is the main agent in procuring funds or appropriations; he is a local magnate; he is pulled hither and yon to make speeches and to attend functions; he is made member of numerous committees and councils; he is a "good fellow" among the alumni; he participates more or less actively in choosing the faculty and in mapping out policies—policies for the college, policies for the service station, policies for the graduate and professional schools. He is the medium of communication between faculty and trustees; unless he approves, the faculty views may not even obtain a hearing. A heavy burden! One of the wisest of American philanthropists, head of a great business organization, long a trustee of a prominent university, once remarked to me: "A man may be president of a transcontinental railroad, an international banking corporation, a far-flung business; but the presidency of a great university is an impossible post." (Flexner, 1994 [1930]: 183)

With generous salaries and presidential palaces where "a professor living on his salary does not breathe freely" (1994 [1930]: 182), presidents have become closer to the trustees and have drifted away from the faculty. For Flexner, "academic dignity will not be restored until a professor is approximately as well paid as a president, lives as well, and is as highly regarded" (1994 [1930]: 183), in other words, when the president goes back to being first among equals.

In *The Uses of the University*, Kerr mentions Flexner's, Veblen's, and Sinclair's books when he refers to the many faces of the multiversity president:

> To Flexner, he was a hero figure, "a daring pioneer" who filled an "impossible post" yet some of his accomplishments were "little short of miraculous"; thus the "forceful president"—the Gilman, the Eliot, the Harper. The necessary revolutions came from on high. There should be Giants in the Groves. To Thorstein Veblen he was a "Captain of Erudition," and Veblen did not think well of captains. To Upton Sinclair, the university president was "the most universal faker and most variegated prevaricator that has yet appeared in the civilized world." (Kerr, 2001a: 23)

Echoes of their comments can be heard in Kerr's long description of the president of the "multiversity" whom he describes as a "many-faced character" (2001a: 22) who is "inspiring in his visions yet cautious in what he does" (2001a: 23):

> The university president in the United States is expected to be a friend of the students, a colleague of the faculty, a good fellow with the alumni, a sound administrator with the trustees, a good speaker with the public, an astute bargainer with the foundations and the federal agencies, a politician with the state legislature, a friend of industry, labor, and agriculture, a persuasive diplomat with donors, a champion of education generally, a supporter of the professions (particularly law and medicine), a spokesman to the press, a scholar in his own right, a public servant at the state and national levels, a devotee of opera and football equally, a decent human being, a good husband and father, an active member of a church. Above all he must enjoy traveling in airplanes, eating his meals in public, and attending public ceremonies. No one can be all of these things. Some succeed at being none. (Kerr, 2001a: 22)

Kerr goes on to say that the university president should "sound like a mouse at home and look like a lion abroad" and be "a seeker of truth where the truth may not hurt too much" (2001a: 23).

Flexner's book is a defense of the "idea of the modern university," that is, the German research university, modeled after John Henry Newman's work *The Idea of a University*, which is a defense of the English liberal arts university. According to Kerr, just as Newman penned his book when the English model was disappearing, Flexner wrote his analysis when the German model was vanishing:

> The Berlin of Humboldt was being violated just as Berlin had violated the soul of Oxford. The universities were becoming too many things. Flexner himself complained that they were "secondary schools, vocational schools, teacher-training schools, research centers, 'uplift' agencies, businesses—these and other things simultaneously." They engaged in "incredible absurdities," "a host of inconsequential things." They "needlessly cheapened, vulgarized and mechanized themselves." Worst of all, they became "'service stations' for the general public." (Kerr, 2001a: 4)

Indeed, as Michael R. Harris (1970) emphasizes, Flexner was a counter-revolutionary who fought against the American land-grant university model of service. His book provides a detailed description of what he considered the excesses of this model, including numerous undergraduate majors and professional degrees of a practical nature, which, in his opinion, interfered with the true education of students, who had to "learn the 'principles' of salesmanship from a Ph.D. who has never sold anything, or the 'principles' of marketing from a Ph.D. who has never marketed anything" (1994 [1930]: 71). Flexner, who is very critical of the "service station" function of the American university and of what he calls its "ad-hoc-ness" (1994 [1930]: 71), concludes that "neither Columbia, nor Harvard, nor Johns Hopkins, nor Chicago, nor Wisconsin is really a university, for none of them possesses unity of purpose or homogeneity of constitution. Their centres are the treasurer's office, into which income flows, out of which expenditures issue, and the office of the registrar who keeps the roll" (1994 [1930]: 179).

Quoting Madariaga (1928b), who believes that most of the information that a businessman needs can be acquired before the student enters the university or after he goes into business, Flexner proposes to eliminate all "the make-believe professions—journalism, business, library science, domestic science, and optometry" and other, in his view, superfluous functions and return to the German ideal of the research university (1994 [1930]: 215). Among other suggestions, he says that "the most formidable 'School'—the Harvard Graduate School of Business Administration—could be detached" and become independent as "a Boston Graduate School of Business" (1994 [1930]: 215). With these changes, "Harvard, Yale, Columbia, and Chicago would at once stand out as universities" (1994 [1930]: 216).

Noting that, with all the buildings and special events, athletics and alumni involvement, less than one-third of the typical university budget was devoted to what he considered proper university expenditures, Flexner questioned whether the university should change its name:

> It has, however, become a question whether the term "university" can be saved or is even worth saving. Why should it not continue to be used in order to indicate the formless and incongruous activities—good, bad, and indifferent—which I have described in this chapter? If indeed "university" is to mean, as Columbia announces, a "public service institution," then the university has become a different thing, a thing which may have its uses, but is assuredly no longer a university. In this event, in order to signify the idea of a real university, a new term may be requisite. (Flexner, 1994 [1930]: 213-214)

Kerr expanded upon the idea and came up with a new term, not for what Flexner called the "real university," but for this new model of university and its multiple "uses," which he called the "multiversity." I believe that *Universities: American, English, German* constitutes the primary source of *The Uses of the University* in terms of style. Flexner's book was an elucidation of ideas contained in three papers he delivered at Oxford University as part of the Rhodes Lectures. Kerr's does the same with the three Goldkin Lectures he gave at Harvard University. Kerr's first lecture, "The idea of a multiversity" draws inspiration from Flexner's first lecture "The idea of a modern university."

Although Kerr uses many of Flexner's materials, his approach is completely different. Rather than fighting this new model of institution of higher learning and questioning its right to be called a university, he renames it and accepts it, albeit with reservations often expressed in witty language reminiscent of Flexner's, Veblen's, and Sinclair's humorous critiques. While these three commentators looked to the past, Kerr looks to the future. Rather than lamenting the loss of the Golden Age, he celebrates the coming of a new one.

### The Leavening: José Ortega y Gasset, Sir Walter Moberly, and Karl Jaspers

What made Kerr turn Veblen's, Sinclair's and Flexner's lament for the past into a vision of the future and what made him choose the term "multiversity" to describe this new model of university? I think that Ortega, Moberly, and Jaspers were instrumental in helping Kerr see what was happening to the American university in a different light. While Veblen's, Sinclair's, and Flexner's American perspectives provided the flour for Kerr's conceptualization of the "multiversity," the ideas of these three European thinkers provided the leavening that gave his interpretation its shape and stature.

*José Ortega y Gasset*

José Ortega y Gasset was a Spanish philosopher of considerable international renown who became particularly famous after the publication of his seminal book *The Revolt of the Masses* in 1930. This work's theory is that society's tone is no longer set by the intellectual elite but rather by the masses, which impose their views tyrannically by creating public opinion. This new world of mass dominance was made possible by liberal democracy, scientific experiment, and industrialism. The "mass-man" uses all the advantages of civilization without being civilized, that is, without being "at the height of the times." Indeed he is a "barbarian." This category includes scholars, who have become so specialized that they do not know very much outside their areas of expertise: A scholar today is a "learned ignoramus" (1993 [1930]: 112). Ortega's theory is that there is a need for unification in order to overcome the fragmentation of research. Thus, he is in favor of a holistic approach to education.

Also in 1930, Ortega published a book titled *Mission of the University*, which Kerr edited with an introduction in 1997. In this work, Ortega expanded some of these ideas and proposed a university for the future. Based on a series of lectures delivered before the student federation of the University of Madrid, this book was the expression of a dream for a new state and a new university. In 1930, the Miguel Primo de Rivera dictatorship was coming to an end, and democracy was in the air, arriving in 1931 with the establishment of the short-lived Republic. Ortega, who was very concerned about the growing influence of the press and its ability to manipulate information and create public opinion, thought that the university should be an "uplifting principle," a "spiritual power" to fight that pernicious influence and stand "for serenity in the midst of frenzy" (1997 [1930]: 81).

Ortega had studied at Leipzig, Berlin, and Marburg and thus was very much a product of the German research university. He was, however, quite critical of its excessive specialization and lack of attention to teaching, believing that these characteristics prevented it from being an acceptable model. In fact, Ortega was very much against the idea of adopting German, English, or any other foreign models for the university. To the contrary, he believed it a fallacy that these nations were great because their schools were good and that other countries could become great by imitating their educational systems. According to Ortega, this erroneous line of thinking was very popular in the nineteenth century:

> The English rout Napoleon I: "The battle of Waterloo was won on the playing fields of Eton." Bismarck crushes Napoleon III: "The war of 1870 is the victory of the Prussian school master and the German professor." (Ortega, 1997 [1930]: 19)

Ortega noted that in fact the opposite was true: great nations produce great school systems, just as they develop great economic and political systems. Therefore, imitating the school systems of successful countries would not achieve the desired results. Ortega knew very well that importing foreign educational models would not transform Spain from a poor and backward nation to a rich and modern one. Indeed, Spain had already experimented with foreign models in the Institución Libre de Enseñanza, an independent institution that successfully combined the English tradition of residential learning with the German research model. Although this institution was very influential in educating the intellectual elite, it had a limited impact on the country precisely because the country was not yet industrialized (Steger, 1979).

Ortega understood that strong economic and political systems produce good educational systems, and not vice versa. Furthermore, he believed that those who imitate others are always behind the times. For Ortega (1993 [1930]), each generation required fifteen years to become established, and the worldview it articulated lasted for another fifteen years. By the time a generation's accomplishments became known and could be imitated, a new generation was developing a different worldview. For all of these reasons, he believed that imitation of foreign models was not advisable. The German research university's model, in particular, was flawed in that it produced what he called "new barbarians," or people who knew a great deal about their own areas of research or professional activity and very little about any others (1997 [1930]: 28).

For Ortega, the most crucial question was "What is a university for, and what must it consequently be?" (1997 [1930]: 18). He concluded that there were four missions: preparation for the professions, training of new scientists, education of leaders, and transmission of culture. Ortega emphasized that, with the knowledge explosion, it was no longer possible for students to learn everything. Therefore, teaching should focus not on the knowledge that can be taught, which is vast, but on what students can learn, which is limited. Thus, he was in favor of a student-centered education that would provide a "general culture" (1997 [1930]: 26), that is, an understanding of "the system of vital ideas which each age possesses" or an awareness of their time and place (1997 [1930]: 60). Although this understanding had to be based on research findings, it was not provided by discovering new knowledge, but rather by integrating existing knowledge into a holistic construct. For him, what the university really needed was a "genius for integration" (1997 [1930]: 70), and its most important function was to bring students up to "the height of the times" (1997 [1930]: 30). This is a Spanish expression that means to be up to date, to be responsive to the changing realities of history, to be cutting-edge. For Ortega, "the man who lives on a plane beneath the enlightened level of his time is condemned, relatively, to the life of an infra-man" (1997 [1930]: 62).

In *The Uses of the University*, Kerr quoted Ortega by name only once, to make a witty comment about student self-government:

> Although José Ortega y Gasset, in addressing the student federation at the University of Madrid, was willing to turn over the entire "mission of the university" to the students, he neglected to comment on faculty reaction. (Kerr, 2001a: 16)

The influence of Ortega on Kerr's book, however, is much greater than this comment suggests and is evident in a number of passages. For example, Kerr's book begins by commenting that Newman and Flexner were behind the times:

> The "Modern University" was as nearly dead in 1930 when Flexner wrote about it as the old Oxford was in 1852 when Newman idealized it. History moves faster than the observer's pen. (Kerr, 2001a: 5)

This echoes Ortega's comment about the impossibility of fruitful imitation: a university that copies a model from another country is, by definition, behind the times.

Kerr indicates that the "multiversity" is not a consciously-created model but "a reality rooted in the logic of history," adding that "it is an imperative rather than a reasoned choice among elegant alternatives" (2001a: 5). Kerr explains that the "multiversity" draws on many historical models:

> The resulting combination does not seem plausible but it has given America a remarkably effective educational institution. A university anywhere can aim no higher than to be as British as possible for the sake of the undergraduates, as German as possible for the sake of the graduates and the research personnel, as American as possible for the sake of the public at large—and as confused as possible for the sake of the preservation of the whole uneasy balance. (Kerr, 2001a: 14)

This analysis rests on Ortega's views about the English and German models and his advice to go beyond them to find an appropriate model for the times. As if this were not sufficiently clear, Kerr goes on to speak about the transformations American society was experiencing and the corresponding evolution of the university, announcing that "by the end of this period, there will be a truly American university," a unique institution "not looking to other models but serving, itself, as a model for universities in other parts of the globe" (2001a: 65). Following Ortega's ideas about education and hegemony, Kerr states:

> Each nation, as it has become influential, has tended to develop the leading intellectual institutions of its world—Greece, the Italian cities, France, Spain, England, Germany, and now the United States. The great universities have developed in the great periods of the great political entities of history. Today, more than ever, education is inextricably involved in the quality of a nation. (Kerr, 2001a: 65)

What Kerr is really saying here, although he probably would not put it in these words, is that the "multiversity" is the educational model of the American empire, which is the empire of what he calls the "knowledge industry" (2001a: 66).

In a subheading titled "Changes Still to Come," Kerr reviews a number of pending matters for the "multiversity," including the need to integrate knowledge and to create "a more unified intellectual world" (2001a: 89). In conclusion, he speculates that the university of the twenty-first century will have to combine aristocracy and democracy, elitism and populism, in order to rise to "the height of the times" (2001a: 91). Interestingly, this direct quote from Ortega's book is attributed in a note to Sir Walter Moberly.

*Sir Walter Moberly*

A British academic who held posts at various institutions of higher learning in the United Kingdom and was chairman of the University Grants Committee, as well as principal of the St. Catherine's Foundation, Sir Walter Moberly was the author of a book titled *The Crisis in the University*, which, published in 1949, not long after the end of World War II, offers a Christian vision of higher education. Following Hastings Rashdall (1936), a theologian and historian who compared the medieval university with the papacy and the empire, Moberly notes that universities are indeed power-houses and wonders how they will adapt to a world of insecurity, advancing the idea that they need "a new deal" (20).

Moberly's book presents an alternative to Flexner's critique of the modern university, drawing heavily on Ortega's theories. In particular, the idea that the university must "rise to the height of the times" is the central motif of the book. Moberly uses this idea to defend a practical vision of the university. Believing that, for better or worse, the post-war world was an industrialized "Great Society" (1949: 96), he expressed quite a positive view of the "red brick" universities, which brought a college education to a wide variety of people in the United Kingdom. The term "red brick" was coined by Edgar Allison Peers (1943), a professor of Spanish at the University of Liverpool, to describe the "civic universities," institutions of higher learning established after 1850 that offered broader access and a more practical curriculum than Oxford and Cambridge. These "red brick" universities included the University of Birmingham and the University of Manchester, where Moberly had held teaching and administrative posts. For Moberly, who was an Oxford graduate, the tradition of Oxford and Cambridge was paternalistic and linked to a feudal, rather than an industrial, model of society.

Moberly pays special attention to the factors that make the university a conservative institution, including its status as a guild, a medieval feature that has survived to the present time. This guild decides what should be its code of conduct, trains and admits new members and protects professional standards, including thinking "of the utmost strictness," for, as Moberly says borrowing from Ortega, at the university "slovenly thinking is taboo" (1949: 123). Left to itself, however, the guild is subject to "lethargy," seeing objections to change very clearly and objections to inaction not clearly at all:

> Dr. Flexner is, in general, warmly eulogistic of Oxford and Cambridge, but he was not without warrant when he wrote, "Progressive efforts are likely to encounter an impalpable, resistant tradition as difficult to penetrate as a London fog." A clever satirical analysis of types of argument current in university politics forty years ago arrives at the triumphant conclusion that "nothing must ever be done for the first time." (Moberly, 1949: 233)

According to Moberly, positions that are critical of occupational training are hypocritical and snobbish, since they still favor training for those occupations with high social prestige, such as law and medicine. He considers such positions "a relic of the aristocratic contempt of the landowner for the tradesman" or "of the brainworker for one who works with his hands" (1949: 168), asking whether law and medicine are more acceptable than "for instance glass technology or industrial fermentation" simply because "they are professions which gentleman have been accustomed to enter" (1949: 191). For him, the criterion for study of a field at the university is its treatment rather than its subject matter: "There is no subject matter which, in itself, is common or unclean" (1949: 191).

Believing that the problem was how to combine the pursuit of excellence with the demands of social justice, Moberly stated that, if the university could not enjoy all the advantages of the cloister, "it should make the most of those of the market place" (305). For him, the university must combine occupational training with culture, if students are to acquire "the freedom of the city" and to become something other than what Ortega called the "infra-man" or the "barbarian" (1949: 172).

Moberly thus used Ortega to oppose Flexner, whose book was very critical of the American university's "extra-mural work," which Flexner considered "sub-university," suggesting that those activities should be undertaken by other agencies. Moberly questioned whether Flexner was right about this or if, on the other hand, universities should take this work more seriously. At the end of the book, Moberly answered this question in unequivocal terms:

> For instance, should universities persevere with the activities represented by their Education and Extra-Mural Departments? They have for some time engaged in these, but for the most part, they have done so rather half-heartedly. Here they should make a decisive choice. If these activities are really "sub-university" in quality or are outside their proper function, they should gradually withdraw from them. Otherwise they should commit themselves to them more fully and energetically than they have yet done. We contend that, for both Departments, the second alternative is the right one. (Moberly, 1949: 306)

For Moberly, the university should be allowed to rise to "the height of the times." Kerr's acceptance of the "multiversity" shows that he had internalized this message. In addition, Kerr found inspiration in Moberly for his comments on the faculty guild, which begin with the quotation:

> "Nothing should ever be done for the first time" was the wry conclusion of F.M. Cornford from his vantage point as a classicist at Cambridge University at the turn of the century when Cambridge was stirring with responses to the modern world. "Nothing is ever done until everyone is convinced that it ought to be done, and has been convinced for so long that it is now time to do something else." (Kerr, 2001a: 72)

Taken from Moberly, who in turn took it from Rashdall, this humorous phrase by Francis M. Cornford expressed the radical conservatism of the institution. Kerr explains that faculty members are torn between the "guild" and the "socialist" views of the university:

> The guild view stands for self-determination, and for resistance against the administration and the trustees; the socialist view, for service to society which the administration and the trustees often represent. The guild view is elitist toward the external environment, conservative toward internal change, conformist in relation to the opinion of colleagues. The socialist view is democratic toward society, radical toward change, and nonconformist. And the political liberal is drawn toward both views. Here is a paradox. Few institutions are so conservative as the universities about their own affairs while their members are so liberal about the affairs of others; and sometimes the most liberal faculty member in one context is the most conservative in another. (Kerr, 2001a: 74-75)

Like Moberly, Kerr favors a university that is responsive to the world's new realities. Like Ortega, he is fond of coining new terms or using old terms with new meanings in order to express key concepts, as he did with the expression "multiversity."

This was not a new term, rather, it had been used by administrators and faculty members at various universities around the country and, as Kerr indicates, "was in the air, and had several more or less simultaneous authors" (2001a: 103). What Kerr did was to use it as a descriptive term and to construct a narrative, a vision, around it. The first time that he mentions this word is a few pages into chapter 1 of *The Uses of the University*, when he states that "neither the ancient classics and theology nor the German philosophers and scientists could set the tone for the really modern university—the multiversity" (2001a: 5). I think that Karl Jaspers was the German philosopher Kerr had primarily in mind. In particular, I believe that Jaspers was instrumental in making him decide to adopt the term "multiversity."

*Karl Jaspers*

Karl Jaspers, a contemporary of Ortega's, with whom he shared an interest in Existentialism, was a psychiatrist who turned from medicine to psychology and eventually to philosophy. His work is often compared to that of Martin Heidegger, although the two had great differences, not the least of which was that Heidegger was associated with the Nazis, while Jaspers, a liberal democrat with a Jewish wife, was persecuted by them. In 1946, Jaspers published a famous book about the general population's varying levels of complicity in the atrocities of the Third Reich titled *The Question of German Guilt*. After the war, Jaspers went back to teaching and was involved in helping to reorganize German higher education. In connection with these endeavors, in 1946, he revised a book he had originally penned in 1923 called *The Idea of the University*. Not unlike Cardinal Newman's masterpiece of the same title, Jaspers' book is a defense of a holistic approach to the university. Like Ortega, Jaspers is concerned with its mission.

The book begins with a straightforward definition of the university as "a community of scholars and students engaged in the task of seeking truth" (1959 [1946]: 1). This is reminiscent of Newman's view of the university as a family or "an Alma Mater, knowing her children one by one, not a foundry, or a mint, or a treadmill" (1996 [1891]: 105). Regardless of funding sources, the university runs its own affairs and enjoys academic freedom. The university combines teaching with research and is "the one place where by concession of state and society a given epoch may cultivate the clearest possible self-awareness" (1959 [1946]: 1). At the same time, state and society expect the university to look after their practical needs by training professionals of various kinds, which is done within academic parameters. The university attains its practical objectives "by an effort of the spirit which at first transcends them only to return to them afterwards with greater clarity, strength and calm" (1959 [1946]: 2). In other words, no matter how practical its objectives, the university works in scientific ways and produces new knowledge in addition to transmitting existing knowledge, because it is "the corporate realization of man's basic determination to know" (1959 [1946]: 2).

Jaspers believes that human beings have "a primary and unconditional thirst for knowledge" that makes them engage in a never-ending quest:

> Modern man remains intensely alive to the ancient wisdom that nothing except the discovery of truth gives meaning to our life (even though we lack final certainty as to what the meaning is and what it implies); that nothing is exempt from our desire

for knowledge; and that, above all, life seeks to base itself upon thought. (Jaspers, 1959 [1946]: 16)

The human craving for knowledge is insatiable because it is guided by a vision of the "oneness or wholeness of reality" (1959 [1946]: 21). Researchers look for the unity underlying plurality, they try to make sense of fragmentary knowledge. The desire for unity motivates the search for knowledge and gives it life and meaning.

According to Jaspers, "by its very name the university is a 'universe'" (1959 [1946]: 46). With its community of professors and students, this institution embodies the unity of knowledge. At the university, all disciplines are in close proximity, which "reawakens a sense of their connection and inspires efforts on behalf of their overall unity" (1959 [1946]: 67). Even the practical occupations are integrated by "defining their place within the whole of knowledge" (1959 [1946]: 80). Although the university resembles a group of schools with little in common, "an intellectual department store with an abundance of goods for every taste," this is "mere appearance since, if true, the university would simply disintegrate" (1959 [1946]: 80). That, however, has not happened. As society has become more complex, the university has evolved to meet its needs, and this will continue to happen, for "nothing can stop the continuing expansion of the university" (1959 [1946]: 88). This constant expansion of the university has created the impression that the university is a collection of unrelated fields, but to ignore new disciplines is a mistake:

> To ignore the presence of these newcomers is nothing but useless snobbery. The idea of the university requires that the university be open to new ideas. There is nothing which is not worth knowing about, no art which does not involve a form of knowledge. Only by unifying these various new lines of inquiry can the university do justice to them. The university is called upon to preserve the scientific spirit by transforming and assimilating the new materials and skills and integrating them in the light of a few leading ideas. (Jaspers, 1959 [1946]: 88-89)

In the middle of this constant growth, the university needs to keep its "aristocratic principles" (1959 [1946]: 97) and require that all new disciplines define their place within the whole of knowledge, because "broadening the scope of the university must initiate a genuine unification of all branches of learning" (1959 [1946]: 88).

Aware that the standing of the university depends on the quality of its students, as well as that of its professors, Jaspers discusses the admissions process in great detail. Stating that intelligence, creativity, and intellectual commitment are inaccessible to objective testing, which can only evaluate some aptitudes and those imperfectly, Jaspers is in favor of evaluating potential, for "the whole courage to educate derives from a trust in such dormant potentialities" (1959 [1946]: 106). In a chapter that contains echoes of Ortega, Jaspers considers the importance of finding the ablest of each generation to lead the masses. Although he thinks that people from disadvantaged backgrounds are severely handicapped and might never be able to overcome their deficiencies, he says that those who have a willingness to sacrifice must be allowed to follow their callings, even though they may be hampered by "imperfect initial equipment" (1959 [1946]: 111). Stating that all selection processes are unfair in one way or another, he favors a system in which the faculty would personally identify meritorious students, with a limited use of exams. Wondering if society is willing to delegate power to the elite and "reserve a place for an understanding beyond its comprehension" (1959 [1946]: 130), Jaspers concludes the book by stressing the importance of academic freedom. For him, as long as professors and students follow scholarly and professional rules when they defend their opinions, all ideas should be entertained. "Seeking truth and the improvement of mankind, the university aims to stand for man's humanity par excellence" (1959 [1946]: 134). This is why the university cherishes academic freedom and "would perish rather than carefully shelter itself from unfamiliar ideas and withdraw from intellectual conflict where fundamentals are involved" (1959 [1946]: 68).

It appears that Jaspers' reflections had a considerable impact on Kerr's ideas, including his famous 1961 comment defending the University of California's decision to allow an alleged communist to speak at Berkeley, which is currently engraved on a bell on the Santa Barbara campus:

> The university is not engaged in making ideas safe for students. It is engaged in making students safe for ideas. Thus it permits the freest expression of views before students, trusting to their good sense in passing judgment on these views. Only in this way can it best serve American democracy. (Kerr, 2003: 131)

This observation echoes Jaspers' argument that the university should not shelter itself from unfamiliar ideas or shy away from intellectual conflict.

Also related to Jaspers' thinking is Kerr's belief that it is important to "preserve a margin for excellence in a populist society" when there is pressure to spend money on behalf of all the people:

> The great university is of necessity elitist—the elite of merit—but it operates in an environment dedicated to an egalitarian philosophy. How may the contribution of the

elite be made clear to the egalitarians, and how may an aristocracy of intellect justify itself to a democracy of all men? It was equality of opportunity, not equality *per se*, that animated the founding fathers and the progress of the American system; but the forces of populist equality have never been silent, the battle between Jeffersonianism and Jacksonianism never finally settled. (Kerr, 2001a: 91)

Although less nuanced than Jaspers' comments on the subject, this statement follows their general spirit.

Finally, Jaspers contributed to Kerr's idea of the "multiversity" with his book, which is a response to Flexner's critique of the university. Unlike Flexner, Jaspers accepts the university's increased complexity as inevitable, thus reinforcing Ortega's and Moberly's ideas about bringing education up to the "height of the times." Jaspers' approach, however, explicitly seeks to find unity in complexity, emphasizing that "university" is related to "unity." In chapter 3 of *The Uses of the University*, under the heading of "Changes Still to Come," Kerr discusses the need to create a more unified intellectual world, to make contact among the cultures of the university and to open channels of communication across its disciplines in order "to answer fragmentation with general theories and sensitivities," adding that, "as knowledge is drawn together, if in fact it is, a faculty may again become a community of masters; but 'a sense of the unity...of all knowledge' is still a long way off" (2001a: 90). This direct quotation from Jaspers—the only one in the book—provides a glimpse of Kerr's thinking process. Convinced that the university's increased complexity was not reversible and aware of the difficulty in finding unity, he borrowed Jaspers' word game equating the "university" with "unity" and established a parallel between "multiversity" and "multiplicity" and a contrast between "university" and "multiversity." Whether or not the term "multiversity" had been used by others, Kerr made it his by charging it with meaning. The "multiversity" both denies and evokes the unity of the "university," thus expressing its current fragmentation and need for integration. Ortega's, Moberly's, and Jaspers' contributions to Kerr's vision of the university were, thus, considerable. If most of the information that Kerr used to describe the "multiversity" was taken from Flexner's, Veblen's, and Sinclair's commentaries, his philosophical approach came from Ortega, directly and indirectly via Moberly's interpretation, and from Jaspers.

### The Flavor: Robert Maynard Hutchins

Veblen, Sinclair, and Flexner provided the flour, and Ortega, Moberly, and Jaspers the leavening, that gave Kerr's book its shape and stature.

But there is more to *The Uses of the University* than flour and leavening. There is a third important ingredient: a flavor between sharp and humorous, with authoritative overtones, which I believe was provided by Hutchins.

## Robert Maynard Hutchins

At the time that Kerr wrote *The Uses of the University*, Hutchins was the most popular American university president, or rather ex-president, for he had stepped down from his position as chancellor of the University of Chicago in 1951 and become what has been characterized as "a prince in exile" (Dzuback, 1991: 229). Hutchins was indeed a charismatic character, very well-known in higher education and beyond. He was intelligent, charming, and witty. He also was very independent, which is probably why his administrative career ended after his struggles at the University of Chicago. As founder and director of the Center for the Study of Democratic Institutions, Hutchins spent all of his time thinking, writing, and speaking about the issues that were of most interest to him, an example that Kerr would later emulate when he accepted the presidency of the Carnegie Commission on Higher Education after his dismissal from the presidency of the University of California. Although for that, he had another important model, UC President Daniel Coit Gilman, who founded the Carnegie Institution of Washington after retiring from Johns Hopkins.

Hutchins had been a very prominent president who published many books and articles on the university during his tenure, including *The Higher Learning in America*, a 1936 study in which he criticized the "service station" concept of the university and its "love of money" (1952 [1936]: 6). Hutchins famously declared that "the justification for the privileges of universities is not to be found in their capacity to take the sons of the rich and render them harmless to society or to take the sons of the poor and teach them how to make money" (1952 [1936]: 58). Like Irving Babbitt (1986) and the new humanists, for whom America needed reflection and wisdom more than it required action and knowledge, Hutchins favored literature over science. He was a relentless champion of general education, understood as the study of the classics, which he believed provided much needed unity to the university. In *The Uses of the University*, Kerr places Hutchins among the greatest American academic leaders. For him, Hutchins was the last of the giants, because "he was the last of the university presidents who really tried to change his institution and higher education in any fundamental way" (2001a: 25).

Hutchins became well-known, in part because of his vision of the great books of Western Civilization as the heart of higher learning, and in part because of his personality. He maintained a focus on his ideas, and he did it with great gusto, energy, and humor. He also was a great defender of academic freedom and made very critical comments about the excesses of the McCarthy era, as can be seen in his 1956 book *Freedom, Education and the Fund*. Kerr, who held similar political beliefs, was in a position to appreciate Hutchins' courage, which he thought was greater than his own.

Although, in the 1963 edition of *The Uses of the University*, Kerr did not use the hedgehog/fox metaphor, he discussed the same idea using Hutchins' distinction between "troublemaker" and "officeholder." Hutchins, by his own admission, was a troublemaker, that is, a hedgehog, a transformational leader, someone who makes things happen, and so was Kerr, who endorsed his views: "The case for leadership has been strongly put by Hutchins. A university needs a purpose, 'a vision of the end.' If it is to have a 'vision,' the president must identify it" (Kerr, 2001a: 24).

Kerr points out that Hutchins' vision of the university was focused on the horizontal contacts of the undergraduate college versus the vertical relationships of the graduate school. Indeed, Hutchins, who was critical of the university's excessive specialization and fragmentation, comparing it to an encyclopedia whose "unity can be found only in its alphabetical arrangement" (1952 [1936]: 95), was trying to find an academic glue that would hold the various parts of the university together, as well as to rethink its purpose:

> My education as an administrator began when at the age of thirty-two I opened Aristotle's *Ethics* for the first time and read, "In practical matters the end is the first principle." I was shocked to realize that in the ten years I had been in universities I had never seriously asked myself what they were for. (Hutchins, 1956: 18)

Whereas Hutchins answers this question by rejecting contemporary developments and going back to the idea of a liberal arts education, Kerr moves forward, enumerating the multiple "uses" of the university, which he renames "multiversity."

As a good hedgehog, Kerr draws on ideas from many sources, which he makes his own, sometimes by affirming them, other times by contradicting them. For example, Kerr's idea of the "multiversity" builds on a humorous remark by Hutchins on the nature of the modern university:

Hutchins once described the modern university as a series of separate schools and departments held together by a central heating system. In an area where heating is less important and the automobile more, I have sometimes thought of it as a series of individual faculty entrepreneurs held together by a common grievance over parking. (Kerr, 2001a: 15)

Many of Hutchins' witty comments are still quoted by administrators, as are Kerr's, both leaders having achieved legendary status in academia.

Robert Nisbet (1992), who greatly admired the work of Robert Sproul as President of the University of California, was very critical of Hutchins, with whom he said Sproul was often "invidiously compared" (107). According to George A. Pettitt (1966), Hutchins and Sproul "did not always see eye-to-eye" (143). The two men started their presidential tenures at the same time and each served for more than two decades. Both faced skepticism from the faculty, Hutchins because of his youth and Sproul because of his lack of academic credentials. But Sproul overcame the faculty's skepticism, while Hutchins did not. According to Nisbet, "Hutchins never understood the nature of a university, or, perhaps understanding it, disliked it," while "Sproul loved the university from the start and came to have an understanding of the institution that could, in performance, have scarcely been improved upon" (107). He believes that this is why Sproul left Kerr a vibrant university, whereas that did not happen with Hutchins in Chicago.

What Nisbet is really saying is that Sproul was a very successful fox, who was able to build a strong university, while Hutchins was a failed hedgehog, because his vision did not prosper. Indeed, Nisbet is very critical of Hutchins' vision, both in terms of his defense of the classics and his attack on sports, which, in Nisbet's opinion, "proved to be quite as grievous a blow to a great university as almost anything else Boy Wonder Hutchins did" (88). For Nisbet, the undergraduate college Hutchins created was as separate from the rest of the university "as would have been a Trappist monastery" (20), and the reading of the Great Books was actually a review of excerpts that were referred to as "Hutchins' Great Snippets" (20).

It is true that Hutchins had limited success at implementing his vision. Very few people today really believe in his Great Books theory, which even at the time it was enunciated was criticized by scholars such as Julián Marías (1972 [1956]), who found the reading list unusually anglocentric. This type of criticism would grow over time, as people began to question the relevance of the Western canon. Yet Hutchins is remembered with interest and nostalgia and continues to be studied and cited. Hutchins still appeals to us in part because of the brave stands he took on academic freedom, which still resonate with academics today, and partly because of his passionate convictions about the curriculum. Although widely believed today to be mistaken in their details, these contained core truths: the love of scholarship should be stronger than the love of money, and the university should have some sort of unity or coherence—a soul. Kerr once said that Hutchins was the person with whom he "disagreed most consistently" and "admired most unreservedly" (Gray, 2009a: 11). Indeed, Hutchins was the last great university president "to see the academic world in terms of a moral compass" (Gray, 1998: 113). Hutchins failed because his hedgehog vision was old-fashioned and because he was not enough of a fox to be able to persuade the faculty to adopt it and make it last, as he suggests himself when he confesses that he lacked patience (1956: 185). Kerr, who had significant fox abilities, including his negotiating skills, was a very successful hedgehog whose vision was adopted and lasted beyond his expectations. He did what Sproul, with all his accomplishments, could not do: match and surpass the "Boy Wonder of Chicago" (Nisbet: 20).

In chapter 6, Kerr compares himself to Hutchins, the only other sitting university president in the twentieth century who spoke openly about the modern research university, and says that both had to pay a high political price for being "indiscreet" (2001a: 160). This is a hedgehog problem. Visions need to be shared, but sharing visions leads to making enemies and shortening political lives, as Hutchins himself saw very clearly.

By introducing the metaphor of the fox and the hedgehog in chapter 9 (2001), and including both Hutchins and himself in the hedgehog category, Kerr subtly echoes his statement in chapter 1 (1963) that Hutchins was the last of the giants and implicitly adds himself to that list. Kerr was indeed the last of the giants, but was he the last of the hedgehogs?

# 4

# Language and Vision in
# *The Uses of the University*

Kerr had a striking ability to use language to express his vision, a talent he shared with Hutchins, who excelled at crafting memorable quotes, such as his wry remarks about the busy and difficult life of the administrator, who "should never do today what he can put off till tomorrow. He should never do anything he can get anybody to do for him" (1956: 175). Although it appeared that he had taken these ideas from Harper, who believed that these two maxims should "regulate the work of the chief officer of a university" (Gray, 2004: 100), Hutchins made them his own by infusing humor into them. The administrator, according to Hutchins, had many ways to lose and no way to win, because "almost every decision an administrator makes is a decision against somebody" (1956: 172). If a decision is made to raise one faculty member's salary, "the administrator quickly learns that such a decision is really a decision not to raise the salaries of the other men in the same department" (1956: 172). That is why most administrators are "officeholders," not "troublemakers." "Officeholders" make fewer decisions and thus offend fewer people than "troublemakers" do.

Kerr also produced many memorable quotations, including his famous 1950s declaration that his most important administrative problems as chancellor of the Berkeley campus were "sex for the students, athletics for the alumni, and parking for the faculty" (Kerr, 2001a: 138), a statement that was considered risqué enough to be picked up by *Time* and *Playboy* (Kerr, 2001b: 126). In the 1982 version of *The Uses of the University* (or chapter 5 of the 2001 edition), he revised this statement to say that, at that moment, the problems were, instead, "athletics for the students who have gone 'straight,' sex for the professors with some of whom the counterculture still finds support, and parking for the alumni as they return for their refresher courses" (2001a: 139). What began as a casual comment at a faculty meeting, where professors complained about parking and which took place just after a panty raid and during a corruption scandal in the Pacific Conference, became a much-repeated sound bite, because it captured the concerns of the times. Kerr later revised the quip to reflect the transformations that were taking place at the university. Jokes like this were a type of storytelling. People repeated them, not just because they were funny but because they helped make sense of events that were unfolding.

Although these stories were memorable, Kerr's greatest linguistic contribution, in my opinion, was the fact that he coined a great number of terms that have become widely used in the academic community. These expressions are not isolated, but rather constitute a complete vocabulary reflecting a holistic vision of higher education. Ironically, this vision is one of fragmentation, as we have seen with the most famous term he coined, the "multiversity." Although I believe that Jaspers' reflections on the university were instrumental in making Kerr choose this term, there were other influences, including Rashdall (1936), who appears to have been his main source with respect to the history of the university from medieval times to the present.

Rashdall begins his monumental history explaining that, contrary to what many people think, "universitas" does not mean "institution for the teaching or for the cultivation of universal knowledge," but merely "a number, a plurality, an aggregate of persons" or a "legal corporation," the corporation of masters or of students (1936, I: 5). So Kerr knew that "university" meant plurality and that Jaspers' reflections on the unity of the university were based on a false etymology. As Kerr says in chapter 4, the term "university" had become associated with the vision "of a unified 'community of masters and students' with a single 'soul' or purpose" (2001a: 102). By coining the term "multiversity," he underscored not only the contemporary fragmentation of the university but also the original meaning of university as plurality. "To discover is to name something correctly" (Ramón y Cajal, 2000 [1898]: 54). Kerr's term was correct, because the university had always been a "multiversity." It was just that it had become more so over time. The university was always complex and was always connected to business. In fact, it was modeled after the merchants' corporations. Again, the only difference was that business had expanded, and the linkages between the university and the corporate world had become stronger and more obvious. Aware of all this, Kerr was comfortable accepting the reality that Hutchins, Flexner, Sinclair, and Veblen had deplored.

In fact, Kerr did more than accept the reality of the "multiversity" and name it. He described it "with exceptional clarity and insight" and without trying to impose any views, "other than to note that popular opinion seemed to be that the university should continue to perform any tasks society assigns to it" (Lucas, 1996: 82-83). Kerr also named its key characteristics, as well as the stages of its development. The most important characteristic of the "multiversity" is that it is the institution of the "knowledge industry" (2001a: 66). Kerr borrowed this term from Fritz Machlup (1962), the author of a comprehensive study of the production and distribution of knowledge in the United States, which he believes falls "into the economist's domain" (3). Quoting Adam Smith, who wrote that "a man educated at the expense of much labour and time to any of those employments which require extraordinary dexterity and skill, may be compared to one of those expensive machines" (1914 [1776]: 90), Machlup sets out to analyze knowledge from an economic point of view, making educated predictions about future developments in higher education.

These are activities dear to Kerr, whose most important book in the area of industrial relations, *Industrialism and Industrial Man*, written with John T. Dunlop, Frederik H. Harvison, and Charles A. Myers in 1960, is a structuralist analysis of industrialization. This book presents industrialization as undertaken by one of the following five types of movers or leading groups: A dynastic elite, the middle class, revolutionary intellectuals, colonial administrators, and nationalist leaders. Each chapter studies some aspects of industrialization in connection with these five types of leading groups. The book, which is a very methodical and comprehensive study of the rules governing "industrialism" and the behavior of what its authors call "industrial man," ends with a chapter on "the road ahead." This road leads to "pluralistic industrialism," which involves tension between the forces of uniformity, linked to technology, and those of diversity, tied to the preservation of identity. "Pluralistic industrialism" has "a split personality looking in two directions at the same time" (1960: 295). This tension, together with the battle between the manager and the managed, will characterize the future:

> These threads of conflict will continue when class war, and the contest over private versus public initiative, and the battle between monistic and atomistic ideologies have been left far behind in the sedimentary layers of history. (Kerr, Dunlop, Harvison, & Myers, 1960: 296)

The book predicts that "industrial man" will identify closely with his occupation, acting more like a "member of a guild than of a class or of a plant community" (1960: 294).

One thing this work stresses is the importance of education in an industrial society, which requires high levels of training for the elite, as well as a solid preparation for all citizens. In fact, the book calls education "the handmaiden of industrialism" (1960: 36) and indicates that in this kind of production system, education is "a leading industry" (1960: 286). What is more, in an industrial society, "the university becomes more the model for the enterprise than the enterprise for the university" (1960: 289). In other words, the university is at the very heart of industrialism. Similar views had previously been expressed by Elwood P. Cubberley, for whom American schools are "factories in which the raw products (children) are to be shaped and fashioned into products to meet the various demands of life" (Cowley & Williams, 1991: 164). With a perspective reminiscent of Ortega's (1993 [1930]), this book explains that education brings equality to the "universal industrial mass" (1960: 289) and helps bring consensus to society. At the same time, "education brings a demand for liberty and can help create conditions in which it is safe to grant it" (1960: 289-290). Thus, industrialism creates "areas of control and areas of freedom, weaving a web of rules and liberating the individual" (1960: 290).

Kerr's vision of the "multiversity" spells out in detail what is expressed in a shorthand manner in *Industrialism and Industrial Man*: that the university is at the very heart of the economy. As such, it follows certain cycles. For example, Kerr spoke about the "federal grant university" as a stage following the "land grant university" and preceding what he called the "private grant university." The "federal grant university" ("riches at the national level"), or "Multiversity I," coincides with "Tidal Wave I," or the great influx of students caused by the baby boom, while the "private grant university" ("poverty at the state level"), or "Multiversity II," coincides with "Tidal Wave II," the second great influx of students caused by the children of the baby boomers coming of age (2001a: 175-177). Tidal Wave II includes three types of students: Market I (traditional students), Market II (non-traditional students) and Market III (retirees) (2001a: 214). Of course, the "land grant university" was federal as well, but the influence of the federal government on the university in the nineteenth century was relatively limited, while it reached very high levels in the twentieth century. Frederick Rudolph (1962) stated that the question "was no longer *whether* the federal government should support higher education but *how*" (490). In addition to relying on Rudolph, Kerr's 1963 vision of the "federal grant university" was influenced by a book about the interconnections between higher education and the federal government edited by Charles G. Dobbins (1963), in which the then-special assistant to the president of the United States, McGeorge Bundy, states that hostility to the federal government's money is "as senseless as tilting at a windmill," because "the windmill is here to stay, and it is no man's enemy" (94). Kerr, who was principled but also practical, did not adopt such a quixotic attitude and accepted the influence of the federal government, albeit with reservations.

Kerr explains the many ways in which the federal government affected higher education, including favoring the sciences over the humanities, graduate education over undergraduate education and research over teaching. Such preferences affected budgets, space, administrators and faculty, and created what he calls the "unfaculty." This term, reminiscent of the characters in the 1957 movie "The Undead," or ghosts who are neither dead nor alive, refers to non-tenure-track faculty members—invisible workers who assume the tasks abandoned by the research-oriented, tenure-track faculty of the "federal grant university." The "unfaculty" is the reverse of what Robert Bendiner (1962) called the "non-teacher," meaning a faculty member who teaches very little or not at all. Kerr's "faculty/unfaculty" terminology is much more powerful than "non-teacher/teacher" because it focuses on the marginal status of those doing much work with little recognition, thus highlighting the internal dislocations of the "multiversity." These have affected the faculty, who are in transition from an "academic guild" system to an "academic contracting" system (2001a: 168-169).

Kerr is in favor of finding a balance between federal needs and institutional desires, advocating an active partnership with the federal government. In fact, in this chapter, which can be read as a response to McGeorge Bundy's essay, Kerr endorses the 1960 American Assembly's proposal to establish a Council of Education Advisers, similar to the President's Council of Economic Advisers, saying that the interaction between the federal government and higher education has to be a two-way conversation. Instead of tilting at the windmill, he wanted to use its energy for his own purposes.

Another set of terms that Kerr coined involved the "city of intellect," as opposed to the university's previous stages as a "town" and a "village." He borrowed this idea from Jacques Barzun's 1959 book *The House of Intellect*, from which he also appears to have appropriated the expression "tidal wave" (96) to refer to massive student numbers. But Kerr also may have been inspired by Daniel Coit Gilman, one of the first presidents of the University of California, who used the same expression to refer to pressing political demands from the state, complaining about "no legislature in thirteen months; and then the tidal wave of what sort of democracy?" (Cordasco, 1960: 52). Barzun (1959) says that "divided against itself, the house of intellect has lost its sense of being a company apart" (10) and laments that the intellectual class has been "captivated by art, overawed by science, and seduced by philanthropy" (27), including federal and private donors, who want to buy knowledge in the same way as they buy "soap and chairs" (206). The university, in turn, wants to obtain prestige, a practice "ratified if not required by the donors" (192). Kerr believes that Barzun's "house of intellect" is inward looking, while the modern university must look outward. It cannot afford to be "a company apart." This is why he favors the term "city of intellect," which he uses to describe the "multiversity" and compare it with Newman's "village" and Flexner's "town:"

> The "Idea of a University" was a village with its priests. "The Idea of a Modern University" was a town—a one-industry town—with its intellectual oligarchy. "The Idea a Multiversity" is a city of infinite variety. Some get lost in the city; some rise to the top within it; most fashion their lives within one of its many subcultures. There is less sense of community than in the village but also less sense of confinement. There is less sense of purpose than within the town but there are more ways to excel. There are also more refuges of anonymity—both for the creative person and the drifter. As against the village and the town, the "city" is more like the totality of civilization as it has evolved and more an integral part of it; and movement to and from the surrounding society has been greatly accelerated. As in a city, there are many separate endeavors under a single rule of law. (Kerr, 2001a: 31)

According to Kerr, the university's spatial organization reflects its history, with the library and the humanities in the central part of the campus, surrounded by the sciences, the professional schools and then industry interspersed with inexpensive housing. For him, "an almost ideal location for a modern university is to be sandwiched between a middle-class district on its way to becoming a slum and an ultramodern industrial park—so that the students may live in the one and the faculty may consult in the other" (2001a: 67).

Kerr continues with the "city of intellect" metaphor by creating a synonymous expression, "ideopolis," and discussing how universities have a tendency to coalesce. Comparing universities with peaks and mountain ranges—a borrowed metaphor (Nevins, 1962), Kerr finds three ranges of important universities: the East Coast, California, and the Big Ten. Each cluster can be seen as a "metropolis," and the reader can imagine the skyline upon reading Kerr's poetic comment that "the constellation is greater than the single star and adds to the brightness of the sky" (2001a: 70).

Kerr goes beyond this national metaphor to an international one when he speaks of two cities of intellect: Eastern and Western. Written during the Cold War, his book ends with a reflection on the power of intellect and its limits. According to Kerr, "the organized intellect is a great machine that has gained extraordinary momentum since the Greeks got it going 2500 years ago." This machine "turns out its countless new pieces of knowledge but with little thought for their consequences—their impact on the environment—like a new insecticide" (2001a: 92). Concerned with nuclear war, Kerr wonders if the intellect can handle the problems it creates in the course of solving other problems. Kerr, who believed that the way of the future was more a "middle class democracy" than the "dictatorship of the proletariat," thought that the two "cities of intellect," Eastern and Western, were not only sources of weapons, but also "a potential bridge between their two societies" (2001a: 94). His tale of two cities ends with a statement to the effect that the intellect can be key to solving the war between "the ideological giants who now rend the world with their struggles" (2001a: 94). Although firmly on the side of the West, his metaphor of this cosmic "city of intellect" is hopeful and conciliatory.

How did Kerr get away with coining so many terms? Why did people take his amusing linguistic creations so seriously? Kerr was famous—president of the University of California and the author of the California Master Plan for Higher Education—and that gave him a great deal of credibility. That is why Harvard University invited him to give the three lectures that constitute the nucleus of *The Uses of the University* and then published the book. His success at promoting his terminology was partly due to his prominent position. But it was also due to his nature as a true visionary. Kerr was a hedgehog. As such, he liked to tell stories, because imagination is about memory. Visions are built by projecting the past onto the future. Brian Boyd (2009) studies the connections among evolution, cognition, and fiction, concluding that telling false stories is necessary to prepare for an unpredictable future, as they help us rehearse possible scenarios. I believe that vision can be understood as the ability to tell credible stories about the future based upon our experience of the past, stories that people feel capable of making come true with their actions.

Kerr not only was a hedgehog, but played the part of the hedgehog in his book, which is full of lists of "changes still to come." He had great confidence in his ability to anticipate the future and was addicted to "the crystal ball." Indeed, each new edition of *The Uses of the University* reviews the success or failure of previous predictions and makes new ones. In fact, Kerr begins the last chapter of the last edition of *The Uses of the University* by discussing his earlier predictions:

> I welcome this opportunity to play, once again, the tantalizing guessing game about the future, although I realize it is a game at which one wins only under very special circumstances. My 1963 lectures came at a time of those special circumstances. Those lectures turned out to be very prescient. I am not convinced that their foresight can be duplicated in the year 2000, but trying to look ahead may have some value, such as helping to identify the types of leaders to choose and the problems they might encounter. (Kerr, 2001a: 198-199)

In the prologue to this edition, Kerr indicates that he no longer possesses the "20/20 vision" he had in 1963 (2001a: vii). According to Kerr, it was harder to make predictions in 2000 than in 1963, because the alignment of forces that was evident in the early 1960s was lacking at the beginning of the new millennium. Instead of compatible forces, he sees conflicting ones, which makes him believe that this is a time for foxes, rather than for hedgehogs:

> In the 1960s many of us had a hedgehog view of the three big forces at work: universal access, progress through science, and increasing productivity; and we were correct. But we also had blinders on and looked straight ahead. We too often ignored the pathologies. And we seldom saw the rise of the student rebellion until too late and then treated it too often as just an interference with the urgent pursuit of our visions. Academic leaders of this new century, or at least of its early decades, may be able to identify no great single vision to guide them or great and compatible forces to dominate them; they may need to look in more directions, to be sensitive to many diverse opportunities and to many threats. They may best be foxes. (Kerr, 2001a: 208-209)

This is both a self-portrait—the hedgehog with blinders who ran into trouble with the student revolts, which a fox, more sensitive to the environment, might have been able to avoid—and a reflection that if times are going to bring more such crises, foxes might be better than hedgehogs at dealing with them. Although foxes do not have a clear picture of history, they might be better at defending themselves and their institutions when there are too many things happening at once, a situation that Kerr believes "is not suited to concentration on one or a very few great visions" (2001a: 209). In this context, "only the fox is alert enough, clever enough, agile enough, not blinded by big visions, survivalist enough to make its way through all the complexities, all the traps" (2001a: 226).

Although Kerr says that there are many opportunities for foxes "to turn challenges into triumphs" (2001a: 229), one gets the impression that he really does not expect many triumphs. Underpinning Kerr's belief that this is a time for foxes, there seems to be a sense that it is also a time of decline. Any major accomplishment would require vision. The fact that Kerr does not see a place for vision must mean that he thought that decline was imminent and unstoppable—just the milieu for foxes. Indeed, Kerr stated that higher education in the United States was "adrift," because the country was "adrift" (2001a: 210). When he looked ahead, his "crystal ball" got cloudy.

What made Kerr believe that he could and should see the future? I think that Kerr's training had a great deal to do with his love of forecasting. That is what economists do, and Kerr, who had a Ph.D. in Economics and was professor of Industrial Relations, was very comfortable speculating about the future of the university. As noted before, his book *Industrialism* concludes with a chapter on "the road ahead." That book addresses the issue of forecasting explicitly: "men attempt to peer ahead, to understand the structure of history, to alter the process of history" (1960: 288). In other words, visions of a future encourage people to choose that future and become true only if they do so. In 1963, Kerr knew the kind of future people were choosing, and he encouraged them to continue on this path. People took his witty linguistic creations so seriously because they rang true. His metaphors articulated a vision that many people recognized and wanted to realize. They were a mirror in which they saw themselves reflected.

But some people today do not see themselves reflected in *The Uses of the University*. The "guarded confusion" Kerr professes is too gloomy (2001a: x). He does not anticipate new sources of inspiration and motivation. He expresses the exhaustion of a paradigm, without hinting at the possibility of a paradigm change. He refers to the disappearance of hedgehogs without looking for them in all quarters. In fact, there are plenty of hedgehogs among women and minorities. There are many hedgehogs among white males for that matter. They just do not happen to get chosen to be university presidents. The mirror of Kerr's metaphors does not reflect everyone equally well. Non-traditional members of academia look for their image in the mirror and find only faint and distorted reflections. What did Kerr think about diversity?

# 5

## Diversity and Inclusiveness in
## *The Uses of the University*

Kerr saw himself as someone from a modest economic background who had done well, which affirmed his belief in the importance of equality of opportunity. He did not seem to realize that he had enjoyed many advantages. First, he was a white male. Would he have become chancellor at Berkeley and president of the UC system in the 1950s and 1960s if he had been a person of color and/or a woman, when even today these institutions continue to be led by white males? Second, his parents were not by any means poor. On the contrary, they had enough money to live comfortably and to send all of their children to top private colleges. Finally, and most importantly, Kerr's parents understood the higher education system. His father was college educated, as were his paternal grandfather, uncles, and aunts. In fact, his paternal aunt had a Ph.D. from the University of Pennsylvania and was the executive director of the American Association of University Women. Even his mother, who was not college educated, had a brother who was a very successful lawyer. In addition, as Kerr points out, his mother's best friend was the local teacher. His family may not have been rich, but it had a great deal of cultural capital and enough money to provide him with a top education. Kerr's situation could not be compared to that of students who come from truly disadvantaged families, such as the children of minority farm workers with elementary educations.

In her study of why certain underprivileged Latinos succeed, Patricia Gándara (1995) discusses various factors, such as having very hard-working and competitive parents who take pride in their work and having family myths about the accomplishments of previous generations, which Kerr obviously had. Gándara excludes from her study all Latinos who have at least one parent with a high school education, because this automatically elevates their chances of success. Kerr had a highly educated father and plenty of college-educated relatives, who provided him with role models in addition to information. Thus, Kerr's self-image as a farm boy who did well was not entirely accurate, for it hid the many advantages that he had enjoyed. Had he been a woman and/or a member of a minority group, and if he had had parents with less cultural capital and fewer economic resources, his life experience might have been quite different.

When we examine *The Uses of the University* from an archeological point of view, we find that the first three chapters, which are the original 1963 text and were never revised, are optimistic and forward-looking, while later additions (1972, chapter 4; 1981, chapter 5; 1995, chapters 6, 7, and 8) are increasingly gloomy, culminating with the strong pessimism of the last edition (2001, chapter 9), noted by David L. Kirp (2003). Kerr himself discussed this evolution in chapter 8 (1995): "I have moved from guarded optimism to guarded pessimism, but I remain an unguarded Utopian: I believe that we can become 'a nation of educated people'" (2001a: 196). Kerr shared this belief with Howard R. Bowen (1982), who had a vision of a "nation of educated people" who would be "taking better care of their health, investing their wealth more effectively, behaving more efficiently as consumers, developing more fully their economic skills, and participating more widely and more wisely in political and cultural life" (Kerr, 2001a: 226).

According to Kerr, Bowen was one of the last optimistic hedgehogs of the 1960s, with whom he shared "tunnel visions of a better world through the efforts of the modern university" (2001a: 226). In 2001, Kerr looked around and saw "many things occurring, not one or two big things, all at once and with and against each other—a natural habitat for the fox" (2001a: 228).

Could Kerr have missed something? After all, he was not in the midst of events and had not been for a very long time. He could no longer easily collect concepts—the building blocks of vision—because he was not working anymore and therefore did not have the same kind of intense exposure to ideas that were in the air. What if he had missed a key piece in the puzzle? Would that not have prevented him from connecting the other pieces into a meaningful narrative?

There is indeed one issue that Kerr seems to have underestimated, if not missed, and that is diversity. The California Master Plan for Higher Education did not anticipate the present-day diversity of California, according to John A. Douglass (2000). In fact, most of the tensions sur-rounding the Master Plan today can be connected to diversity in one way or another. The Master Plan was a remarkable achievement, but Kerr's hedgehog vision had one blind spot: he did not anticipate that this plan would segregate the student population along the color line, which was indeed the problem of the twentieth century, as W.E.B. DuBois (1903a) predicted over one hundred years ago. By reducing access to the Univer-sity of California and redirecting students to California State University and the community colleges, the Master Plan created obstacles to the preparation of minority elites, or, as DuBois (1903b) called them, "the talented tenth."

According to Mary Clark Stuart (1980), diversity is an area that does not seem to have fully entered Kerr's field of vision, although he was in many ways a pioneer in terms of his thinking about equality of op-portunity. For example, he eliminated segregation in student organiza-tions and created the university's first student outreach programs during his presidency (Douglass, 2007). Kerr probably did not completely understand the depth of feeling surrounding diversity or its increasing importance to the state, the country, and the world. This is not to say that Kerr did not know, or did not care about, the demands of a diverse society. He did, but he considered this to be one of many factors affect-ing higher education, whereas a growing number of people today see it as one of the most important challenges facing the university and the broader community.

Kerr's comments about gender and ethnic diversity in *The Uses of the University* seem to support this view. First of all, women and minorities have a very low profile in the 1963 version of the book (chapters 1-3), which does, however, discuss equality of opportunity. Although this was a topic of great interest to Kerr, he appears to have been thinking mostly about equality of opportunity for people of low socio-economic backgrounds. Gender and ethnicity are not discussed until chapter 4 (1974), and then only to say that their consideration had been introduced at the university by the federal government in the 1960s. This idea is further expanded in chapter 5 (1982), where Kerr indicates that, thanks to the efforts of the federal government, more women and minorities are attending college and obtaining faculty positions, "but most of them come from the higher income groups. Progress in increasing attendance from low-income groups has been meager" (2001a: 129).

Chapter 5 begins by reviewing some of the events that had taken place since 1963, including the establishment of affirmative action. Kerr then

identifies six recent changes, the last of which is that a higher proportion of students are women and minorities. But immediately after that,
he states that "none of these is a fundamental change" (2001a: 123).
The chapter continues with an analysis of "fundamental changes at-
tempted—and failed." One of these does involve diversity:

> Some changes of the 1960's were based not on academic but on political concerns
> and were forced into practice by student pressure, changes such as programs in Black
> studies, Native American Studies, and Hispanic studies. Faculty members generally
> never liked them; in fact, barely tolerated them. Born in the passion of student activ-
> ism, they have mostly withered, or at least wilted, in the silent embrace of faculty
> committees. (Kerr, 2001a: 127-128)

These programs, however, have not withered. On the contrary, they have
prospered. Kerr acknowledged this miscalculation in the 1995 edition
(chapter 6):

> I was clearly wrong about one internal reform: the development of African-American
> Studies, Hispanic Studies, Asian Studies, Native American Studies, and Women's
> Studies—if these are looked upon as internal rather than external reform efforts; actu-
> ally they were both. These areas of study have taken off in recent years. One campus
> I know well has more than one hundred courses in these areas in its catalogue. I think
> this is because, once these areas were opened up, students chose them in substantial
> numbers (sometimes encouraged by requirements), and then budgets and faculty
> positions followed closely on student choices of courses. I did not anticipate this
> because such courses have few vocational or professional uses, and students had been
> generally moving in vocational and professional directions. The search for supportive
> academic and social environments has been much greater than I anticipated. Also,
> these developments had much external support. (Kerr, 2001a: 161)

This explanation shows that Kerr had failed to understand the students'
feelings. Although he had a strong intellectual commitment to the idea
of equality of opportunity, he had trouble putting himself in the shoes
of women and minorities. It was difficult for him to understand their
emotions, their need to learn about themselves, and their interest in
discovering what was holding them back. He thought that gender and
ethnic studies were divisive. He also wondered whether diversity led in
the direction of greater social integration "or rather from the once externally enforced segregation toward more self-chosen internal separatism
on the campus, and toward the teaching more of competitive and even
antagonistic cultures than of an understanding of comparative cultures"
(2001a: 167).

In the same chapter, Kerr laments the disintegration of the guild
status of the faculty, listing affirmative action among the contributing
factors. So, as recently as 1995, Kerr seemed clearly uneasy about the

consequences of increasing gender and ethnic diversity in the academy. But he continued to think about this, and in the prologue to the 2001 edition, he provided a critical comment about his 1995 views:

> Looking back, I now note their generally pessimistic tone: the demise of "liberal education" for undergraduates, the fractionalization of the campus by fields of study, by ideologies, by gender and ethnic status. At the same time, however, it was clear that the American university had become the supreme research institution in the world. (Kerr, 2001a: viii-ix)

Kerr understood that more needed to be done in the area of diversity and inclusiveness and, in chapter 9 (2001), placed extending more opportunities to women and minorities on a list of unfinished business items from the twentieth century. In the same chapter, he enumerates fifteen factors affecting higher education that would be of interest to him if he were a fox in the twenty-first century. These include "the changing demographics among state populations" (2001a: 227).

If diversity were considered a fundamental change—not one of a long list of factors affecting higher education but one of the top three or four—would a different picture emerge? Could diversity be the missing piece of the puzzle? Did Kerr concede to the shrewdness of the fox because his hedgehog vision was becoming blurred? Would he have arrived at a different conclusion if he had realized that the ultimate destination was "a *diverse* nation of educated people?"

# 6

# The Plot of *The Uses of the University*

Kerr never updated the original text of *The Uses of the University*. Instead, he added chapters over the years. He probably did not want to tamper with the original version of the book—the first three chapters—because it had become a classic; thus, the archeological nature of his book shows several layers of thinking. It is interesting to speculate about how the original text of the book (the first three chapters) could have been rewritten in light of comments he made in later chapters and in his other works and considering what we know about current conditions affecting the university.

If we go back to the 1963 text of *The Uses of the University*, we see that Kerr's analysis was very concise. He studied the transformations the university was experiencing by reviewing its history and focusing on three aspects of its evolution, namely, its new mission (knowledge production for a knowledge-based economy), its new funding pattern (the "federal grant university"), and its new structure (the fragmentation of the "multiversity"). These three developments had resulted in a very complex institution, which he calls the city of intellect, or "a city of infinite variety" (2001a: 31), as opposed to the two previous stages of the university, which he describes as a town and a village, respectively. Kerr did not propose an "idea" of the university, but rather discussed its multiple "uses," which was "a recognition of the breakdown of any substantive principle of unity" (Touraine, 1997: 269).

According to Kerr, life in the multiversity is complex. The students are "older, more likely to be married, more vocationally oriented, more drawn from all classes and races than the students in the village, and they find themselves in a most intensely competitive atmosphere. They identify less with the total community and more with its subgroups" (2001a:

31). Faculty members also have changed. They are "less members of the particular university and more colleagues within their national academic discipline groups" (2001a, p. 33).

Kerr notes that, although the "multiversity" has many problems, it has a great deal to offer, including "consistency with the surrounding society." Indeed, "it has no peers in all history among institutions of higher learning in serving so many of the segments of an advancing civilization" (2001a: 33-34). Critics such as Robert Paul Wolff (1997) have warned that the "multiversity" does not always meet "human need," although it might be quite responsive to "market demand" (36). They also have found Kerr's comments about the "multiversity" excessively positive, indeed celebratory. Kerr, however, thought that he was just describing and accepting an imperative:

> "The Idea of the Multiversity" has no bard to sing its praises; no prophet to proclaim its vision; no guardian to protect its sanctity. It has its critics, its detractors, its transgressors. It also has its barkers selling its wares to all who will listen—and many do. But it also has its reality rooted in the logic of history. It is an imperative rather than a reasoned choice among elegant alternatives. (Kerr, 2001a: 5)

Kerr's "multiversity" was very much "at the height of the times," but the times are changing, and market demands and human needs are changing too. In addition, some previously unarticulated "human needs" are being expressed and, thus, becoming "market demands." Accordingly, the three key aspects of the university that Kerr analyzed in 1963 are undergoing profound transformations. Rewriting *The Uses of the University* today would require a new vision, a vision for a world that contains multiple fractures, in which it is imperative that we find common ground, not by giving up what is different and unique about each of us but by using it to advance the common cause of knowledge, wisdom, and the pursuit of happiness.

## Mission

One of the most consequential transformations taking place today is that the United States and other industrialized countries are becoming more diverse, as they function as magnets for people from less prosperous areas, including their present and former colonies. This is a fundamental change that is influencing society and affecting the mission of the university. The knowledge-based economy has turned out to be a transnational economy in which both goods and people circulate easily. Successful participation in this economy will require strong leadership on the part of the university, which will have to help manage this development by providing access on a much larger scale than previously experienced or envisioned. As James J. Duderstadt, Daniel E. Atkins, and Douglas Van Houweling (2002) have suggested, the country needs a "learn grant act" to develop human talent, as the land grant acts helped develop the natural resources of the country. Much of the talent that is currently being wasted belongs to women and minorities.

The issue of access to higher education by diverse populations, however, is a very difficult one. As Vest (2007) notes, "in our time, nothing has been so bitterly contested as the role of race, and diversity, more broadly, in the admission of students, and it has not been resolved through orderly political and administrative processes" (20). Vest, who has very clear ideas about the importance of educating diverse leaders, urges the university to strive for innovation and to nurture access, in order to stay true to the mission of creating opportunity. But progress in this area has been uneven. In one of his last publications, Kerr discussed the existence of "backward movements since the Master Plan of 1960," such as huge differences among neighborhoods in terms of the availability of high school advanced placement courses and transfer programs in community colleges, stating that this had increased "inequality of opportunity" (2002: 5).

Indeed, "inequality of opportunity" has increased, in part, because the quality of California's schools has deteriorated over time. In 1960, California was one of the top five states in expenditures per student. By 1990, it was one of the bottom five states, which made the preparation of underprivileged students very weak (Douglass, 2007). In addition, higher education has become more expensive. In fact, the entire country has been in a downward spiral with respect to higher education since the 1970s, with people losing access to public universities, which are becoming privatized and, thus, more expensive and out of reach for many students (Goldin & Katz, 2008). This is exacerbating competition among different social groups for access to higher education.

Kerr had acknowledged before that there were problems. For example, in his 1997 introduction to Alain Touraine's book, *The Academic System in American Society*, he conceded that American institutions of higher learning, including the University of California, reproduced the existing social order and that Touraine was "onto something very important: that a gigantic worldwide struggle is underway over the location of power in society" (xix). He agreed with Touraine that this struggle ran along horizontal lines, such as gender and race, more than along vertical ones, like class.

In fact, Kerr seemed to have sensed from the start that he had missed something, for on December 11, 1963, less than three weeks after John F. Kennedy's assassination and exactly six months after the president's famous June 11 address proposing what would become the Civil Rights Act of 1964, Kerr gave a speech noting that the university had provided "equality of opportunity" but perhaps had not "actively searched for the means to increase opportunity for equality" (Douglass, 2007: 76). This comment built on the president's statement about students of all races being entitled to equality of opportunity to develop their talent, ability, and motivation and to make something of themselves. Had the Master Plan been drafted after these important events, it might have been different, but it was negotiated and approved in 1960, during the presidency of Dwight D. Eisenhower, when there was less attention paid to diversity issues. Besides, in 1960, when the University of California was expanding fast, there appeared to be room for everyone in its classrooms. This, however, changed quickly as the population continued to grow and, without a corresponding investment in public research universities, competition for admission to the most selective campuses increased. Gardner, feeling pressure, made room for women and minorities by shrewdly bending the rules, but he did not articulate a new vision. Thus, his efforts, though successful, did not result in lasting change. At present, UC is dealing with the aftermath of Proposition 209, a 1996 initiative petition amending the state constitution to prohibit public institutions from considering sex, race, or ethnicity in their admissions and hiring decisions.

By a process of trial and error, the university is painfully trying to develop a new modus operandi. According to Sheldon Rothblatt (2007), this seems to be building on the idea of worth, associated with social democracy, which is different from the idea of merit, associated with liberal democracy. Merit is related to measurable ability. Worth has to do with strength of character. The appearance of the concept of merit is a relatively new phenomenon in the history of universities, which historically have favored the idea of worth. The tension between these two concepts is built into the California Master Plan for Higher Education, which reconciles populist and elitist ideals (Organization for Educational Co-operation and Development, 1990). This was a compromise between merit and worth, providing a balance between selectivity and access. The problem is that this balance did not last. The competition for prestige in which American universities engaged during the second half of the twentieth century heavily favored the concept of merit, so the idea of worth had to be reintroduced through the back door of special admissions.

The question went all the way to the Supreme Court twice, first with the 1978 *Regents of the University of California v. Bakke* decision and then with *Gratz v. Bollinger* and *Grutter v. Bollinger*, where the Court ruled in 2003 that race could be considered, together with other factors, in university admissions decisions. This issue was also at the heart of the controversy about SP 1 and SP 2, the 1995 UC special policies that prohibited consideration of race in admissions and hiring, respectively, as is evident in Reverend Jesse Jackson's speech at a Board of Regents meeting:

> In many ways judging merit is like defining virtue. It is subjective. Who decides what is meritorious? We cannot let merit be defined narrowly by grades and test scores, which are not intrinsically indicators of success, worth or service. The desire for the minority student to go back home and become a teacher in the ghetto, or for a woman to become a rape crisis counselor, are these not virtues that should be considered? Even if we accept grades and test scores as the basis for merit, and we should, how can we be sure that culturally biased tests could measure worth? Grades and test scores have never been the sole criteria for admission. (Pusser, 2004: 148)

The modus operandi UC is trying to develop at present relies on increasing the importance assigned to worth. But UC needs more than a modus operandi. It needs a new vision of balance that includes what Kerr missed. It also needs more resources in order to educate everyone.

At the undergraduate level, the greatest challenge is institutional capacity (having enough room for all promising students) and the admissions process (having an effective system to identify promise) (Daryl G. Smith, 2009). Recent changes seeking to abandon mechanical criteria which sort applicants according to a few potentially biased indicators, and instead to consider candidates individually by evaluating both past accomplishments and leadership potential as recommended by William G. Bowen and Derek Bok (1998), show a great deal of promise. In particular, there should not be overreliance on aptitude or intelligence tests, on which many scholars, such as David E. Drew (2005), in fact believe "no educational decision should be based" (4). In addition to making the admissions process more flexible, the university needs to increase capacity by creating new campuses as C. Judson King (2006) has suggested.

At the graduate level, the largest challenge is geographical expansion. The need for graduate education is as great today as the need for a college education was after World War II. Providing access to graduate education for a larger and more diverse student population in more locations will be crucial in the years to come. In the case of California, the opening of a new UC campus at Merced, in the heart of the ethnically diverse San Joaquin Valley, is a step in the right direction. More campuses in other underserved locations will be needed in the future. At the same time, having the California State University offer professional doctorates in areas of need makes sense, as these advanced degrees today are what professional masters were in 1960. A serious conversation about today's requirements for graduate and undergraduate education is much needed.

California is perhaps the most diverse and most knowledge-driven state in the country. Unless diversity and knowledge become firmly connected, and the middle class is able to expand, the state will not be able to sustain its economic prosperity and intellectual preeminence. The mission of the public research university is to establish this connection by giving diverse populations access to the highest levels of knowledge.

## Funding

While access to the highest levels of education by people from nontraditional backgrounds of various kinds is becoming paramount, the funding patterns of American universities are evolving to rely more on endowments and tuition and less on public support. This reflects a worldwide trend, as state funding is decreasing in virtually all countries (Lawrence, 2006). At the same time, the number of private universities is growing around the world (Altbach, 2007). The pattern of de-funding and de-democratizing public universities is particularly acute in the United States, which, compared to other industrialized countries, has lost considerable ground in the last few decades (Goldin & Katz, 2008). This has resulted in the demise of the middle class, which is shrinking due to lack of public investment (Newfield, 2008).

In Kerr's terminology, in the United States, the "federal grant university" is becoming the "private grant university" (2001a: 188). This is an important change that is affecting the behavior of the research university and its leaders as much as, or more than, the infusion of federal money did decades ago. The "private grant university" receives funds from industry, as well as individual donors. According to Vest (2007), thanks to the close relationship between academia and industry, in the United States there is a dynamic innovation system. Indeed, "50% of the growth of the U.S. economy during the last sixty years has been due to technical innovation, much of which has originated in university research" (41).

The relationship between academia and industry has continued to evolve. On the one hand, universities have become players that have patent rights to their inventions and engage in technology-transfer activities. On the other hand, companies have limited their in-house research and development, which has made them more dependent on the work of universities. The fact that academia and industry are growing closer generates discomfort. Although their interactions have been quite successful, there is a potential for problems or the perception of problems. The biggest threat to academic freedom today comes from industry, whose influence on academia needs to be monitored closely (Altbach, 2007).

In addition to funding from industry, universities are receiving an ever-increasing amount of resources from individual donors, which truly makes them deserve Kerr's label of "private grant universities." Private universities, of course, have always depended on philanthropy, but public universities are now turning to philanthropy too, as states decrease their contributions. Vest (2007) points out that presidents and chancellors of public universities are fond of saying that their institutions have gone from being state-supported, to being state assisted, to being state-located. According to Duderstadt (2007), one university president took the metaphor one step farther and referred to "state-molested" universities, as the less money states provide to their universities the more they seem to want to meddle in their affairs (145).

Public universities are getting better at fund-raising. In fact, their endowments are growing at a faster pace than the endowments of private institutions. Public universities are learning not only to obtain funds from donors, but to extract more money from students by charging higher tuition, particularly in the professional schools, which in many cases have become virtually privatized. Michigan and Virginia, for example, are largely privatized, and now the University of California is taking steps in the same direction.

As tuition and fees are increasing, salaries and benefits for low-paid campus workers, such as food workers and janitors, are being kept low, oftentimes by outsourcing these jobs, giving rise to protests. This process is aggravated by the fact that academics themselves are divided into two classes, a shrinking body of tenure-track faculty and an army of lecturers and researchers with no job security and lower compensation and prestige. Indeed, according to Altbach (2007), half of all new faculty positions at American universities are not tenure-track. The pyramid is topped by a small group of highly-paid executives who are resented by everyone. This structure, with its loss of well-paying jobs and widening gap between rich and poor, reflects that of the country at large, resulting in alienation and eroding the campus' sense of community.

Kerr distinguishes four periods or stages in the evolution of the American research university: (1) Origins (1810-1870), (2) Slow growth (1870-1940), (3) Rapid expansion and extension of activity (1940-1990), and (4) Constrained resources (1990-2015 and beyond) (2001a: 164-166). Stage 3 is the era of the "federal grant university" or "Multiversity I" ("riches at the national level"), which coincides with "Tidal Wave I," or the great influx of students caused by the baby boom. Stage 4 is the era of the "private grant university" or "Multiversity II" ("poverty at the state level"), which coincides with "Tidal Wave II," the second great influx of students consisting of the children of the baby boomers (2001a: 175-177). According to Kerr, the "Multiversity II" lives in a Hobbesian world "of every man against every man" (2001a: 178). This "free-for-all scenario" might become even more so in the future (2001a: 217). Given the knowledge-based nature of the economy, we need the "multiversity" more but, due to competition for resources from the health care and criminal justice systems, we are less able to afford it. There is a "clash of prospects:"

> It will be a sad situation if, over the long run, public investments in prisons continue to take a higher relative priority than investments in universities; and if, internally within the universities, preservation of the status quo takes priority over an aggressive commitment to access, to quality, and to autonomy. (Kerr, 2001a: 196-197)

At present, it appears that public universities are indeed becoming privatized. Education is increasingly perceived more as a private good than a public service. At the same time, a counter-trend to make education affordable to students from modest means is emerging.

Harvard and other elite private universities have moved to eliminate or reduce tuition for students from low income and middle-class families in a simple, easy-to-understand way (Kelly, 2007). Besides giving students who are not rich a break, this approach has the advantage of clarity, offering the same comfort public universities' low tuition used to give students of modest means who did not want to get in over their heads financially. According to Jeffrey Selingo (2008), a survey conducted through the The Chronicle of Higher Education/Gallup Panel, shows that 42 percent of Americans believe that the most important higher education issue for the country's president to address is controlling college costs. This is deemed more important than providing more financial aid, showing that, when it comes to tuition costs, people really like clarity. The high tuition-high aid formula is arcane and off-putting. Students and their parents want to know the cost of tuition up front, and they want this cost to be moderate. This new model, pegging tuition to income in a relatively straightforward manner, may be the way of the future. This model also could be the beginning of a trend towards more need-based, rather than merit-based, aid, the latter having favored the well-to-do enormously in recent times. Indeed, tying tuition to income might meet the Carnegie Commission's recommendation, based on a cost-benefit analysis and endorsed by Kerr, to have students bear one-third of the costs of education and society the other two-thirds.

It appears that public and private universities, which have divergent orientations with respect to the type and volume of their research production (Geiger, 2007), are converging with respect to teaching (Brint, 2007), as they are moving towards a model in which only students who can prove financial need get subsidies, and the others pay full-price or close to it. In the case of the publics, this subsidy will have to be provided by the state, at least in part. The problem is that, due to tax reductions over the past few decades and numerous other commitments, states do not have much money. Since expenditures on higher education are considered discretionary, universities, which were in a very precarious financial position before the current economic crisis, are facing imminent disaster.

In some cases, the scarcity of state resources has pitted state schools against one another, as they are forced to fight for crumbs from the state budgetary table. For example, the University of California and the California State University have recently opposed a proposal to guarantee the community colleges a certain level of funding. The community colleges are very under-funded and deserve this increase and more. The problem is that this would create yet another entitlement and further decrease the pool of discretionary funds from which the University of California and California State University get their budgets. This is a shameful situation. It will take particularly strong leadership at the university, state, and national levels to develop a new model for providing access to higher education, which has been decreasing in recent decades. This must include more public funds to rebuild the middle class through an expansion of affordable, high-quality education.

There are only two likely courses of action. The first is to continue along the same path, with fewer and fewer discretionary funds and more and more squabbles over this limited pot of money. This path inevitably will result in enhanced privatization, in order to preserve quality, or increasing massification, to preserve access. Neither privatization nor massification can lead to greatness. A few years from now, the University of California will probably be fighting not just with the community colleges or with the California State University but with itself. One can easily imagine a situation in which the UC system is dismantled and each campus required to fend for itself. Such sentiments already exist in the system, as the recent unsuccessful proposal by twenty-three UC San Diego department chairs to close some of the smaller campuses shows (Gaines, 2009).

The UC system has always had a great deal of internal competition, and that has been good. But if state support continues to decrease in relative terms, and the benefits of membership in the UC system become less obvious, the system might break up into independent, semi-private universities. This would not be good for anyone. All campuses would lose, the state would lose, and the country would lose. The trend towards dismantling the UC system and the California Master Plan for Higher Education should be resisted at all costs. Although adjustments are needed, the hedgehog concept of systemic excellence is a productive one and should not be abandoned. As C. Judson King (2009) has noted, with its high level of technological innovation, the University of California has played a central role in developing the economy of California. To let the UC system disintegrate would be suicidal for the state, as would be neglecting CSU and the community colleges. The three public systems should unite and lobby relentlessly for more support for higher education.

That is the alternative path and, in my view, the only one that can restore and enhance greatness. Recent developments involving a plan to increase funding for the impoverished State University of New York (SUNY), chronicled by Stanley Fish (2007), give hope that the public may be beginning to realize that change is needed. It is not surprising that this realization occurred at one of the less well-supported state systems, like SUNY. But the current economic crisis has resulted in devastating budget cuts for other states' public universities, including the University of California, which is facing the largest financial challenge in its history. Events have brought it to a crossroads. The state must now decide whether to make a large investment in higher education or to rescind the California Master Plan for Higher Education and let its public universities decline, particularly its research institutions. These are the same choices that the country as a whole faces: privatization of institutions of higher learning, with a corresponding decrease in access, massification, with a concomitant decrease in quality, or a significant investment of resources in public institutions, with a mandate to educate each and every member of American society to the best of his or her ability to learn.

## Structure

While the knowledge-based national economy and the "federal grant university" described by Kerr in his 1963 text formed a marriage made in heaven, the knowledge-based transnational economy, which requires expanded access, and the "private grant university," which offers less need-based aid, do not necessarily mesh well. Tensions between mission and funding are making universities very difficult to lead. The "multiversity" is much more unruly than it was when Kerr first defined it. In addition, its structural fragmentation has continued, making the need for integration of its various components, as well as of its mission and funding, more obvious and more urgent. To lead the "multiversity" in the coming years will require a great deal of shrewdness and a truly uplifting vision.

According to Vest (2007), "the multiversity" is morphing into what, borrowing a term from Douglass (2002), he calls "a global meta-university"; a university of "globally created and shared teaching materials, scholarly archives, and even laboratories," which "could grow to undergird and empower campuses everywhere, both rich and poor" (108-109). The main characteristic of this new stage in the evolution of the university is openness, which is facilitated by the new information and communication technologies connecting scholars around the world instantaneously. For Vest, this is one of the most important changes that have taken place since Kerr penned *The Uses of the University* in 1963. Of course, in later editions of his book, Kerr discussed technology, which he realized would play an important role in the future of the university. In particular, in the 2001 edition, he called information and communication technology "the fourth revolution in the technology of education and the first in 500 years," the other three being the replacement of parents by teachers, the development of writing, and the invention of the printing press (2001a: 219). Each of these revolutions added to, rather than replaced, previous technologies, and the same will be true today. Dismissive of predictions regarding the disappearance of classroom teaching as we know it, Kerr notes that "education is not only about the transfer of factual knowledge, but also about learning to reach conclusions with others" (2001a: 220-221). This is, of course, true, but Kerr, not being very conversant with technology, may have underestimated its ability to facilitate bringing people together.

Speculating about the future, Charles Van Doren (1991) sees a new Golden Age in which "humans and computers, in intimate cooperation with one another, could embark upon a course of learning undisturbed by other, more disturbing, impulses" (412). Vest (2007), like Kerr, believes that the educational process is based on human interaction and indicates that when people try to make predictions about the future, "the rate of technological progress is almost always dramatically underrepresented, and the rate of social progress is almost always dramatically overpredicted" (92). One thing many people envisioned at the beginning—video lectures—has turned out to be much less important than other uses of technology, such as computer-based tools and simulations, electronic journals, massive search engines, digital archives, and video and web interactions. These changes have resulted in the creation of learning communities including members from all over the world.

Vest (2007) envisions a way in which universities will develop great synergies through the use of technological tools. For example, "architects located on multiple continents use video and Web interactions to come together as juries for architecture studio projects" (94). Another important example is the MIT OpenCourseWare (OCW) program, which makes MIT class materials available on the Web, free of charge, to scholars all over the world. Vest, who as president of MIT, helped establish this program, believes that it is a potentially democratizing force which could have enormous impact, as shown by the following examples:

> An Arizona high-school teacher motivates and supervises group study of MIT OCW computer-science materials within his after-school artificial-intelligence club. A group of then-unemployed programmers in Silicon Valley used MIT OCW materials to master advanced computer languages, upgrading their skills when the job market became very tight. An educator at Al-Mansour University College in Baghdad utilized MIT OCW aeronautics and astronautics course material in his air-traffic control research. The computer-science department of a university in Legon, Ghana, is updating its entire curriculum, using MIT OCW materials to help benchmark and revise its courses. In another country, an underground university based largely on MIT OCW educates young men and women who, because of their religion, are forbidden to attend universities. (Vest, 2007: 97)

These examples give us a glance at the potential for transformation contained in this single technology. While MIT's OCW courses are being translated into Mandarin and Spanish, other universities around the world have developed, or are developing, their own open courseware. For example, the Michigan Virtual University offers access to the courses of some state universities (Duderstadt, Atkins, & Van Houweling, 2002). The effects of this movement are difficult to calculate, as are those of other open archiving, indexing, and publishing projects, such as JSTOR, ARTstor, the Google Print Library Project, the Million Book project,

DSpace, and the Public Library of Science. Even more exciting are the possibilities associated with web-based labs, such as MIT's iLab, which allows scholars around the globe to run expensive experimental equipment at MIT.

Vest (2007) believes that openness will emerge as "a dominant ethos of global education" (108). This ethos is not paternalistic, but democratic, based on sharing available resources. Duderstadt, Atkins, and Van Houweling (2002) express similar ideas, stressing that all of these new technologies have the potential to create "a profoundly democratic revolution" (274). For Vest (2007), "a global meta-university is arising that will accurately characterize higher education a decade or two hence in much the same way that Clark Kerr's multiversity accurately characterized American research universities forty years ago" (108). The University of California is moving towards the model of the "meta-university." For example, its campuses are connected internally through such instruments as the California Digital Library, which is considered the University of California's eleventh library. The CDL assists campus libraries in sharing resources and provides leadership in using technology to develop library collections and services. Another way in which the University of California is connected to the rest of the world is through Internet2, an advanced networking consortium of U.S. universities, laboratories, corporations, and government agencies, as well as many international organizations. As President Richard Atkinson, who led these initiatives, states, "globalization is challenging universities to rethink their organization and responsibilities so that they can respond creatively to the new world they have helped to bring about" (2007: 109-110).

In the "meta-university," which is reminiscent of the "transversity" (Scott & Awbrey, 19: 1993), the "multiversity" overcomes its fragmentation by going global (Marginson, 2010). How this connectivity will affect, and be affected by, mission and funding remains to be seen. One thing is certain: the connected "multiversity," like the economy, will not be national, but international. Indeed, like a mature industry, as Levine (1997) calls it, American higher education is looking for new markets. American universities are rushing to set up outposts abroad, opening programs and campuses all over the world but most particularly in countries with limited access to education (Lewin, 2008). A recent example is the agreement signed by Saudi Arabia's new King Abdullah University of Science and Technology with Stanford University, the University of California, and the University of Texas, which will collaborate on research projects and help to recruit the faculty and develop the curriculum (Fisher, 2008). Another example is the recent hiring by the United Arab Emirates University of Wyatt (Rory) Hume, former provost of the University of California system, who now holds the same position there (Mills, 2008).

According to Joseph Alois Schumpeter (1949), capitalism destroys earlier versions of itself. There is a process of constant mutation and creative destruction that goes beyond the traditional idea of competition. Each innovation creates a new structure and destroys the previous one. This dynamic, whose pace seems to be accelerating, will surely affect higher education in the coming years, just as it has in the past. Indeed, the diversification of institutions of higher learning in the United States, including the creation of for-profit universities, is an example of this kind of competition, which does not consist of doing the same thing better or more cheaply but of doing different things, of finding a niche.

A case for new types of institutions has recently been made by Kamaljit S. Bawa, Ganesan Balachander, and Peter Raven (2008), who believe that developing countries need "knowledge institutions" that deal with local problems such as poverty alleviation and environmental sustainability. Examples of new "knowledge institutions" include the Ashoka Trust for Research in Ecology and the Environment (ATREE) in India and the EARTH University in Costa Rica. These new types of institutions should have "flexible mandates, freedom from bureaucratic control, and a focus on specific problems," as well as ties to various governmental and nongovernmental agencies, community organizations, and universities throughout the world. These scholars think that philanthropists seeking to fund projects in the developing world "could be convinced that support for these new institutions will provide stable long-term solutions, even when immediate results from social welfare programs may seem more attractive" (136). In other words, what they suggest is not to duplicate the comprehensive research university model, which they think is of limited use in some parts of the world, but rather to create new institutions of higher learning that are context-specific and could be funded by donors who want to have a direct impact on improving life in the region. Thus, their proposal ties structure with funding and mission in a particular way.

Most universities around the world, however, are trying to duplicate the comprehensive university model, which they see as the only competitive one in the prestige race that started in the United States and is spreading throughout the globe with the help of newly-created international rankings. The competition for prestige results in homogenization of research universities and tends to increase costs, as each institution wants to offer the same things as the others, only bigger and better, in order to become a world-class university. This is particularly visible in doctoral education, which is becoming global (Nerad, & Heggelund, 2008). Ph.D. programs are becoming standardized not only in Europe but also in other countries around the globe. In the short-run, I think that we should expect a great deal of additional homogenization, as universities around the world imitate the American research university and engage in the prestige race. At the same time, the institutional diversity that characterizes higher education in the United States is also likely to be imitated in other countries. In fact, according to Altbach (2007), a differentiated academic system, such as the one articulated by the California Master Plan for Higher Education, is a prerequisite for the rise of research universities and crucial for the well-being of developing countries, which should have a variety of institutions of higher learning. Thus, the legacy of the American higher education system is a double one: diversification of systems and homogeneity of research universities.

## Wild Card

Discussing the future of the American research university in chapter 9 of the 2001 edition of *The Uses of the University*, Kerr mentioned some wild cards, including wars and depressions. That concept could be expanded, using the 1963 text, where he says that each nation, when it becomes dominant, tends to develop the leading educational institutions of its time. This idea comes from Ortega, who stated that great countries produce great educational systems, not the reverse—a sobering thought. In 1987, Henry Rosovsky wrote that between two-thirds and three-quarters of the world's best universities were located in the United States: In higher education, "made in America" still is "a fine label" (63). According to Derek Bok (2006), however, American universities, although still very highly ranked, are showing signs of becoming self-satisfied. Douglass (2006) goes one step further and declares that America's once-dominant role is waning as other countries improve their higher education systems, pointing out that, for the first time since the 1800s, the United States is not the first country in the world in terms of the percentage of its population that goes on to a post-secondary institution. Participation in post-secondary education for those eighteen to twenty-four years old declined from 38 percent in 2000 to 34 percent in 2005. By contrast, many industrialized countries are approaching or have exceeded 50 percent. In California, participation in post-secondary education directly after graduation for students of public high schools declined from 55 percent in 1970 to 48 percent in 2000, with most such students going to community colleges. In addition, in relative terms, the United States is educating fewer scientists and producing less science than before. Thus, it is not surprising that productivity rates in many industrialized countries are approaching or exceeding those of the United States.

One reason for the decline in the numbers of college-going students is cost (Goldin & Katz, 2008). Going to college is more costly than it used to be. Interestingly, the salary gap between college graduates and high school graduates is greater in the United States than in other industrialized countries. Thus, in the United States, relatively fewer students attend university at a higher cost and then get jobs at higher salaries, than in other industrialized countries. It is a role reversal of sorts. As Newfield (2008) has noted, the egalitarian country is no more. The American research university is now an enterprise by the elite, of the elite and for the elite. Its primary focus is prestige, academic and social.

Robert L. Geiger (2004) discusses the paradox of the marketplace, which has made education more expensive at American institutions of higher learning:

> The marketplace has, on balance, brought universities greater resources, better students, a far larger capacity for advancing knowledge, and a more productive role in the U.S. economy. At the same time, it has diminished the sovereignty of universities over their own activities, weakened their mission of serving the public, and created through growing commercial entanglements at least the potential for undermining their privileged role as disinterested arbiters of knowledge. (265)

As a result of the marketplace organizational model of higher education, the American research university has become the best in the world, if not the most democratic. What is more, it has become a model for other countries, which are building new institutions and programs in its image. If the marketplace model is failing and the American empire is declining, nobody could tell that from looking at its research universities: "Vast campuses, the finest and most convenient libraries in the world, laboratories and research centers from which the world expects the most long-awaited discoveries and whose scientists win most Nobel Prices in science, constitute one of the most striking aspects of American power" (Touraine, 1997: 2). Whether or not this will continue will depend on how the country fares in the coming years, including its ability to rebuild the middle class and generate widespread prosperity, and that is the wildest card of all.

What is clear is that, when the United States declines, which like all empires, it inevitably will do, it will leave behind, as one its most important legacies, the "multiversity," a model for institutions of higher learning for other countries. The United States at present is not in good shape. It has serious economic, political, and social problems. It may be premature to declare that the country is in decline, however, as its leadership may be able to energize its citizens and begin to solve some chronic challenges. Kerr warned against being too optimistic in good times and too pessimistic in bad ones. In the 1970s, the country was in a gloomy and defeatist mood and so were its universities, about which many negative books were written. Kerr quotes eighteen titles such as *Death of the American University, Fall of the American University,* and so forth (2001a: 157). But the American university did not fall and did not die. On the contrary, it reached new heights as the country experienced a boom in the latter part of the twentieth century. Perhaps this was so because, as Kerr says, "the best step in conquering the future is to worry about it—to fear it" (2001a: 212), and there was a great deal of worry at that time about the decline of the university and the country. Shapiro (2005) notes that the university needs to feel constant uneasiness about the future:

> Such anxieties and the honest self-examination they ought to occasion are essential ingredients in a university's capacity to build and maintain its excellence. In the decades ahead, anxiety, courage, energy, adaptation, leadership, and change are the price of continued distinction and relevance in higher education. (Shapiro, 2005: 39)

A healthy fear of the future and courageous and adaptive leadership can bring positive change to the university. The best chapter in the history of the American university might still remain to be written.

According to Kerr, "as society goes so goes the university," and conversely, "as the university goes, so goes society" (2001a: 194). Higher education has been moving west ever since it was born in the Middle East (Pedersen, 1997: 40). In his book *Higher Education Cannot Escape History*, Kerr comments on this:

> The greatest centers of world-orbit scholarship have historically shifted greatly from the Greek world to the Muslim world, and from the Muslim world to the Western European; and, within Western Europe, from Italy to the United Kingdom to France to Germany, and then, outside Europe, to the United States. One of the most interesting speculations in the intellectual world is where leadership may next be moving, if, in fact, it does move from the United States. (Kerr, 1994b: 16)

Indeed, as power moved west to Greece, Rome, the Muslim world, Spain, France, England, and the Americas, so higher education moved.

Even within the United States, we have seen a movement from the East Coast to the West Coast, giving the University of California its current preeminence. All indications are that power, and with it higher education, is now shifting to Asia in a sort of slow trip around the globe. Perched at the edge of the West, the University of California is in an ideal position to pass the torch to the people across the Pacific. However, the westward drift is slow and it might be premature to let go of the torch just yet.

# Part II

# History of American Higher Education

# 7

# The Strands of History

The first chapter of *The Uses of the University* begins with a comparison between present and past, in which Kerr affirms the importance of understanding history:

> The university started as a single community—a community of masters and students. It may even be said to have had a soul in the sense of a central animating principle. Today the large American university is, rather, a whole series of communities and activities held together by a common name, a common governing board, and related purposes. This great transformation is regretted by some, accepted by many, gloried in, as yet, by few. But it should be understood by all. (Kerr, 2001a: 1)

Before analyzing contemporary developments, Kerr felt the need to go back to the beginning of higher education, which he traced to antiquity, finding examples of the twin traditions of interest in knowledge for its useful applications and interest in knowledge for its own sake. Kerr reviews the birth of the university in the Middle Ages and its decline in the Early Modern era. He then discusses its rebirth in nineteenth century Germany, with the infusion of research, and the transplantation of this model to the United States, where it fused with existing English-style colleges that focused on teaching, and the new American land grant universities that stressed service to society. This resulted in a unique institution in which all the strands of history came together with great benefit.

Kerr notes that "looked at from within," universities have changed a great deal, but "looked at from without," they have changed very little. Commenting on Heraclitus' saying "nothing endures but change," Kerr states that "everything else changes, but the university mostly endures":

About eighty-five institutions in the Western world established by 1520 still exist in recognizable forms, with similar functions and with unbroken histories, including the Catholic Church, the Parliaments of the Isle of Man, of Iceland, and of Great Britain, several Swiss cantons, and seventy universities. Kings that rule, feudal lords with vassals, and guilds with monopolies are all gone. These seventy universities, however, are still in the same locations with some of the same buildings, with professors and students doing much the same things, and with governance carried on in much the same ways. (Kerr, 2001a: 115)

This often-quoted paragraph about enduring institutions shows the strength of the university, as well as its ability to serve a changing society and stay true to itself.

In order to understand the university's current challenges, it is important to be familiar with the unchanging, as well as the changing, traits of higher education from its inception to the present. There are three key issues or principles that have affected higher education over time. The first is that education follows the economy. This is what I call the "follow the money" principle. As Ortega (1997 [1930]) notes, great nations produce great educational systems and not vice versa. Each stage in the evolution of education has been linked to a revolution in the economy. The second rule is that, although it is true that knowledge is money, knowledge is also pleasure, and sooner or later academics fall under its spell. This is what Veblen (1918) calls the "trait of idle curiosity" and the "instinct of workmanship," which makes people see the quest for knowledge as an "end in itself" (10). Scholarship is its own reward, and academics diligently pursue their research projects even when there is no practical application to their work. I call this the "follow the pleasure" principle. The history of higher education is a chronicle of the tensions between economy-driven educational systems and pleasure-driven scholars who use those systems to pursue knowledge for its own sake. Finally, when we explore the issue of access of marginal peoples to higher education, we find that, oftentimes, marginal peoples become even more marginalized when their society's higher education system experiences an improvement, because this tends to favor the elite and thus reduce access. This is what I call the "better can be worse" principle. With these three principles in mind, I will review the course of Western higher education, from the dawn of history to the present, with the goal of providing a framework in which to place the history of the University of California. In this review, I will pay special attention to the connection between education and empire by comparing the evolution of higher education in the English and Spanish colonies of the Americas.

## Culture and Agriculture

The roots of the quintessential American research university that is the University of California, and of all other institutions of higher learning in this country, are to be found in the European educational system, which ultimately originated in the schools of the ancient civilizations of the Fertile Crescent. According to Jared Diamond (1997), the Fertile Crescent—a large area of the Middle East that enjoys the presence of water—was blessed with a unique combination of plants and animals that allowed hunter-gatherers to become farmers. The first farming settlements date to the tenth millennium BC. Complex societies developed in subsequent millennia, when a grain storage economy was established, and it became necessary to have managers who could keep track of the surplus (Lucas, 1994). Writing appeared in order to meet a need for record keeping. Thus, the first literate people—scribes—were literally "bean-counters" who recorded grain transactions on clay tablets.

This happened for the first time among the Sumerians and their successors, the Akkadians, in Mesopotamia—the area between the Tigris and Euphrates rivers that coincides roughly with today's Iraq. This is considered the cradle of Western civilization, because it was here that writing was developed in the fourth millennium BC. The first known formal schools date from the third millennium BC and were called "tablet-houses." Whether conducted in a temple or a palace, formal education was rigorous and included training in all known subjects, such as accounting, geometry, grammar, literature, history, law, music, and etiquette, among others. The same type of formal education is found in ancient Egypt, which also had a grain storage economy with a large and important scribal class. There is evidence that this included an elite body of priests-scholars who devoted themselves to advanced studies, among other things, probably because knowledge is attractive.

If the education of the Sumerians, Akkadians, and Egyptians was centered on the temple or the palace, the education of the Greeks was focused on the agora or marketplace because the economies of their city-states had produced an urban middle class that needed speaking skills to compete in a system of self-government. In the fifth century BC, the sophists provided those skills. Unlike the pre-Socratic philosophers, whose cosmologies speculated about the nature of reality, the sophists, who were professional educators, held that human impressions and standards are subjective and conventional and, therefore, ephemeral. Specializing in rhetoric, the sophists taught students to defend all sides of an argument, so that they could prosper by becoming good orators. Since the education they provided resulted in better incomes for their pupils, the sophists were able to charge high fees. Not surprisingly, this kind of practical and relativistic education elicited a challenge from the philosopher Socrates (c. 469-399 BC) whose goal was to uncover universal truths that would help people behave properly. While Socrates, like the sophists, taught in the marketplace and other public spaces, his disciple Plato (c. 428-348 BC) opened a teaching facility for his school—the academy. In it, he developed his vision of a harmonious social order ruled by philosopher kings. Aristotle (384-322 BC), who also had his own teaching facility—the lyceum—went beyond Plato's interest in producing enlightened leaders and pursued knowledge for its own sake, writing on a wide range of subjects, from physics to ethics. While Plato focused on speculation and logic, Aristotle based his work on observation and classification, establishing the basis of scientific knowledge. Thus, an educational system that was devised to serve the economy eventually led to independent thinking, including the ability to be critical of the economy that produced it. This pattern would recur throughout history.

Greece's intellectual influence grew during the Hellenistic period, reaching many areas such as Alexandria, where a great library was built. This was called museum or "temple of the muses." A research center where scholars sometimes lectured, the museum, which received public funding, was an early version of a state-supported institution of higher learning (Cowley & Williams, 1991). A rival research center was its counterpart in Pergamon. When the Egyptians declared an embargo on papyrus in order to prevent Pergamon from increasing its collection, the Romans turned to parchment. Thus, this rivalry between institutions of higher learning resulted in better communication technology.

The Romans absorbed the culture of the peoples they conquered, most particularly the Hellenistic Greeks from whom they took their educational system, which was focused on rhetoric. This reached new heights with Cicero (106-45 BC) and Quintilian (c. 39-96 AD) and was a key element in the development of Roman law, which constitutes the basis of many existing Western legal systems. With the advent of Christianity, education in the Roman Empire started to change to include catechumenal instruction. Christian schooling grew after the fall of Rome, replacing secular instruction in the early Middle Ages, a long period of cultural retrenchment in which scholars took refuge in relatively isolated monasteries.

Although little is known about diversity in antiquity, in general it is safe to say that most people who had access to higher education were men of considerable wealth, although intelligent and ambitious men of modest means often managed to study. In some cases, slaves were highly educated, working as accountants, teachers, and the like. In general, women had many fewer opportunities to study than men did, but they were not totally excluded from higher education. There were quite a few learned women during the Greco-Roman period, during which females were admitted to some schools or else tutored at home. The Christian church also undertook to educate women in its convents, which provided new opportunities for female learning.

## The Birth of the University

After the fears of the year 1000, which many people believed was going to bring about the end of the world, Europe started to recover from centuries of disorganization and isolation. Technical innovations, including the invention of the wheeled plow and a switch from a two-year to a three-year crop rotation, increased food production, resulting in a cash economy and the development of cities and an urban merchant class (Pedersen, 1997). The need for a body of experts to manage this new economy became obvious, and the educational system changed to meet it. First, in the eleventh century, the cathedral schools expanded their curricula to include secular learning, in addition to religious instruction. Then, in the twelfth century, a new institution was created to provide the kind of education that was required, the "studium generale" later called "universitas," which means "corporation." This new institution, modeled after the merchants' corporations, was an association of teachers or an association of students. In Bologna, the university was managed by students, who hired and fired the faculty and set the rules. By contrast, in Paris, the faculty was in charge of the university. Salamanca was somewhat influenced by Bologna. Oxford followed Paris. These differences are still visible today, as students in Italy, Spain, and Latin America have more institutional power than those in France, England, and the United States.

The universities were created as international institutions. The language of instruction was Latin, and students came from all over Europe, organizing themselves within the university by "nations." Universities granted three main degrees: Bachelors, Masters, and Ph.D. In a businesslike fashion, these attested to the level of knowledge acquired, representing an exchange of an investment of money, time, and effort for a certificate that would allow the recipient to collect the benefits of that investment. Time to degree was very much what it is today, with graduate students helping the faculty teach undergraduates the way today's teaching assistants do. An interesting factor affecting time to degree in the Middle Ages was that Ph.D. students were expected to give a lavish party after their graduation. This was so expensive that some students had to delay graduation until they saved enough money to finance the event.

Universities were established in rapid succession throughout Europe between the thirteenth and fifteenth centuries, thus, by the end of the Middle Ages there were over seventy such institutions of higher learning. Initially, universities did not own facilities but rather rented space and could move to other parts of the city or to other cities, which produced much consternation, as neighborhoods and cities did not want to lose the business they brought. Eventually, they became established in particular locations and built classrooms and dormitories. A very important institution was the college, which was both a residential and teaching facility. In continental Europe, colleges lost their teaching function and their importance over time, but they retained and increased their central importance in England, where they were at the heart of the teaching enterprise, a feature that carried over to the United States.

The university of the Middle Ages was a teaching institution, and its emphasis was on the professions: it offered degrees in law and medicine, theology for the clergy, and liberal arts for educators. In terms of the content of its teaching, much came from the Greeks and the Arabs via the Iberian Peninsula, which disseminated scientific knowledge to the rest of Europe. During the early Middle Ages, European knowledge could not compete with that of the Moslem world, which was very advanced. For Mohammed, "the ink of the learned" was "as precious as the blood of the martyrs" (Cowley & Williams, 1991: 32-33). Higher education bloomed from Damascus to Córdoba, and students endeavored to learn from the most famous teachers, who granted diplomas. In contrast, diplomas in the medieval university were not granted by individual instructors but rather by the institution. Although the university was originally vocational and utilitarian and linked to the church, it evolved into a secular institution in which free-thinking was allowed and encouraged, a safe heaven for ideas where teachers and students could enjoy the principle of "idle curiosity."

Although poor men could sometimes attend the university by working, often as servants of rich students or assistants to faculty members, women of all social classes were excluded from participating. Until the creation of the university, women had had access to schooling, including attending some co-educational schools, but their ability to receive an education comparable to that of men suffered when the creation of a small number of high-powered centers of learning took men away from their hometowns. Women usually were not allowed to leave their families to attend the university, nor were they normally accepted at the university. With the best men gone, the quality of education for those left behind, including women, declined. Naturally, some women still received decent schooling, and some even managed to study and teach at the university, but they were the exceptions. Thus, while the university opened new professional opportunities for men, it marginalized women further by creating a bigger gap between their educational opportunities and those afforded to men.

After the plagues, wars, and famines of the late Middle Ages, the economy changed from local to national, and then to global, with the creation of nation-states and the discovery of new territories. The guilds became less important, as the number of independent businessmen increased, giving way to a new and more cosmopolitan merchant class engaged in international trade. At the same time, government became more complex, for the new nation-states were creating large bureaucracies, which provided job opportunities for members of the nobility and commoners alike. This resulted in the cultural revival called the Renaissance, which shifted society's focus from God to man and brought back the classics. Indeed, people looked for autonomy and security through the mastery of language (Rüegg, 1992). The printing press played an important role in the development of the textual culture of humanism. The struggles of the Reformation and Counter-Reformation undermined the ideal of a unified Christian Europe and provided the basis for nationalism.

The medieval university had been focused on preparing men for the professions, including the clergy. In the Early Modern era, however, there was a need for worldly citizens who could shine both in business and in society. A well-rounded education similar to that of the Greeks or Romans became desirable for these new secular men of affairs. Thus the *studia humanitatis* or humanities were added to the *studia divinitatis* or theology. As Sheldon Rothblatt (1993) notes, with this change the liberal educational canon was established. Later, the sciences were added to the humanities. During the sixteenth and seventeenth centuries, scholarly innovations took place largely in newly-created academies and learned societies of various sorts, which focused on the new disciplines. The university was slow to change, expanding the curriculum to include humanities and sciences, and moving from Latin to the vernacular, only after these transformations had occurred elsewhere.

The Early Modern era was full of contradictions. On the one hand, it was revolutionary in terms of geographic and intellectual discoveries. On the other hand, it was conservative, as social mobility decreased and the tensions of the Reformation and Counter-Reformation made people's attitudes more rigid. Education reflects these contradictions. The university, which continued to be important since the degrees it issued were necessary to obtain lucrative posts, was quite rigid and old-fashioned, while there were many distinguished scholars teaching students in the academies or tutoring them at home. Interestingly, although women did not attend the university, except under extraordinary circumstances, a significant number were educated by the many excellent private tutors available at that time. Therefore, the intellectual decline of the university, which took scholars out of it and into society, favored women. At the same time, the number of rich students increased, since the children of the nobility started to attend the university in greater numbers as a higher degree became a requirement for gentlemen. Accordingly, men of modest backgrounds had fewer opportunities to attend the university than in the Middle Ages.

## The University Goes to America

One event that had a great impact on European society in the Early Modern Era, and in fact resulted in the creation of new societies with their own challenges and opportunities, was the discovery, conquest, and colonization of America. This took place during the period in which universities were declining and intellectual activity was emerging in academies and learned societies. The first to bring European higher education to the New World were the Spaniards, who established universities in America shortly after the discovery. As Harold R.W. Benjamin (1965) has noted, the number of medieval universities was limited, and many universities that we consider old today were established in the sixteenth century, so the founding of the first Latin American universities took place at the same time as that of many European universities. The first university in the New World was the University of Santo Domingo, established in 1538 by means of a papal bull. Run by Dominican friars, the University of Santo Domingo, seat of the first colony in the New World, had four schools: Arts, Theology, Law, and Medicine.

In the sixteenth century, the Spaniards conducted many interesting pedagogical experiments in the Americas. Demonstrating the axiom that great countries produce great educational systems, the most creative period for education in the Hispanic world was the sixteenth century, at the height of the Spanish Empire. During this time, the University of Salamanca was one of the most active universities in Europe, and the University of Alcalá and other universities were established. The conquest of America took place during this period of splendor of Spanish culture.

Spain found large Native American states with sophisticated cultures in the Americas. The Indians had rigorous schools to prepare the children of the nobility for public service, including both rhetorical and military skills: "head and heart," as the Aztecs conceptualized it (González & Padilla, 2008: 4). Following the philosophy of assimilation that they had developed with the Moslems during the Reconquest in the Iberian Peninsula, the Spaniards set out to acculturate the Indians. This was accomplished by offering a Christian education to the children of the native nobility. According to George I. Sanchez (1970), immediately after the conquest of Mexico, Hernán Cortés asked Emperor Charles V to send clergymen to convert and educate the Indians. The Spaniards' approach was to train the Indian nobility and run the empire with their help. Spain was in the middle of its Golden Age and had great writers and scholars. As Felipe Fernández-Armesto (2003) indicates, the first viceroys of Mexico sponsored artists, including Aztec painters. Indeed, the viceroys were patrons of learning who supported the creation of schools, as well as the establishment of printing presses, which published books on such topics as religion, law, medicine, philosophy, mathematics, and Indian languages.

The first school in the Americas was the school for Indian children founded by Fray Pedro de Gante in Texcoco in 1523. This very active educator later directed the great Indian school of San José de Belen de los Naturales in Mexico City, whose curriculum included Spanish, Latin, music, and fine arts. While some students were prepared for posts in government, others were taught trades such as shoemaking, carpentry, and tailoring. A system of peer mentoring was developed, and advanced students helped younger ones and served as teachers in neighboring towns. There were many other Indians schools in Mexico during the first eighty years of the colony. These included the rural schools of Vasco de Quiroga, who, influenced by Plato's *Republic* and Moro's *Utopia*, created several community centers providing instruction in agricultural techniques and trades, as well as an elementary education. Although very sophisticated and experimental, none of these schools offered university-level training.

Emperor Charles V wanted to bring the sons of the Indian nobility to Spain for purposes of higher education, but this plan never came to fruition. Instead, an institution of higher learning—the first in the New World—was established in Mexico City in 1536, two years before the establishment of the University of Santo Domingo: the Colegio de Santa Cruz de Tlatelolco, directed by the famous historian Fray Bernardino de Sahagún. The curriculum included religion, Spanish and Latin grammar and literature, logic, philosophy, science, and Indian medicine, as well as Indian languages for those studying to become priests. The faculty included Spanish scholars trained in European universities and, later, also homegrown Indian scholars. The school's graduates obtained leadership positions as teachers, mayors, and governors. There were other institutions of higher learning, such as the Colegio de Tiripitío, founded by Fray Alonso de la Veracruz in 1540 in Michoacán. The result was a highly-educated Indian elite. An unusual situation arose in which the Indians "furnished teachers to the conquerors before half of the conquistadores were dead" (Castañeda, 1938: 11).

The sophisticated teaching offered at these institutions of higher learning was resented by some Spaniards, who were jealous of the fact that Indians had access to such fine instruction while they had to go to Spain to obtain similar training. At the same time, mestizos, those of mixed Spanish and Indian ancestry, were in a precarious position, not having access either to Indian schools or to a Spanish education. Although there were some schools for them, these were insufficient. Requests were made for "a university of all the sciences where the natives and the sons of the Spaniards might receive instruction" (Castañeda, 1938: 13). Thus, in 1551, Emperor Charles V ordered the establishment of the University of Mexico to educate Spaniards, Indians, and mestizos. This caused the decline of the Indian schools. The missions the Spaniards established across North America in the eighteenth century revived Indian education, but training there was mostly vocational (MacDonald, 2004). The era of the high-quality Indian schools ended with the arrival of the university.

The creation of the University of Mexico owes a great deal to Hernán Cortés, the conqueror of Mexico, who made provisions for it in his will. Although his plans were not implemented, his desires were shared by such important people as Fray Juan de Zumárraga and the viceroy, don Antonio de Mendoza, (Lanning, 1940). One argument used to convince the king of the need for such an institution was that it was important to educate the Indians, just as had been done with the Moors after the end of the Reconquest with the creation of the University of Granada. Spaniards were very aware of the connection between education and empire. In fact, one of the letters sent to the king by a group of Franciscans in support of the university argued that Spain did not become important until it became learned and that Greece and Italy had lost their preeminence in antiquity because they had lost their scholarship (Méndez Arceo, 1952). This comment reflects the great esteem in which Spaniards held culture. This regard was well-documented by contemporary observers such as the humanist Pablo Giovio, who declared that in Spain people who did not like studying were not considered noble (Méndez Arceo, 1952). Like most superpowers, the Spanish Empire placed a great deal of importance on education.

According to Lanning (1940), the University of Mexico, which started instruction in 1553, included faculty with degrees from Paris, Salamanca, Alcalá, and Valencia and was modeled after the University of Salamanca. Salamanca was one of only four universities authorized to teach Greek, Hebrew, Arabic, and Chaldean by the Council of Vienna in 1312, a decision for which there were missionary motives, particularly in the Iberian Peninsula (Pedersen, 1997). In Mexico, however, these languages were of little use and were not taught. Instead, Indian languages were included in the curriculum, as they were essential to the imperial enterprise. Indeed, one of the reasons given for establishing a university in Mexico, instead of sending students to Spain, was to prevent them from forgetting the Indian languages the knowledge of which was so crucial (Méndez Arceo, 1952). Many jobs required knowledge of Indian languages, and this was a firm requirement, so the University of Mexico and the other Latin American universities were the first in the world to teach non-classical languages (Lanning, 1940).

There were many other full-fledged universities in Latin America besides the University of Mexico. The University of Lima was founded by Charles V in the same year that the University of Mexico was established, and it also admitted Indians and mestizos from the beginning (Góngora, 1979). By the early seventeenth century, the Spaniards had created universities in Chile, Argentina, and Bolivia. In addition to full-fledged European-style universities, Latin America also boasted a variety of other institutions of higher learning, including the many colleges managed by the Jesuits, who focused on the study of the classics and of science. In all, there were twenty-three universities in the Spanish colonies, according to Lanning (1940). After independence, the influence of France on Latin American universities became very strong, resulting in the creation of independent research institutes (Shils & Roberts, 2004). Thus, Latin American universities followed Spain and France, while Anglo-American institutions imitated England and Germany.

According to John Roberts, Agueda M. Rodríguez Cruz, and Jurgen Herbst (1996), Latin American universities were formally open not only to Indians and mestizos but also to blacks and mulattoes, although relatively few members of these groups attended. As time went by, the numbers of non-white students at these institutions of higher learning decreased. New regulations made their presence more difficult. There is evidence that, at least in some cases, in order to enter the university, students had to show that their ancestors were old Christians and had not engaged in trade (Benjamin, 1965). Although these regulations were aimed at keeping Jewish and Moslem *conversos* out of the university, they reflected a negative attitude towards all minorities. The crown, however, continued to protect the Indians with regulations, such as one clarifying that the Indian nobility was to be considered equivalent to the Spanish nobility, thus supporting class rather than race distinctions (Lanning, 1940). In spite of these efforts, by the nineteenth century, Indian students had become a rarity at Latin American universities, which catered to the upper classes of European origin. The independence of the Latin American republics only made things worse for Indians, who lost the protection Spain had offered them as subjects of the crown.

The situation in the English colonies was very different. First of all, these colonies were established later than the Spanish colonies, so by 1636, when Harvard was established, the University of Mexico had already graduated 8,000 students (Sánchez, 1970). According to Castañeda, by 1776 when the United States became independent, this Hispanic institution had granted 1,162 doctoral and masters degrees and 29,882 bachelors degrees, and there were many other colleges and universities throughout Latin America. Whereas Latin American institutions of higher learning were comprehensive universities funded by the state or by the church, the colonial colleges of the United States were neither full-fledged universities nor well-funded (Herbst, 1982). These colleges had to resort to philanthropy in order to survive. According to Rudolph (1962), the American colleges had a missionary spirit and were used to settle the land, "re-creating a New England town in the West" (53). The American colleges were, thus, not unlike the Spanish missions. Both were frontier institutions. The difference is that the American colleges educated whites, while the Spanish missions trained Indians, and the United States failed to create a national university in the capital, while the Spanish colonies had full-fledged universities in all major cities—and many major cities predated the arrival of the Spaniards—from the start.

Why did the strong and well-funded Latin American universities decline, and why did the weak and penurious colleges of the United States develop into powerful institutions of higher learning? In order to find the answers to these questions, we have to follow the money—or the power. The Spanish Empire, whose period of splendor extended roughly from the discovery of America in 1492 to the death of Felipe II in 1598, entered a period of decline in the seventeenth century, which lasted three centuries. Burns (2003) compares Felipe II with his English counterpart, Elizabeth I, finding that she was a transactional leader whose focus was survival, while he was a transformational leader, a Catholic prince whose grand plans for the conquest and conversion of England went awry with the destruction of the Armada, marking the beginning of the end for the Spanish Empire. Véliz (1994) goes further, comparing not the individual monarchs but their empires, concluding that the British Empire had a fox mentality, while the Spanish Empire had a hedgehog outlook. Being a holistic construct, both the Spanish metropolis and the colonies were affected by the decline. Indeed, many of the colonies and their universities were not developed until the empire was already decaying. By the time educational systems were established in some parts of the empire, they were already quite old-fashioned. For example, the Jesuits, who had offered cutting-edge education in sixteenth century Mexico, continued using the same instructional methods all over Latin America for a very long time.

Thus, what was creative and progressive in the sixteenth century eventually became rigid and obsolete, because it did not change. The large Latin American universities became fossilized and conservative. The Indians, who had shared classrooms with the Spaniards during the founding period of the universities, disappeared, giving way to *criollos* or American-born people of Spanish ancestry. Independence, which was a *criollo* revolt not an Indian upheaval, increased the marginalization of the Indians, as they lost the support of the crown and its institutions. Once more, an advance in education—the establishment of full-fledged universities—hurt marginalized peoples. The Indians, who had enjoyed the benefit of great schools devoted to them, were eventually excluded from the new institutions. Women also went through a similar exclusionary process, as their access to education diminished with the dissolution of the Indian schools, to which they had had access. Convents provided education to women and, although it appears that they did a good job, they did not offer the same level of training as the schools that disappeared or the universities from which women were excluded.

The situation in the English colonies in North America was somewhat different. On the one hand, the lands the English occupied did not have great Indian states like the Aztec or Inca Empires. On the other hand, the English did not have a tradition of conquest and acculturation comparable to the one the Spaniards had developed over many years of interactions between Christians and Moslems on the Iberian Peninsula. Thus, the English did not focus on conquering and acculturating Indians and using them as labor, but rather on conquering the land, eliminating or marginalizing the Indians, and doing the work themselves or with the help of black slaves imported from Africa. Therefore, the English colonists were not truly interested in educating the Indians, although they expressed a desire to do so. As Bobby Wright (1991) points out, their attempts "were lamentable failures" (433). Colleges such as Harvard and Dartmouth received money to educate Indians, but "did not follow through on these plans and promises for very long" (Pfister, 2009: 26). Indeed, in the case of Harvard, the money was used to educate colonial students who planned to become missionaries instead of the Indians themselves (Thelin, 2004).

The colonial colleges were white institutions. The few experiments in Indian education made by colonial colleges ended in disaster. Most of the Indian students died from illnesses or became alienated. One of the Indian leaders complained that the English clergy was too harsh and should follow the example of the Catholic missionaries, who knew how to treat the Indians and did not speak roughly to them or flog them (Wright, 1991: 442). The harsh discipline of Protestant schools greatly upset the Indians, who were very indulgent with their children (Pettitt, 1946: 6). This was quite different from the situation in Latin America, where there was less cultural dissonance between the Spaniards and the Indians. The Council of Indians, which had agreed to send their sons to the schools, believed that the schools had ruined their lives and withdrew their support. According to James Axtell (1976), the colonists liked the Indian lifestyle much more than the Indians liked the colonists' way of life, which is why so many white captives refused to return when given the opportunity, while this was not the case with Native American captives. As a result of this set of circumstances, the English colonies lacked the lively Indian schools in which the Spaniards successfully educated the Indian elite who helped them run the empire. They also lacked large universities.

Unlike the Spaniards, who were Catholic and had a holistic under-standing of the world, the English were Protestant and had pluralistic views. Thus, they founded many different colleges, as each religious branch wanted to have its own institution to train its clerics and educate the laity. Due to geographical dispersion, all colleges had to take students from other denominations, so there was a fair amount of tolerance. In fact, it was not uncommon for colleges to include minority sectarian representation on their boards of trustees. Of necessity, American colleges were eclectic and open-minded. They were also subject to few regulations, which allowed them to grow freely. In terms of the composition of their student bodies, these were originally relatively democratic, as they included students from modest backgrounds along with the children of the mercantile class, who were the majority. Thus, access to education for poor white students in the colonial era was relatively good. As noted by David Allmendinger (1974), there were geographical differences, with New England's hilltop colleges such as Amherst, Williams, and Dartmouth enrolling students of more modest means, often from small farms, than Harvard, Yale, and Princeton, many of whose students came from the mercantile class, and the Southern colleges, whose students were the sons of large plantation owners. But even at the colleges that took many poor students, there was a strong awareness of social class. As Thelin (2004: 23) points out, college rolls listed students by social rank, instead of alphabetical order, and academic robes were different for "servitors," or scholarship students, and "commoners," or regular students. If, in spite of these hurdles, poor white males had reasonable access to a college education, Indians, blacks, and women were almost totally excluded.

The curricula of the English colonial colleges was based on those of Oxford and Cambridge, which were the models for Harvard, founded by scholars from those institutions, and combined medieval learning and Renaissance studies in the classics (Rudolph, 1962). Modern languages and sciences were added over the years. These colleges were mostly residential institutions, although many students lived in boarding houses and the like. The purpose of the liberal arts education they offered was to train clerics and gentlemen who could handle any occupation. Their founding took place during the period in which England was beginning to create what would become a vast empire. This imperial system was resented by the colonists, who eventually obtained their independence from England to found the world's first secular democracy. Education was considered very important to building the new country, and the number of colleges grew after independence. George Washington's dream of creating a large national university, which would be publicly supported, was never realized (Wheeler, 1926), although there were various attempts, including one by Andrew Carnegie, who ended up creating the Carnegie Institution of Washington instead (Cordasco, 1960). According to Thelin (2004), the only true national institutions ever established were the West Point military academy and the Annapolis naval academy, along with the Smithsonian Institution. Instead, there was a proliferation of small colleges. Colleges were corporations. In fact, America's oldest corporation is not a commercial business but Harvard College, which was indeed the "Alma Mater of a nation," as proclaimed by a bumper sticker (Thelin, 2004: 1).

American colleges had an ambiguous status, neither fully private nor fully public (Herbst, 1982). A legal case involving Dartmouth College clarified the distinction between public and private and encouraged the "college building boom" (Thelin, 2004: 73). According to Arthur M. Cohen (1998), what the Dartmouth decision clarified was that "once a corporation had been established, it had a right to manage its own affairs, hold property, and exist indefinitely" (60). Indeed, its charter was considered a contract. Because private colleges could not expect much help from the state, they were forced to rely on philanthropy from the start, which created a culture of fund-raising. The authority of the president of these institutions was enormous, as was the power of the board of trustees, a feature they inherited from some European universities, including the Scottish universities (Cowley & Williams, 1991). Unlike the large European universities, where the rector was considered "first among equals," the president of the American college was a manager and fund-raiser, an entrepreneur, rather than a faculty member performing a coordinating function. The high degree of power and visibility of the president, who is a public figure, remains one of the characteristics of all American institutions of higher learning today and explains the fact that many former presidents, including Kerr and Gardner, write their memoirs and that there is a market for such books.

## Science and Technology

Although most of the science and technology giving rise to the industrial revolution came from outside of the university, once this transformation was underway, society turned to higher education for the creation of new knowledge. Thus, the research university was born in 1810, with the establishment of the University of Berlin. According to Cowley and Williams (1991), after the Napoleonic wars destroyed and humiliated the German states, putting an end to the Holy Roman Empire, the philosopher Johann G. Fichte called for a total revamping of education, including the introduction of a research component in all academic fields offered at the university. This was a nationalistic effort, an attempt to unify the German peoples, who at the time were fragmented and defeated. Writing when Berlin was occupied by French troops, Fichte (1968 [1808]) envisioned the emergence of a nation-state with a coherent and inspiring national educational system. He personally contributed to this effort, for along with Wilhelm von Humboldt, he played a leading role in the creation of the University of Berlin and was its first rector. Björn Wittrock (1993) believes that Humboldt's project prospered precisely because the Prussian government had left Berlin, which made change possible. Humboldt's idea of the university was holistic, as was Fichte's. Both wanted to combine teaching and research. Accordingly, the University of Berlin took over the existing Academy of Sciences and made it an integral part of the institution. The other German universities followed suit, and soon they became models for the other European countries, which developed equally large national systems of public higher education. As Bill Readings (1996) notes, the nation-states wanted universities that would offer a unifying worldview through culture. Thus, the invention of the national literature department and its role as the spiritual center of the university.

Meanwhile, the United States was busy establishing small private colleges, less concerned with creating a unifying culture than with offering its citizens opportunities for advancement. Since having a college in town was good for business, there was competition to establish new ones all over the land. Thus, on the eve of the Civil War, education was flourishing in the country in terms of numbers of colleges, but none of these colleges offered advanced instruction. Whereas the University of Mexico and other Latin American universities offered Ph.D. programs from their inception, so that students did not have to travel to Europe to obtain this degree, in the United States, the Ph.D. degree was not available. As a result, people had to go to Europe to study. One of the countries of choice was Germany, putting American scholars in direct contact with the research revolution taking place in that country. The large Latin American universities continued the tradition they had inherited from Salamanca, which was appropriate for the agrarian society of the time of the Spanish conquest. But the small North American colleges were transformed when they came into contact with the ideas from

Berlin, which were well-suited to a country built during the industrial revolution. In the United States, university building and nation building went together, which is why, in the mid-nineteenth century, newspapers and magazines published many articles about the future of higher education. These articles advocated the establishment of "a truly modern American university" (Thelin, 2004: 87). For example, *The Nation* wrote that the country's "intellectual progress" bore "no sort of proportion" to its "progress in the accumulation of wealth and in the mechanical arts" (Cordasco, 1960: 63). It was becoming clear that education was an indispensable companion to empire.

After the end of the Civil War, the university experienced many changes, although progress was uneven. Northern institutions of higher learning prospered, while many Southern universities were destroyed or destitute. Thus, the South fell behind the North in terms of higher education, a state of affairs remaining today, when Southern universities are still trying to catch up with those in the North. A fundamental change in the post-war period was the combination of the German research model with the American teaching model, which was accomplished by adding a graduate school to the undergraduate college in a sort of layer-cake structure (González, 2001).

The first research university in the United States was Johns Hopkins, established in 1876, not coincidentally "with the largest philanthropic bequest ever seen in the United States at that time" (Thelin 2004: 112). As Veysey indicates, what made innovation possible in the later part of the nineteenth century was "the blunt fact of the surplus capital that was newly available" (1965: 3). Shapiro (2005) points out that the post-war period "marked the ascendancy of the United States as the largest and most dynamic economy of the world" (56), noting that the university had very little to do with the economy, whose technological innovations came from the artisan tradition, not from academic knowledge. But when the economic boom began, society turned to the university for the production of new knowledge and the training of professionals. Along with the huge bequest, the leadership of Daniel Gilman at Johns Hopkins was very important. Frustrated by his struggles—first at Yale, which had become conservative after creating the first Ph.D program in the country, and then in the Golden State, where there was a powerful faction opposing his vision for the University of California—Gilman moved to Baltimore. There, he was allowed to create the institution of his dreams, Johns Hopkins University, a faculty-centered institution focused on graduate education, with the graduate fellowships, labs, and libraries that have come to be associated with research universities (Geiger, 1986). Harvard, Columbia, and other universities followed suit, and the research model spread quickly.

One important innovation that greatly facilitated this change was the introduction of electives, an effort led by Harvard's first non-clergyman president, Charles Eliot. With this device, Eliot managed to accomplish what George Ticknor, a distinguished Hispanist and the first German-trained American scholar, had failed to do: open Harvard's doors to disciplines other than the classics and bring a spirit of inquiry. The elective principle revitalized not only Harvard but the entire system of higher education in the United States. It acknowledged that, with the knowledge explosion, students had to specialize and transformed "the English college in America by grafting upon it German ideals" (Rudolph, 1962: 305).

At the same time, the need to bring higher education to more segments of the population and to offer a practical curriculum, including new professions, resulted in the creation of the land grant universities, emphasizing agricultural and mechanical training. During the post-Civil War period, government became interested in the university, which it saw as a tool for economic and social progress. The United States conceptualized public education as a single educational ladder, from elementary school through college. According to Shapiro (2005), the land grant movement was part of a larger trend that included such developments as the transcontinental railway, a national currency, and national taxation. This development was part of the aftermath of the French Revolution of 1789, which brought a belief in progress and empirical knowledge. The nineteenth century also brought the idea "of revolution, or change, as a permanent condition" (Shapiro, 2005: 50). This had a great impact on the structure of higher education. The German research university was part of this trend, as were progressive changes in the *grandes écoles* of France and the Scottish universities.

During the early years of the American land grant university, women students had an important presence at the university. While advocates of land grant universities "estimated that agriculture and applied sciences would be the locus of expansion in higher education, the professional field that enjoyed the most growth, first in student enrollments and then in employment, was education" (Thelin, 2004: 86). In addition, "Home economics, sometimes offered as a part of the agriculture units, was one of the most successful new fields" (Thelin, 2004: 136). The areas of science and technology took longer to grow. Thus, women helped institutions of higher learning to expand by providing large enrollments at a crucial stage of their evolution (Clifford, 1995: 98). With the Morrill Acts of 1862 and 1890 and the Hatch Act of 1887, public universities developed into large institutions focused on applied knowledge and service to society, in addition to teaching and research. As exemplified by "the Wisconsin idea," public universities used their resources to address the problems of their states. Their practical orientation constitutes an original contribution of the United States to the development of the university. By the end of the nineteenth century, land grant universities had developed the tripartite mission of teaching, research and service discussed by Lyman Abbot in 1906 (Rudolph, 1962). These three missions of the university brought with them three administrative structures. While teaching had been associated with colleges since the Middle Ages, research was linked to departments and service with extension offices, new structures created at this point to meet the needs of the university. If research and service were new, teaching was updated with the introduction of electives, a recognition that knowledge had become too extensive to expect that any program of studies could cover it all. This was coupled with a movement that emphasized process over content. Rather than teaching a fixed body of knowledge, universities began to focus on teaching mental discipline or the ability to learn. This very American trend spread quickly over the United States along with the German ideals of "freedom to teach," the professor's right to pursue his or her research interests, and "freedom to learn," the students' right to pick subjects of study, which was at the heart of the elective system. Academic freedom insured that both teachers and students could express their ideas openly.

While presidents served for a long time, allowing them to shape their institutions, faculty members were organized according to rank, became specialized and joined national and international organizations. This greatly increased their mobility, as universities started to shop for specialists in various fields in order to improve their reputations. Generalists gravitated towards the many colleges that chose not to become universities. These colleges stressed attention to the education of the whole person and the intimate atmosphere made possible by their small size. Honors programs, which created even smaller learning communities with an emphasis on "human considerations" (Rudolph, 1962: 458), enhanced this intimacy. American higher education thus developed along two different lines: that of the original undergraduate colleges, which survived as liberal arts colleges, and that of the undergraduate-plus-graduate school model of the American research university. The result was a very original system, which is probably the most diverse in the world in terms of the variety of institutions it includes and the activities these institutions offer. What started as a weakness—the lack of full-fledged universities—turned into a strength, as such universities were created at the precise point when research was introduced and the country was booming. At the same time, the many liberal arts colleges that did not make the transition to research universities served to enhance student options. It was the right system in the right place at the right time. Students could choose from among a wide range of institutions, including not only research universities and liberal arts colleges, but also regional and urban universities and colleges for people who did not have the resources to attend other institutions of higher learning. There was reasonable access for white male students of modest means, particularly at the public institutions. Access for women and blacks at mainstream universities was more limited. But there were women's and black colleges for individuals who might not fit easily in other institutions.

The tradition of women's colleges had started before the Civil War and continued afterwards even as institutions of higher learning were becoming coeducational. The philosophy behind them was that women would be more likely to succeed if they received the undivided attention of their teachers. Indeed, coeducational institutions did show a tendency to marginalize women, and even today, there are students who prefer women's colleges for this reason. The situation of blacks was somewhat different. Very few blacks attended college before the Civil War and those who did were in the North. After the Civil War, numerous institutions of higher learning for blacks were established in the South. The Morrill Act provided funds for black state universities and colleges. Thus, the HBCUs were born. Some Indian schools were also established at the end of the nineteenth century, including the Carliste School in Pennsylvania and the Hampton Institute in Virginia, although the latter ended up enrolling mostly blacks. When the 1896 "separate but equal" ruling of *Plessy v. Ferguson* permitted the exclusion of blacks from mainstream universities, these schools became crucial.

A very important debate about the education of blacks at the time took place between Booker T. Washington and W.E.B. Du Bois. This debate reflects the tensions between advocates of liberal and vocational education in the United States during that period. Attempting to lead the black community after the death of the legendary activist Frederick Douglass, Washington took the view that blacks should obtain a vocational education that would allow them to make a living, rather than attending college, which he thought was unrealistic for most. The institution of higher learning he founded—the Tuskegee Institute in Alabama—had an eminently practical approach to education. A former slave who had received industrial training, as he explains in his famous book *Up from Slavery*, Washington (1951 [1901]) believed that progress had to be gradual. For him, the first order of business was for blacks to recover the knowledge of trades that had been lost after emancipation, as he explained in his 1903 article "Industrial Education for the Negro." His "Atlanta Compromise," a speech in which he asked for certain benefits for blacks, but not equality, appeased whites, but made many blacks, including Du Bois, very unhappy.

A Fisk graduate with a Harvard Ph.D. who conducted advanced studies in Germany, Du Bois believed that blacks needed access to the highest levels of learning and that the only way for them to prosper was to build a cadre of leaders who could guide the community and lift it out of ignorance. In his 1903 article "The Talented Tenth," a sociological analysis of black college graduates, Du Bois reviewed data showing that these people were occupying key professional positions, including clergymen, teachers, doctors, and lawyers, noting that this included the faculty at Tuskegee. For Du Bois, when it came to education, it was necessary to begin at the top, for someone must teach the teachers who must teach the rest. This view was directly contrary to Washington's plan to start with elementary and vocational education before moving to secondary and college education.

Indeed, in his famous 1903 book *The Souls of Black Folk*, written in a prophetic style, Du Bois repeats the same arguments in a more literary way. After stating that the problem of the twentieth century was the problem of the color line, he discusses the troubled vision of blacks, who see as through a veil because they look at themselves through the eyes of others. Thus, it was important for black people to gain self-consciousness, which can only be accomplished through education. Although he acknowledged Washington's good intentions, he was very critical of his approach, which he considered misguided in its acceptance of second-class citizenship for blacks. Calling Washington a "compromiser between the South, the North, and the Negro" (40), Du Bois explained that Washington was asking black people to give up their political power and their insistence on civil rights, including the right to a higher education, without which the economic development he preached was impossible. Exposing this paradox in Washington's position, Du Bois pushed for "1. The right to vote. 2. Civic equality. 3. The education of youth according to ability" (42). For Du Bois, the industrial school could not be the answer to the question of how blacks should be trained, for they needed an education that would enhance their humanity by putting them in touch with the best creations of the human spirit and allowing them to "dwell above the Veil" (74).

Washington and Du Bois represent not only two different points of view but also two leadership styles. As Robert J. Norrell (2009) explains, Washington was a fox who tried to survive by shrewdly accepting second-class citizenship in order to make progress incrementally and through the back door. As a typical fox, he got along well with people and was very good at obtaining money for his cause. I believe that Du Bois was a hedgehog who had a vision of equality that he was not willing to compromise or conceal, even if that alienated many people. Both performed a great service to the black community and to the country. They are a good example of why society needs both foxes and hedgehogs. Without shrewdness, we are stuck. Without vision, we are dead. The positions that Washington and Du Bois took constituted a preview of the current debate about access. While in many cases, it might be wise to encourage minorities to attend community colleges and regional and city universities, their presence is crucial at elite liberal arts colleges and research universities, not only as students but as faculty and administrators, including presidents.

## The Golden Age of the American University

A chief characteristic of American higher education in the twentieth century was the importance of competition, which has continued to expand up to the present time. As Lucas (1994) points out, universities compete for federal and private grants, for reputation as reflected in rankings, for faculty and for students. Within universities, individual departments and programs compete for funding, space, and administrative support. Faculty members compete for promotions, raises, space, grants, and honors. Students compete for entrance, grades, fellowships, loans, and jobs or admission to graduate school. There are many different kinds of institutions of higher learning, and each competes with the other institutions in its group. The result is a very large and diverse group of institutions of higher learning with all levels of difficulty, from the most selective to the ones that take all applicants. This free-market mentality has resulted in excellence in research, teaching, and service, combined with open access. American universities have reached new heights due to their reliance on competition. At the same time, this system contains the seeds of its own demise, as competition, carried to its logical conclusion, is capable of undoing the accomplishments of the last decades.

The twentieth century started with a trend towards coordination and standardization through associations and rankings. This explains the building of student unions, which provide internal focus, and the creation of the Association of American Universities, which offers external links, as well as the central role of the federal government, including research grants and the GI Bill. All of these changes transformed universities, which bloomed after World War II, in the Golden Age of American higher education, a period marked by the "three P's" of prosperity, prestige and popularity (Thelin 2004: 260). After its victories in Europe and the Pacific, the United States invested a great deal of money in research and education, following the call of Vannevar Bush's 1945 manifesto *Science, the Endless Frontier*, which appealed to the country's pioneering spirit. The competitive research grants advocated by Bush became the model by which the federal government adjudicated its funds. The result of this system was better research, but only a relatively small number of universities were in a position to compete for these grants, which had the effect of increasing the distance between elite and non-elite institutions of higher learning.

As the century progressed, the support public universities received from the states housing them decreased while, ironically, state surveillance increased. Meanwhile, the influence of the federal government and private business grew steadily. Thus, public universities came to depend on the federal government and private business for their funding, while remaining subordinate to state governments, which became more controlling as they withdrew financial support, as if to compensate for lack of funding with their supervisory zeal. At the same time, education started to be considered a private good rather than a public service, and tuition became more expensive. While democratization led to expansion, expansion led to competition, which resulted in an anti-democratic trend.

As institutions of higher learning started to grow at the turn of the twentieth century, they developed a need for administrators to run their multiple offices in a businesslike manner. This created a division between the faculty and the leadership, an "us and them" situation that persists today. It also brought an increase in the power of presidents, who began to be selected not from the clergy, but from among laymen who could deal with the business world. At the same time, boards of trustees also became populated by members of the corporate world, while rich alumns became active in the lives of their institutions, coinciding with the expansion of college sports. The influence of business and other external constituencies on the university has continued to the present time. The process of privatization that so many people decry today started over one hundred years ago and was painstakingly described by Veblen, whose 1918 book remains the best analysis of the process to date. Not coincidentally, there were many assaults on academic freedom during that period, when many faculty members lost their jobs for expressing ideas that donors and politicians found inconvenient. In response to this problem, in 1915, faculty members created the American Association of University Professors, which drafted a Statement of Principles concerning academic freedom and tenure. The depression era brought some paranoia about communists, which resulted in quite a few faculty members losing their jobs. The paranoia subsided during the war, only to become stronger than ever during the McCarthy era, when the careers of many professors were destroyed and institutions of higher learning suffered purges of various kinds. These included the University of California, which was shaken by the loyalty oath controversy.

During the early twentieth century, there was a great deal of curricular experimentation at institutions of higher learning. In part, this was because the new research universities did not replace the old undergraduate colleges but rather complemented them. "The Age of the University" was also the "Age of Collegiate Life" (Thelin, 2004: 154). This released a great deal of creative energy. Among other things, there was a reaction against the elective system established in the previous decades, as well as against the increasingly vocational orientation of these institutions. Universities stressed the fact that students were there primarily to "find themselves." The adoption of school mascots and songs gave students a sense of identity and belonging. Coursework was organized around an area of concentration or major, with distribution requirements to ensure that all important disciplines were included. This led to a debate about general education. Particularly noteworthy experiments are Frank Aydelotte's honors program at Swarthmore, Alexander Meiklejohn's freshman survey and senior capstone courses at Reed, and John Erskine's studies of primary sources at Columbia, which was the inspiration for Robert Maynard Hutchins' famous great books courses at Chicago. Hutchins was one of the most outspoken critics of vocational education. For him, education needed to focus on the ideas embodied in the classics.

After World War II, there was renewed interest in general education, which was seen as a tool to defend freedom during the cold war. The launching of Sputnik, however, made specialization very important, as the country engaged in a scientific race with the Soviet Union. This negated the desire to enhance general education, which never regained the importance it once had. It also enhanced the importance of graduate education, as many students decided to pursue the Ph.D. These graduate students, working as teaching assistants, played a very important role in educating the large numbers of undergraduates who attended college in the second half of the twentieth century.

While colleges and universities were trying various approaches to education, new types of institutions were developing. In particular, the two-year college that had appeared in the nineteenth century spread quickly during the first decades of the twentieth when the number of students attending college grew. These institutions were both a way to provide access to higher education and a way to control it, since they allowed successful students to transfer to universities and provided vocational training for the rest. Normal schools also experienced a great transformation during this period, when they evolved into state colleges. After the war, these institutions continued to evolve, first into state colleges and then into state universities. At the same time, universities developed departments or schools of education, which produced research about pedagogy and the context of teaching. Another change affecting all institutions of higher learning is the use of technology, which has enhanced access. An important recent development is the rapid creation of for-profit universities, which offer no-frills education at convenient times and locations, with or without the help of technology. These "fast food chains" of higher education are very popular among people with a strong vocational orientation. Their share of the market is expected to grow, as the process of privatization continues to unfold.

In terms of enrollments, there was continuous growth during the twentieth century until academic year 1975-1976, when enrollments declined by 175,000, but the numbers continued to grow afterwards, with public institutions expanding their enrollments much more than the privates (Thelin, 2004). According to Martin Trow (1970), higher education, which had gone from an elite to a mass orientation with relative ease, had problems transitioning from mass to universal. The proliferation of institutions of higher learning produced confusion as to the meaning of a college education. There was a sense that quantity had replaced quality. The creation of portable fellowships created competition for students and made institutions of higher learning more dependent on the federal government, which was then in a position to demand that they conform to its dictates, including affirmative action regulations.

Throughout the twentieth century, access to college was possible for students from modest backgrounds. But members of certain immigrant groups, particularly Jews, suffered considerable discrimination in the 1920s and 1930s, when elite institutions of higher learning established quotas to reduce their presence in the student body, which would have been extremely high if admissions had been based on grades alone. Their situation improved after WWII, when universities became more welcoming to students from non-traditional backgrounds. Indeed, the GI Bill brought to the university over two million such students, whom the universities received with open arms. The GI Bill's success was made possible by the "high school movement" that developed between 1910 and 1940, making a great percentage of the population educated enough to aspire to go to college (Goldin & Katz, 2008). Even so, accommodations were made, and admissions requirements became flexible. As a Harvard recruiting brochure announced, "intellectual brilliance is not required for admission—or for success after admission. Character, experience, promise, all around performance are vital" (Thelin, 2004: 264). Interestingly, because of the high volume of applications and the lack in many cases of high school transcripts and college preparatory records, universities started to rely on tests for admissions and placement decisions. The GIs, most of whom were white males focused on careers, made American campuses more conservative and less diverse in terms of gender and race, although not in terms of social class.

With respect to women and minorities, their numbers did not increase a great deal until the civil rights movement. Engaged in the prestige race, universities did not pay much attention to them until they were forced to do so by the student revolts of the 1960s, which caused a great deal of upheaval at the University of California and many other institutions around the country. Thelin (2004) states that the university's problem was not, as some people believe, that "its center had failed to hold," but rather that it "had no center at all" (316). Towards the end of the century, the number of non-traditional students, including part-time and older students, expanded.

Students enjoyed periods of tranquility, which alternated with moments of upheaval. In particular, there was a fair amount of student activism during the 1920s and 1930s. After two decades of conformism, students became very politically active in the 1960s, at the time of the "New Frontier," the civil rights movement and the Vietnan War. The free speech movement at Berkeley set the tone for similar revolts all over the country. Although the issues students chose to embrace were different on each campus, they all had in common an anti-establishment spirit. They were a rejection of middle class values. The 1960s student movements were unique in that, for the first time, a youth counterculture was established. After the end of the Vietnan War, during the economic crisis of the 1970s, protests died out and students began to focus on getting jobs, as these became harder to obtain. Students started to see themselves as consumers who were paying a great deal of money for their educations and therefore were entitled to good grades, as well as good instruction, services, and facilities. Their parents, who in many cases were footing the bill, became more involved in their educations, which now had turned into a significant economic investment. These "helicopter parents," who descend upon campuses to make demands on behalf of their children, can be seen as the final consequence of a process of privatization.

With the increase of women and minority university students in the second half of the twentieth century, the curriculum changed to include ethnic, women's, and gay studies. This new emphasis on multicultural-ism was not well-received in some quarters, giving rise to the "political correctness" controversy. While some professors studied the histories and cultures of non-Western civilizations, as well as those of women and minorities within the Western World, others believed that this approach was an attack on Western values. Over time, this debate died out, as the changes became institutionalized.

While the university was becoming more inclusive in terms of gen-der, ethnicity, and sexual orientation, its growth was uneven. As Kerr notes, while enrollments in the community colleges grew tremendously between 1960 and 1980, the percentage of all enrollments in Research Universities I went from almost 20 percent to under 10 percent. Unlike what happened in some European countries, which dumped all increased enrollments on their pre-existing universities, the United States directed the growth in enrollments to new public institutions such as community colleges and regional universities. As Kerr says, "the elite institutions in the United States remained elite; some became even more elite in their admission standards" (2001a: 117). Kerr adds that the rest of the system absorbed the impacts of growth and accommodated "the lesser professions and occupations" (2001a: 117). What he does not mention is that by reducing the relative percentage of elite universities and making the pre-existing ones even more elite, the American system relegated women, minorities, and the poor to lesser institutions. Thus, something that was good—making elite universities more selective while providing universal access—was a mixed blessing for women and minorities, who got access to higher education but, for the most part, were tracked to non-selective institutions of higher learning.

As Lucas (1994) indicates, the history of higher education shows that there is only a small perdurable number of questions: "The educational institution's role in society, and whether its contribution is to serve society or to challenge it; the possibility of objectivity and impartiality in knowledge; the appropriate balance between curricular commonality or integration and diversification and specialization; issues of inclusion and exclusion, and so on" (299-300). Although there are many variations, these questions and the kinds of answers they have elicited have been constant. Lucas (1994) advises against contemplating the past with nostalgia, as does Thelin (2004), who states that neither students nor faculty would like to exchange places with their counterparts from one hundred years ago. Thelin (2004) believes that the status of American higher education as a "mature industry"—a term coined by Levine (1997), which is reminiscent of Gray's "institutional maturity" (1983: 16)—should be acknowledged and accepted so that the university can focus on values and revisit the issues raised by Flexner (1994) and recently reviewed by George M. Marsden (1994) and Julie A. Reuben (1996). It is important to remember, however, that as Goldin and Katz (2008) have pointed out, there is still room to grow in American higher education, since the United States in recent times has fallen behind other industrialized nations in terms of the percentage of the population that graduates from college. In addition, learning was not more disinterested in the past than it is today.

From the first formal schools in Mesopotamia onward, society, and students in particular, have turned to education for economic reasons. Similarly, faculty members and administrators have been affected by the social developments of each period. Their academic freedom was always limited. Criticism of the establishment was always problematic. In fact, professors might enjoy more protections today than ever before in history. With respect to the curriculum, there have been constant tensions, as new disciplines and trends displaced or replaced old ones. Noting that knowledge is never neutral and that the curriculum tends to reflect the cannon of the establishment, Lucas (1994) wonders whether the current push to mainstream the contributions of women and minorities is an exception to this rule or whether it simply represents the ascendancy of these groups. I believe that it represents the latter, as this trend started with the upheavals of the 1960s, when marginalized people began to make demands.

Money talks, and in the United States, women and minorities are economic and political forces, whose numbers and power are only going to increase. Historically, democratic periods in higher education have been followed by periods favoring an aristocratic approach to access. At the same time, periods of practical or vocational orientation have been followed by periods which favor knowledge for its own sake. According to Veblen (1918), the natural progression is to go from a vocational orientation to a focus on knowledge for its own sake. A similar trend appears to be present with respect to diversity. Any new development in the history of higher education has originally been open to a relatively large number of students, only to become less accessible over time as it becomes institutionalized and fashionable. This generates a counter-trend of people demanding access, eventually giving way to a new system. I believe that we are now at a point where access to the highest levels of education is limited, and society is asking for change.

# 8

# The Hinge of History

The preface to the 1963 edition of *The Uses of the University* states that "universities in America are at a hinge of history: while connected with their past, they are swinging in another direction" (Kerr, 2001a: xi). Noting that the university is one of the oldest extant institutions, Kerr discusses the novel position in which it finds itself in society where, as a knowledge producer in a knowledge-based economy, it has a centrality it never enjoyed before. In the 1994 edition of *The Uses of the University* (chapter 6 of the 2001 edition), Kerr reflects that "the hinge of history" can been seen "even more dramatically in 1994 than in 1963" (2001a: 141) pointing out the great increase in research and service and the decrease in teaching that faculty members have experienced during that period, trends related to the success of the German research model and the American service model, and the decline of the British teaching model, focused on liberal education. According to Kerr, in 1963, "the 'Hutchins' College' at Chicago and the 'Red Book' at Harvard were still much discussed as means of reviving 'liberal knowledge' for undergraduates" (2001a: 144). By 1994, it had become clear that liberal education was not truly compatible with the research and service model of the university. Thus, the failure of the "cluster colleges" at Santa Cruz, an unrealized liberal education dream of Kerr's, as this campus became part of the "multiversity," just like all the other campuses of the University of California.

There are indications that Harvard, Yale, Princeton, Stanford, and other elite private universities are moving farther away from the liberal education ideal. These elite private institutions combined the liberal arts college atmosphere with the research university by having small undergraduate enrollments and large graduate and professional schools and research programs. Expansion of the latter, however, is causing balance problems and forcing the Ivy League schools to increase undergraduate enrollments (Farrell, 2007). As these schools devote their wealth to enlarging their facilities and adding faculty members to enhance their research enterprises, they will have to expand their student bodies in order to maintain the right ecosystems. This will also allow these highly-selective institutions to take more students from diverse backgrounds without giving up the income that rich students bring to their campuses. With these changes, differences between private and public research universities should diminish, as Kerr (2001a) anticipated when he stated that Michigan had become an Ivy and Harvard a land grant. In both cases, the prevailing model emphasizes research and service over teaching, and graduate over undergraduate education. Thus, the liberal education dream was a short-lived mission of the university in the United States, as Laurence R. Veysey (1965) points out.

Veysey's book *The Emergence of the American University* is one of the most interesting studies about the various missions of the American university. Written as a doctoral dissertation at UC Berkeley in 1961 and published in 1965, this book does not quote *The Uses of the University* or mention Kerr at all. Conversely, Kerr's book, which came out in 1963, does not refer to Veysey's work, then still a dissertation. Yet these studies have a great deal in common. Both take a broad view of the American university's development, which they see as a layered structure. For Veysey, American institutions of higher learning had four distinct periods, each with a different mission, and these periods unfolded in rapid succession. The colonial colleges' first mission was to provide mental discipline, as well as to enhance piety. Thus, during that era, professors were generalists. Their goal was not to teach disciplines in depth, but rather to introduce the students to certain habits of thought. The next stage was that of utility, which became popular in the second half of the nineteenth century, when universities became the companion piece to expansion. At that point, there was an idea "that the university should take its orders directly from the non-academic mass of citizens" (Veysey, 1965: 64). During this period, there was a democratic trend resulting in some universities not charging tuition nor giving letter grades, as was the case with Stanford's early years. The University of California also held democratic ideals, expressed eloquently by Wheeler (1926), who said that "a university is a place that rightfully knows no aristocracy as between studies, no aristocracy as between scientific truths, and no aristocracy as between persons," adding that "all that can make one student better than another is cleanness of soul, cleanness of purpose, cleanness of thought, and cleanness of life" (66).

Eliot's advocacy of the elective system at Harvard was connected to this philosophy of utility and democracy. At the same time, he focused on excellence, a word that had been almost absent from the language of Harvard's reports before his time but had a strong presence in the documents produced during his presidency. As an alumn commented, his inaugural message was "no more old fogyism," and indeed, Eliot went on to change everything (Lewis, 2006: 34). The next element or mission was research, linked to science, which was imported from the German university and successfully established in the United States by Gilman at Johns Hopkins. This brought the graduate school. Competition for prestige centered on the quality of graduate programs and faculty publications. Unlike teaching, research is quantifiable, and universities started to collect and distribute lists of faculty publications early on. Finally, a fourth perspective or mission was added, also at the end of the nineteenth century, as an alternative to the others, and that is what Veysey calls liberal culture, a concept that was explained by such scholars as Irving Babbitt (1986 [1908]) and Hugo Münsterberg (1913). The liberal culture vision of the university was defended by a small but militant group of scholars who favored the study of humanities as the best means to educate "gentlemen" in the tradition of Oxford and Cambridge.

According to Veysey (1965), "the academic outlooks which were most European in their perspectives were those of culture and research, whereas both mental discipline and utility exhibited a more self-satisfied parochialism" (197). If we consider the entire history of the university, however, we realize that only the mission of utility was truly an American invention, since mental discipline was the original mission of the medieval university focused on the *trivium* and the *quadrivium*. In fact, what happened to the American university is that it added the missions that had taken centuries to ferment in Europe in a very short period of time. The European university went from focusing on mental discipline in the Middle Ages to adding the humanities or liberal culture in the Renaissance to adding science in the nineteenth century. The American colonial colleges, which started with a medieval focus on mental discipline, added science (the new mission imported from Germany) and utility (a unique American contribution) at the same time, causing a shock to the system. Liberal culture was introduced at that time as an antidote to change, a way of rescuing and improving the original mental discipline mission and perhaps also, as Shapiro (2005) suggests, to provide "a spiritual vision to replace the loosening glue of the belief in God" (74). Thus, the language of religion was used to defend liberal democracy. At the same time, the university was modeled after business. The result was a creative tension that greatly assisted the development of the American university into an original institution seemingly able to pursue all of the missions at once. In part, it did so by specialization: small colleges focused on the mental discipline and liberal culture mission, while large universities paid more attention to research and utility. But all institutions of higher learning contained some elements of these four missions. For example, Woodrow Wilson, who as president of Princeton famously said that a college was "not a place where a lad finds his profession, but a place where he finds himself" (Veysey, 1965: 242), was nevertheless in favor of public service as a mission of the college.

Veysey (1965) notes that, although the American university enjoyed enormous freedom in its creative stage, it soon developed a structure that quickly solidified and became typical of all American universities. This structure consists of "an undergraduate college basically English in conception" linked to a "Germanic graduate school" ( 311). The ties between the two are loose and mostly financial, as are the bonds between them and the other parts of the university. "Bureaucratic administration was the structural device which made possible the new epoch of institutional empire-building without recourse to specific shared values. Thus, while unity of purpose disintegrated, a uniformity of standardized practices was coming into being" (Veysey, 1965: 311). At the end of the nineteenth century, there were two countertendencies in American higher education: fragmentation and centralization. The latter was achieved through bureaucratic structures, such as accreditation organizations, professional associations, ranking systems and even newly-created ceremonies, as shown by the work of the intercollegiate commission on academic dress that formulated the rituals that have become a standard feature of academia in this country.

Veysey (1965) compares academia with industry, stating that "the university and the factory both had to harness the energies of disparate groups" (315-316). This was done through bureaucratic regulations in both cases. The cohesion of the institution depended on the incentives it provided its various component groups and its "tendency to blend and reconcile," achieved by a new breed of administrators who came to power at the end of the nineteenth century. These administrators were "outstanding empire-builders," as well as "harbingers of the mood of intellectual reconciliation" (Veysey, 1965: 360). These are the leaders that Kerr calls the "Giants in the Groves:" Gilman, Eliot, Harper, etc. (2001a: 23). But even the greatest of the giants could not reconcile everything. In order to deal with "the problem of the unreconciled" (Veysey, 1965: 418), or the lack of consensus, universities developed academic freedom, which protected those faculty members who resisted standardization. By placing administration in the hands of professional managers and establishing protective mechanisms for non-conformists, the American university gave the faculty a great deal of flexibility. The prestige system allowed them to develop careers and to excel.

According to Veysey (1965), the development of the American university was not the result of a single, large vision, although there were many visionary leaders at its institutions of higher learning. Rather, it came about by a happy string of serendipitous events, which gave way to a unique institution. In other words, it was a fox-like process that shrewdly combined the contradictory visions of many hedgehogs. No single vision prevailed. Thus, the failure of the idea of a national university and the replacement of culture by excellence (Readings, 1996). Culture is a unifying factor, a set of beliefs that everyone must share, while excellence allows diversity. Unlike the universities of the European nation-states, which were focused on national culture, American institutions of higher learning offered a mosaic of visions, a multiplicity of options, which gave the new empire the tools it needed to carve out a place for itself in the society of nations. This multiplicity is evident in the very structure of the university, which, as Shapiro (2005) notes, has "a distinctively American flavor" (72), showing a sharp separation of graduate, undergraduate, and professional education, in addition to the existence of various types of institutions of higher learning. In the course of the twentieth century, the American university, with it focus on excellence, did a brilliant job of providing access to higher education for the majority of the country's citizens. Its most famous success story was the California Master Plan for Higher Education, which promised a place in one of its public institutions of higher learning to any student who wanted to attend. This became a model for other states, which followed suit. No country on earth could boast of the level of access to post-secondary education as did California and the rest of the United States during the Golden Age of the twentieth century.

As Vest (2007) says, American universities became "the envy of the world," which was driven home for him when he had dinner with the rector of Humboldt University in Berlin, who asked his advice about how the American research university model could be successfully transplanted to Germany. The irony, of course, is that the American research university is a successful transplant of the research university model of Humboldt. I had an identical experience when I was invited with a group of fellow American graduate deans to visit Humboldt and other German universities, as well as the Deutsche Forschungsgemeinschaft, and provide advice about how Germany might improve its graduate programs (González, 2002). So I can easily envision a future in which American universities will ask the help of consultants from the countries that are currently adopting the American research university model. The torch of knowledge changes hands periodically. In the twentieth century, the United States was the undisputed carrier of this torch. The flame is still bright, but there are strong winds.

In the prologue to the last edition of *The Uses of the University*, Kerr said that universities in America were again at a hinge of history, adding that this time, however, he saw "the hinge flapping in the winds blowing from many directions—no zephyrs, alas" (2001a: vii). The winds might take the torch elsewhere or they might not, at least not yet. The winds might settle down in one direction, and the odds are good that it will be in the direction of expanding access to the research and liberal culture missions of the university to non-traditional students, adding one level of innovation and criticism to the American higher education system. As Shapiro (2005) says, the university has a "dual role as both society's servant and society's critic" and should live "in an unresolved state of anxiety with the status quo" (15). This is about to change again:

> New challenges to the human condition are arising; The challenges of demography, the national and international distribution of income, new infectious diseases, new forms of communications, the environment, new technologies, political and cultural fragmentation amid forces pressing for globalization, and even challenges to the role of rationality in helping us achieve a better understanding of the human experience. Indeed, it is hard to avoid the feeling that we are on the brink of another transformation. (Shapiro, 2005: 87)

Shapiro (2005) believes that the university's capacity for peaceful interactions across cultural divides and its ability to challenge the familiar are "indispensable assets for the future now unfolding" (119). The American higher education system's greatest strength—the multiplicity of options—was also its greatest weakness, however, for, although it afforded access to marginal people, it did so in a segregated fashion. Well-to-do white men have had much more access to the research and liberal culture missions of the university than women, minorities, and the poor, who are concentrated in institutions where the predominant mission is utility. In theory, the system is open to all and, as Shapiro (2005) notes, "there is an unusually large variety of entry points, relatively speaking, to the so-called elite programs" (2), but in practice, access to the most prestigious institutions—those dealing with the research and liberal culture missions—is limited to certain social groups.

In *Troubled Times for American Higher Education*, a book in which he does quote Veysey, Kerr speculates about the future of higher education in the United States, pointing out that, on average, national academic leadership since the sixteenth century has lasted about eighty years. This suggests that the United States' preeminence might be waning, although he thinks that "it might remain first for the dimly foreseeable future, but first among more nearly equals" (1994a: xiii). For Kerr, American institutions of higher learning differ from those in other countries in their emphasis on affirmative action for faculty and students and their interest in multiculturalism in the curriculum, and he believes that this trend is bound to increase as the population continues to change. He describes the introduction of affirmative action policies into higher education as an "intrusion" related to the labor market (1994a: 66). Tensions in this new society are not vertical but horizontal. Rather than the poor against the rich, we now have black against white, female against male, etc. The forms of warfare are no longer the broad, encompassing ways of "the revolution" but rather are "guerrilla-type actions" about specific issues (1994a: 13). Kerr, however, does not believe that these tensions will be as strong as other people think and expresses optimistic views about the power of education to address them:

> I have been impressed with the importance of looking at all individuals in a multidimensional way—not at any one characteristic alone, particularly if that characteristic is not of the individual's personal choosing. I have also been impressed that society, as far as is possible, should equalize opportunity so that individuals advance and retreat on the basis of their talent and effort and not their inherited status. I have also been impressed with the role of education in affecting how individuals look at other individuals, and in helping to level the playing fields of economic, political, and cultural life. (Kerr, 1994a: 152)

Kerr believed that opportunities previously afforded to white males had been extended to women and minorities and that the focus now should be to concentrate on the disadvantaged in both categories in an effort to find and develop talent. Although he was overly optimistic about the rate of progress, I think that his instincts were fundamentally correct: We need to identify and grow talent in all populations. In particular, we need to find and develop a new generation of diverse leaders who can understand today's challenges and opportunities. At the same time, we must be aware that, as Kerr warns, only a return to economic prosperity and political preeminence can move higher education in the United States to a new level of accomplishment. Now, as always, the fate of higher education depends squarely on the fate of the country.

# Part III

## History of the University of California

# 9

# The Hedgehog Concept

In their book *Built to Last*, Jim Collins and Jerry I. Porras (2004 [1994]) compared a set of highly-successful companies with a group of similar or "twin" businesses that had not done as well and found that the former had a small number of core values that guided them through thick and thin and explained their success. Instead of relying on "time telling" or the vision of individual leaders, these companies depended on "clock-building" or a collective vision that sustained them over time (22-42). Most of these visionary companies chose their leaders internally and, although they did not begin with a great idea, they did have a strong sense of purpose. Their achievements came after much branching and pruning, and their struggles are on-going.

In *Good to Great* (2001), which he considers a prequel to *Built to Last*, Collins examines companies that made the leap and sustained their success for at least fifteen years. All of these businesses went through the same stages. First, at crucial moments of their development, they had what he calls "level 5 leadership" (17-40), that is, a combination of personal humility and professional will. These leaders started by getting "the right people on the bus" (41-64) before they confronted "the brutal facts" (65-89) and developed a "hedgehog concept," which Collins defines as "a simple, crystalline concept that flows from deep understanding about the intersection of the following three circles: what you can be the best in the world at...what drives your economic engine...what you are deeply passionate about" (95-96). Collins notes that there is a big difference between pre-hedgehog and post-hedgehog states:

> In the prehedgehog state it's like groping through the fog. You're making progress on a long march, but you can't see all that well. At each juncture in the trail, you can only see a little bit ahead and must move at a deliberate, slow crawl. Then, with the

Hedgehog Concept, you break into a clearing, the fog lifts, and you can see for miles. From then on, each juncture requires less deliberation, and you can shift from crawl to walk, and from walk to run. In the posthedgehog state, miles of trail move swiftly beneath your feet, forks in the road fly past as you quickly make decisions that you could not have seen so clearly in the fog. (Collins, 2001: 110-111)

The companies that failed to go from good to great almost never emerged from the fog, showing a desire to grow for the sake of growth that was lacking in the successful concerns. The latter were focused on a vision, and had a culture of discipline, allowing them to stop doing things that were not relevant to their purposes. Their vision did not come to them suddenly, but rather was an iterative process that took years. This is what Collins calls the flywheel of success, as opposed to the doom loop of failure.

In *How the Mighty Fall* (2009), Collins examines the five stages of decline, namely, "hubris born of success," "undisciplined pursuit of more," "denial of risk and peril," "grasping for salvation," and "capitulation to irrelevance or death" (27), pointing out that most of the fallen companies he studied had external CEOs, while most of the successful ones had internal ones. For him, executives who fail to undertake succession plainning set their enterprises on a path to failure.

To build an enduring company of iconic stature requires strong homegrown leadership, together with core values and a sense of purpose beyond economic profit. In other words, after a process of buildup and breakthrough, the enduring companies understood what was unique about their contributions and stayed faithful to their essence. Their focus was not merely on making money but on rendering a service to society.

These principles apply to all kinds of institutions, not just to business corporations. Collins (2005) addressed this issue in detail in a book titled *Good to Great and the Social Sectors*. His stated intention was not to suggest that the social sector should be run like a business, but that all institutions, whether businesses, churches, hospitals, or schools, follow the same rules when it comes to what separates good from great. Indeed, the *Good to Great* principles most certainly apply to universities, particularly to the University of California.

In *The Rise of American Research Universities: Elites and Challengers in the Postwar Era*, Hugh D. Graham and Nancy Diamond (1996) evaluated institutional performance in new ways. Rather than ranking universities according to perceived quality, they counted numbers of federal research dollars, scientific journal articles, and fellowships in the arts and humanities. They divided these by the number of faculty members at each institution, in order to determine research productivity. One of this book's most interesting findings is the high performance by the faculty of all campuses of the University of California, whose extraordinary rise stands out as the most spectacular academic success story of the twentieth century. With ten campuses of top quality, six of which are members of the prestigious Association of American Universities (AAU), the University of California is a unique institution that many consider the best university system in the world.

How did the University of California achieve such high status? Obviously, the size and wealth of California have contributed to UC's success. Great countries produce great educational institutions (Ortega, 1997 [1930]), and the State of California is the largest and richest state in the country. Indeed, according to Kerr, its history consists of a series of "gold rushes:" gold, oranges, and grapes, motion pictures, military-industrial development, electronics, and biotechnology (2001b: 416-417). The conditions were certainly right for the creation of a great institution of higher learning, but this did not necessarily have to happen.

Other large and prosperous states developed good universities but not the kind of top-of-the-line university system that UC is (Kerr, 1994a; Feller, 2007). New York, perhaps because of its proximity to the Ivy League institutions, did not fund its public universities well and therefore could not develop a comparable system, nor has Texas developed a similar system, in spite of its prosperity and its location. In fact, "in 1971 the State of Texas supported at least thirty-seven public sector institutions under as many as fifteen different governing boards, six of which controlled systems" (Rothblatt, 1997: 293). Texas can be considered California's "twin" state, the closest in many respects, including size, wealth, and distance from the private universities of the East Coast. California might just as easily have created universities the same way Texas did. It could have built a few excellent state universities, but not a top-level public university system with across-the-board quality.

The University of California's success has to be attributed to extraordinary insight and commitment on the part of its members and supporters over an extended period of time. The University of California has been a visionary institution that has followed the same set of core values throughout its history. In particular, it has brought together democratic goals and aristocratic ideals. These were enunciated at the time of its founding in 1868, when the private College of California became a land grant university, combining the characteristics of both types of institutions.

These principles were affirmed when the California Master Plan for Higher Education, which provided a formula for the state's public institutions of higher learning to combine selectivity and access, allowed the University of California to develop and implement its "hedgehog concept" of an elite public research university system. Like the enduring companies of iconic stature studied by Collins and Porras (2004 [1994]), the University of California understood what was unique about its contributions and stayed faithful to its essence. Its focus was not on being good or even on being great, but on being great in a way that would match and promote the greatness of the Golden State, which is the most powerful expression of the American Dream.

According to Henry F. May (1993), the University of California reflects the dual character—traditional and innovative—of the United States as defined by George Santayana with an architectural metaphor: "a neat reproduction of the colonial mansion—with some modern comforts introduced surreptitiously—stands beside the sky-scraper" (3). As Pelfrey (2004) notes, Californians had a dream of high-quality universal public education, which combined tradition with innovation, and were willing to pay for it. Indeed, "nothing could be more American—or more Californian—than the expectation that a UC Berkeley or a UC San Diego could be the equal of a Harvard or a Cambridge" (93). According to alumn Joan Didion, the University of California seems to be "California's highest, most articulate idea of itself, the most coherent—perhaps the only coherent—expression of the California possibility" (Pelfrey, 2004: 3).

Although the idea of creating a public institution of higher learning is as old as the state, the University of California was not established until the College of California's terms—that its campus be used to establish "a complete university" with the help of land grant funds—were accepted. The President of the College of California was Henry Durant (1870-1872), who was a Republican with a New England notion of "refinement," which quickly came into conflict with the state's "Democratic, industrial and agricultural forces" (Otten, 1970: 35-36). A Yale scholar, Durant insisted that the new university teach the liberal arts in addition to agriculture and engineering. He was the first permanent president of the university, following John LeConte's one-year tenure as interim president. Durant's successor as president, another Yale scholar, Daniel Coit Gilman (1872-1875), was an unusually creative leader who had to fight very hard to defend the institution from those who wanted it to be a vocational school rather than a "complete university." In the three years he was president, Gilman laid the foundations for the future by setting the standards to which the University of California should aspire, doubling the size of the library collection, increasing the number of faculty, and creating graduate fellowships—a great novelty back then. Frustrated by the political attacks he suffered, Gilman, who favored pure science over applied technology (Rothblatt, 1997: 430), left to become the founding president of Johns Hopkins University, which was the first American research university.

Gilman was a visionary academic leader, who, according to Abraham Flexner (1946), wanted to influence minds since well before his California adventure. In his youth, he wanted to be a preacher, and in a sense he became one, for he "never lost a chance to express his conception of a university" (62). At the same time, Gilman was a doer, who paid great attention to detail in order to make his dreams happen. He created many different programs at the institutions where he worked during his youth, in addition to shaping the University of California and then establishing both Johns Hopkins University and the Carnegie Institution of Washington.

Gilman clearly was a path-breaker. At Yale, the first American university to offer the Ph.D., he was involved in developing this program, as well as in caring for the library. When Yale hired a more conservative president, Gilman, who appears to have been a candidate for the position, left for California, where he had trouble with the state's politics. As he confessed, he felt that he was building "a superior structure" that rested "over a mill which may blow up any day" (Cordasco, 1960: 48). Indeed, it did blow up on him, for he had to endure vicious personal attacks. By the time Johns Hopkins came calling, he was ready to go. As he stated, "However well we may build up the University of California, its foundations are unstable because dependent on legislative control and popular clamor" (Cordasco, 1960: 61). Gilman referred to this popular clamor as a "tidal wave" (Cordasco, 1960: 52).

Compared to the open, rough waters of California, Johns Hopkins was a pond. There, Gilman could finally implement his vision of a university with graduate and undergraduate programs, active research, good libraries and laboratories, journals, speakers, etc. Flexner (1946) reflects on Gilman's intellect, noting that he was not an investigator. His ideas were not original. Rather, he took them from multiple sources and adapted them to the needs of American higher education. He had a genius for "integration," rather than for "discovery," in the terminology coined by Ernest L. Boyer (1990). According to Flexner (1946), Gilman was a great educational executive, a great strategist who, like Napoleon, "concentrated all his forces at the weakest point and pushed forward boldly" (82). This is the vision of a hedgehog.

Gilman, who was easily the best academic leader in the country at the time, was followed by what Verne A. Stadtman (1970) calls "the era of powerless presidents" (88-106), including John LeConte (1869-1870 & 1875-1881), who came back as president and continued the struggle to turn the University of California into a research university. Although not well-suited for administration, he did not lack vision. He certainly made more progress than Stadtman (1970) suggests, because, during his tenure, the university became a public trust with an unusual degree of autonomy—a fact that would greatly facilitate its academic success. After LeConte, there were three short-lived presidents—William Thomas Reid (1881-1885), Edward Singleton Holden (1885-1888), and Horace Davis (1888-1890). They, in turn, were followed by Martin Kellogg (1890-1899), whose long tenure Stadtman (1970) calls the "quiet, constructive years" (175-178). Kellogg seems to have been a very smooth and experienced fox. He made the regents so comfortable that they eventually granted his office more autonomy, allowing his successor, Benjamin Ide Wheeler, a young and energetic hedgehog, to move the university forward. According to May, Wheeler was determined to transform the University of California into a research institution, and he could be ruthless in the pursuit of this goal. As with Gilman, his vision was not expressed in his writings, but in his actions. His first and best-known statement—"it is good to be here"—expresses the sentiments of the other members of the university and of the people of California (Wheeler, 1926: 43).

At the beginning of the twentieth century, with the rise of the Progressives and their faith in education as a great social equalizer and with the aid of philanthropy, California saw the creation and rapid rise of Stanford University. Not to be outdone, Wheeler energetically proceeded to expand the University of California. Wheeler, who was a Cornell professor educated in Germany, understood the importance of its land grant and research missions and transformed the university into an engine of prosperity for the state (May, 1993). While doing so, he realized important innovations, such as separating the university from other institutions of higher learning and developing a unique budgeting method.

According to Douglass (2000), Wheeler contributed to putting in place the tripartite division of higher education consisting of the university, the normal schools, and the junior colleges. The concept of the junior college as a bridge between high school and higher education emerged in the late nineteenth century, and its most ardent proponent was William Harper, president of the University of Chicago. While David Starr Jordan at Stanford tried, to no avail, to implement Harper's ideas, Wheeler succeeded in doing so. The first such junior college was created in Fresno in 1910, and many others were founded in the ensuing years. At the same time, the number of normal schools expanded. In addition, during a budget crisis, Wheeler successfully negotiated an enrollment-based budget, which was to become a distinct feature of the University of California. He also did a great deal of fund-raising, establishing strong ties between the University of California and the business sector.

Wheeler, who was a hedgehog with a vision of California as the bridge between East and West and the center of the modern world, built the elite public research university Durant, Gilman, and LeConte had dreamed of. During his tenure, the University of California hired many top-notch faculty members and brought a string of distinguished speakers from around the country, which enhanced its visibility (Nisbet, 1992). Indeed, Wheeler, who was a hands-on president, personally hired all members of the faculty according to his vision of what the University of California ought to be. Consequently, during his tenure it was ranked among the best American Universities by Edwin Emery Slosson, who, in 1910, placed the University of California after Harvard, Yale, Princeton, and Stanford.

Slosson declared that the University of California had inherited the virtues of both parents and none of their defects:

> I know of no other university which cultivates both mechanics and metaphysics with such equal success, or which looks so far into space, and, at the same time, comes so close to the lives of the people; or which excavates the tombs of the Pharaohs and Incas while it is inventing new plants for the agriculture of the future. (Slosson, 1977 [1910]: 149)

Slosson (1977 [1910]) noted that the faculty respected each other's ideals and lived in "an unusual degree of harmony" (155). Indeed, ten year later, in 1920, immediately after Wheeler's resignation, this very cohesive faculty body, inspired in part by the publication of the AAUP's *1915 General Declaration of Principles*, demanded and won a great deal of autonomy with the recognition of the academic senate (Pusser, 2004: 18). This body is "unique in its scope and the extent of its powers and privileges" (Taylor, 1998: 112). The faculty already had some degree of power before 1920. For example, in 1915, the University of California was the first state university to receive a budgetary appropriation for research and to create a faculty committee to allocate the funds (Geiger, 1986). Wheeler was an autocrat, who, as Sinclair (1923) points out, had faculty members sit according to their salaries at the Charter Day banquet, which they resented. Out of such squabbles emerged what is probably the most powerful academic senate of any university in the country, due to its system-wide nature. Among other things, the senate controls faculty appointments and advancements. There is a ladder system, and all faculty members undergo a performance review every few years.

This system, which is unique to the University of California and pre-dates its tenure system, was a major factor in its success, as it created a culture of discipline, with clear academic standards for all its members. Whether tenured or untenured, all faculty members are subject to periodic reviews. Salary raises depend on promotion to the next step. All campuses, large and small, are subject to the same requirements. This resulted in a very cohesive and competitive institution with high-powered and proactive faculty members who share governance with the administration.

Growth, governed by rigorous academic standards, continued under David Prescott Barrows (1919-1923), William Wallace Campbell (1923-1930) and, most particularly, under Robert Gordon Sproul (1930-1958), the first Californian to serve as president. Sproul "combined the loyalty of an alumnus with the shrewd eye of an accountant" (Thelin, 2004: 246). He was given positions of responsibility very early on, becoming comptroller at age twenty-nine, vice president at thirty-four, and president at thirty-nine. Although he was not an academic, Sproul understood the institution and cared about it, guiding it during a very long period that included the Depression, the Second World War, and part of the Cold War. Sproul, who was a classmate and friend of Earl Warren, the governor of California, was able to secure abundant funds for the university and to expand it according to previously-established parameters. During this period, the university's importance increased tremendously, due in part to its heavy involvement in the defense industry. Among other activities, the university operated the Los Alamos laboratory, which produced the first atomic bomb.

During Sproul's presidency, the university grew to include other campuses and facilities, yet he continued to run everything centrally, sticking to the idea that, no matter how large it became, UC had to be "one university" (Pelfrey, 2004: 39). This is why he created the all-university conferences (Pettitt, 1966). A micromanager by nature, Sproul made a large effort to keep the system united and of high quality by traveling from campus to campus and making all important decisions personally. His profile, as described by Pettitt (1966), is that of a very competent fox: he was very good at dealing with people and at obtaining money for the institution, in addition to having great public speaking ability. Sproul truly loved the University of California and turned down impressive job offers elsewhere, including the presidency of a bank. He energetically advanced the institutional core value, enunciated by the founding fathers, of an elite public research university, insisting on having a competitive faculty with good facilities. His tenure represents the end of the period of "buildup" in Collins' terminology. The country started to pay much attention to the University of California during this period. Indeed, in 1948, *Life* magazine published an article by Ralph Crane in which the author described UC as "the biggest university in the world" (Thelin, 2004: 286).

In 1958, Sproul, who had been president for twenty-eight years and, according to Otten (1970), "was probably the only president who did not resign under extreme duress" (188), was replaced by Clark Kerr (1958-1967), a scholar who was very focused on academic achievement. As first chancellor of the Berkeley campus, Kerr had set enrollment caps, which had never before been accomplished at any public university. Like the leaders of the enduring companies studied by Collins and Porras (2004 [1994]), Kerr did not want growth for the sake of growth. He understood the power of "no." As he reflects in his memoirs, people used to say that he had "the fastest 'no' in the West" (2001b: 26). When he became president of the massive University of California—"the thousand-mile university" (Pelfrey, 2004: 41)—he continued his efforts to rationalize growth, extending them to the entire system—and, in fact, to the whole state, with the Master Plan.

Douglass (2000) points out the differences between Kerr's diplo-matic style and Sproul's autocratic ways. Upon arrival, Kerr proceeded to decentralize functions and to give independence to the campuses, while maintaining the idea of "one university" by setting the same high standards of quality for all of its member institutions. Thus, the cur-rent system was born. The idea of systemic excellence, as opposed to campus excellence, was a "breakthrough" in Collins' terminology, the moment when the institutional core value of excellence morphed into a "hedgehog concept." This "hedgehog concept" was articulated in the California Master Plan for Higher Education, which assigned a uniformly high level of academic quality to the entire University of California system, in order to differentiate it from the other state institutions of higher learning.

During Sproul's presidency, the normal schools had been authorized to offer liberal arts curricula to non-teachers, thus becoming state colleges. After World War II, when a college education became as common as a high school diploma had been before, the so-called Strayer Report was produced. This "first master plan" (Douglass, 2000: 184), recommended expansion of junior colleges and creation of more state colleges, which now would offer masters degrees, while assigning exclusive responsibility for professional and doctoral degrees to the university.

Kerr made significant concessions to the state colleges, such as agreeing for them to grant some professional masters degrees. In exchange, he proposed that the state draft a master plan in order to provide universal access to higher education without duplicating efforts or compromising quality. The Master Plan Survey Team established a very selective admissions policy, according to which the university and the state colleges would draw from the top 12.5 percent and 33.3 percent of California high school graduates, respectively, shifting the remaining enrollments to the junior colleges. This division of labor was very cost-effective and resulted in a high level of funding per student for the University of California, which allowed it to compete with the best private universities in the country.

The proposal called for an independent board of trustees for the state colleges and a state coordinating council. Whether the state colleges should offer doctoral degrees was left for the coordinating council to decide. Concerned about the possibility of mission creep, Kerr did not accept this aspect of the agreement, proposing instead the creation of joint doctoral programs between the university and the state colleges. Anxious to secure Kerr's support for an independent board of trustees, the state colleges agreed, and a deal was struck. Kerr's "plan to end all plans" was endorsed by the Master Plan Survey Team and approved with minor modifications by the legislature in 1960. The Master Plan was an instant success, and Kerr made the cover of *Time*.

This could have been the end of the story, but it was not. As Taylor (1998) states, the Master Plan made the idea of systemic excellence possible, but the academic senate was instrumental in shaping the institution. The University of California could have failed to benefit from the funds provided by the state by distributing them across the board, but it did not. With the culture of discipline it had developed earlier, it used the money it received from the state to reward faculty performance and to enhance institutional competitiveness. The administration did not have to tell the faculty what to do. Faculty members had a tremendous amount of motivation, which they used to implement the hedgehog concept of becoming the best university system in the world, a goal about which both faculty and administration have been passionate.

What drives the academic engine is that both faculty and students are subject to common standards, which is unusual, as Mark G. Yudof (2008) has noted. This is what President David S. Saxon called "endemic excellence" (Pelfrey, 2004: 55). Today, people talk about "UC quality faculty" or "UC quality students." The students must be among the best high school graduates in the state, and the faculty must meet the exacting requirements of a system-wide tenure, promotion, and merit system with periodic pre- and post-tenure evaluations. In addition to common standards for faculty and students, the University of California has a highly-coordinated administration, which speaks with one voice. The chancellors of the individual campuses cannot interact directly with the legislature. Only the president of the system can do that. Thus, the president really represents the entire University of California, which is a true system. The three circles of the "hedgehog concept"—"what you can be the best in the world at…what drives your economic engine…what you are deeply passionate about"—intersected to produce the institution of iconic stature that is the University of California.

Douglass (2000) reflects on the accomplishments and limitations of the Master Plan, which, he believes, balanced the goals of selectivity and access. Due to the division of labor among the University of California, California State University (the former state colleges) and the community colleges (the former junior colleges), the state's cost per undergraduate student has remained low, while the quality of research and graduate education has reached new heights, as shown by national rankings and the international reputations of Ph.D. programs. As Douglass (2000) points out, however, the Master Plan did not envision the growing diversity of California's population and the consequent fact that the three-tiered system, drawing applicants from schools of varied circumstances and uneven resources, would organize students along the color line—the higher the level, the whiter the student body. As a result, the University of California has "catered to the better-off classes and the white majority" (Otten, 1970: 205).

While the institution was growing at a fast pace, there was room for people from other backgrounds, but problems arose when space became tight and choices had to be made. As Pusser (2004) has noted, the zero-sum admission process is a relatively recent phenomenon. Until the early 1970s, Berkeley and UCLA accepted many of the eligible students who applied. Tensions developed when access to the elite campuses became difficult and the perception of its benefits grew. The Master Plan did not anticipate this problem. According to Sheldon Rothblatt (1992), equality of opportunity and equality of outcome "were not polemical issues at the time the Master Plan was first devised" (1992: 23). Indeed, as we will see, in its eagerness to stick to its core value of excellence, the University of California slowly but surely sacrificed diversity in the first half of the twentieth century.

# 10

# The Trouble with Hedgehogs

When, in 1910, Slosson ranked the University of California among the top universities in the country, he urged it to keep itself free of discrimination in order to fulfill its destiny as a great cosmopolitan university, stating that, due to the many nationalities of its members, the University of California was in the best position "to buckle the belt of civilized nations around the globe" (163). The University of California seemed to him like a preview of things to come:

> There is a new form of university coming, which is foreshadowed in the University of California. Greater and more influential than a State or a national university will be the international university of the future. (Slosson, 1977 [1910]: 180)

Slosson (1977 [1910]) obviously was very taken with California's institutions of higher learning, as he expressed very positive views about both the University of California and Stanford University, which he found more open-minded than Harvard, Yale, and Princeton. For example, comparing Stanford and Princeton, he said that Stanford did not exclude from the university persons "who do not belong to a particular race or sex" (122).

Slosson (1977 [1910]) was even more impressed by the University of California in this respect. Among other things, he reports his encounters with Japanese and Chinese students and tells pleasant anecdotes about them, stating that he did not hear at Stanford or the University of California the kinds of negative comments about them that he had heard at Harvard. Although he acknowledged that there was discrimination, he quaintly said that this was not "any stronger in the Californian universities than anti-Semitism in Princeton, Pennsylvania, and Columbia" (162). He noted that in 1908, there were registered at the University of California seventeen students from China, eighteen from Japan, and nineteen from India.

Indeed, the presence of students from other parts of the world was noted with excitement by Agnes Edwards Partin (2006), a freshman who in one of her first letters to her family in the fall of 1917, wrote that her English class was "quite interesting. There is a girl from Russia, a Japanese, a Hindu of some sort and two other boys who speak with a foreign accent" (12). Of course, as Douglass (2007) points out, there was a great deal of discrimination against Asians in California during this period. Nisbet (1992) explains that most of the students of color found at the University of California were foreigners funded by their well-off families or by their governments. For example, he recalls that in the 1930s, there was a Mexican student by the name of Raúl Magaña, of whom he says that "he was well known for both his acute intelligence and his beautiful sister, Isabella, who came up from Mexico City two or three times a year to visit her brother and to shop at some of San Francisco's fine stores" (62). Nisbet (1992) goes on to comment on this student's linguistic ability by saying that his English was excellent and adding that he heard from "those qualified to judge that his native Spanish was pure enough to warrant Library of Congress recording" (62). Implicit in this comment is the mistaken belief, very widespread in this country, that Mexican Americans and other Latinos cannot speak either English or Spanish well. This student, who ended up as a very successful lawyer in Los Angeles, is presented as an exception. He is an exotic character, rather than a member of a minority group.

Nevertheless, the University of California was more welcoming to students of color than other institutions of higher learning. Jews were also better treated there than at the universities of the East Coast (Nisbet, 1992). Indeed, Wheeler, who was ahead of the times in hiring ethnic minorities, appointed a Jew, Monroe Deutsch, as his provost and hired Jewish faculty members, including some women (May 1993). I believe that this atmosphere was due, in part, to Wheeler's international predilections, which are reflected in his condemnation of racial prejudice:

> A fixed prejudice is a case of arrested development. Like the petty village aversions, racial and social prejudices generally affect what is near at hand, what one sees and does not know. The man who has made up his mind that he dislikes Jews or Chinese or some other blood has introduced into his life a persistent source of narrowness, blindness, and poverty. He has raised a barrier between himself and the exceeding richness of human fellowship. (Douglass, 2007: 68)

In his visionary speeches, collected in a volume titled *The Abundant Life*, Wheeler (1926) talked constantly about intercultural communication, stressing the importance of seeing the world "from others' eyes" (56). Wheeler was also very proud of the large number of poor students the university admitted and the fact that it did not charge tuition (May, 1993). This attitude greatly impressed Slosson (1977 [1910]), who also noted the high number and top performance of women at the University of California, where, according to the administration, they raised the average grade "to an abnormal height" (167).

Maresi Nerad (1999) points out that when, in 1870, two years after the University of California opened its doors, eight female students enrolled, the regents had to pass a resolution to admit women. Apparently, many people disapproved of this action, which was defended by *The University Echo*, one of whose editors was Josephine Lindley, the first woman student ever to register. An editorial believed to have been authored by Lindley states that "men cry out against woman's extravagance and trifling, yet they are the first to condemn the opening of paths to her," stressing that "every young lady should be fitted to *do* something in life" (Ferrier, 1930: 332).

By 1900, 46 percent of the university's students were women, a higher percentage than at any other co-educational university in the country, and by 1915, there were more women than men in the College of Letters and Science, "which began to resemble a women's college" (Nerad, 1999: 20). This is what Slosson saw and marveled at during his visit. It seemed like a new world to him, a preview of things to come. After that promising start, however, women and people of color failed to make significant gains. Like other elite research universities, the University of California became a very exclusive institution.

Geraldine J. Clifford (1995) explains that the feminization of teaching in nineteenth century American schools, due in large part to the increasing abundance of more lucrative jobs for men, resulted in women going to college in great numbers. This helped newly-established American universities grow at a fast pace, in addition to giving them some unique features, such as the presence of schools of education. Most women students at Berkeley were trying to become teachers, for whom there was a great demand in California. Indeed, in 1907, women accounted for 967 of the 1070 teachers in the San Francisco schools. After this initial enrollment boom, Berkeley started to focus on prestige, experiencing "two divergent cultures" (Clifford, 1995: 80). One was democratic, oriented towards meeting local teaching needs. The other was aristocratic, focused on satisfying national research standards. As Berkeley proceeded to strengthen its elite research university status, the presence of large numbers of women, who had been instrumental in getting the university up and running, became an embarrassment.

According to Nerad (1999), women students at the University of California sustained losses as the administration proceeded to marginalize them by moving them from the College of Letters and Science to Home Economics. While Stanford set quotas for women, capping their number at five hundred, the University of California created a ghetto for them. In both cases, there was a fear that the presence of a large number of women students would prevent the university from being able to compete with the most prestigious institutions, which were more male-oriented. This attitude was shared by other university presidents around the country, such as Henry Tappan, who was worried about the effect that having women students would have on the "perception" of the quality of the University of Michigan (Douglass, 2007: 24). When it became clear that, contrary to people's fears, co-education was not harmful to college women, who thrived on campus, it was considered "harmful—or rather, threatening—to college men" (Thelin, 2004: 186). As Veblen (1918) warned, the principles of competitive business resulted in the elimination of all scholarly work that did not bring prestige to the university. Kerr's 1955 decision to close Berkeley's Department of Home Economics, studied in detail by Nerad (1999), must be understood in this context.

Kerr was not the only academic leader to have negative views about Home Economics as a discipline. Indeed, some of the scholars he admired expressed similar views in their books. For example, Veblen (1918) was critical of "schools of 'domestic science,' 'domestic economy,' 'home economics' (in short, housekeeping)" (191) and Sinclair (1923) was disparaging of universities that offered courses on "millinery" and other such subjects, including the University of California, which had a "costume laboratory" and a course in "jewelry" (320). Flexner (1994 [1930]), who was against all "vocational" schools, makes devastating remarks about departments of "domestic science," which were blooming at major research universities at the time:

> The departments of domestic science or household arts at Columbia and Chicago boast staffs that undertake to deal with nutritional problems and to offer advanced degrees (A.M., Ph.D.) indifferently to persons who write theses on underwear or on topics in the field of physiological chemistry. A course on catering is found side by side with research in food and nutrition. It is of course absurd to suppose that either

competent teachers or competent students can be found in departments of this kind. (Flexner, 1994 [1930]: 153)

These comments are repeated by Moberly (1949), who says that professors should not encourage students to study unimportant subjects simply because it has never been done before, noting that the United States led the way in extravagances.

Kerr's decision to close Berkeley's Department of Home Economics did not happen in a vacuum. It was part of the University of California's relentless quest for prestige, and he writes proudly about it in his memoirs:

> Actually, the problem with home economics at Berkeley was that it was a miscellany. We took its best part, nutrition, and made that into a high-quality specialty. The most popular home economics course had been "Marriage" with ten lectures, the first on "courtship" and the last on "venereal disease." The students relabeled the course "From Courtship to Venereal Disease in Ten Easy Lessons." It was popular, in part, because there were no reading assignments and nobody flunked; and the subject matter held substantial student interest. But the course was a source of embarrassment to the department and the campus. (Kerr, 2001b: 87)

The elimination of Berkeley's Department of Home Economics was part of a trend affecting major research universities and was the logical conclusion of Kerr's plan to place the University of California among the top institutions of higher learning in the country.

Nisbet (1992) discusses the unusually high quality of this department, which was due to the leadership of its chair, Agnes Fay Morgan, a German-educated chemist who was very active in research but could not find a faculty position in any chemistry department in the country. "For the reason we don't have far to search. She was, in a word, female" (Nisbet, 1992: 71). Morgan and her faculty did much interesting research and made important discoveries, but, in spite of their academic success, Kerr felt compelled to close their department. The theory behind this was that women could study other subjects and did not have to limit themselves to Home Economics, but as a practical matter, this move reduced female presence at the university, including women faculty. As Nerad (1999) notes, the highly-accomplished female scientists of the Department of Home Economics had to endure seeing how the strong nutrition program they had developed with very little support from their colleagues was taken away from them and put under male leadership, while the department's applied programs were sent to Davis. After this, the number of women faculty on the Berkeley campus declined from 6 percent in 1950 to 3.5 percent in 1968. The cost of excellence was diversity. The university leadership, in its efforts to create a first-rate university, eliminated everything that it believed would make the university appear less competitive. Women, who had entered the university with innocent optimism, were progressively marginalized and would not regain strength until the affirmative action era.

People of color also suffered setbacks. For example, during World War II, Japanese-American students from Berkeley were sent to internment camps, which considerably reduced the number of non-whites on campus. Indeed, the best student of the class of 1942 was taken away before he could pick up his diploma and his medal. This is what the May 13, 1942, *Oakland Post-Enquirer* reported:

> When the University of California awards the medal to the senior having the highest scholastic average at today's commencement exercises, the recipient will not be present to receive it. He is an American-born Japanese and has been evacuated! A student in the college of chemistry and enrolled in a premedical course this semester, [Akio] Itano, who is 21, maintained a straight "A" average for four years at the university in Berkeley. He is a member of the Phi Kappa scholastic honor society; Sigma Xi, chemistry honor society, the university Y.M.C.A. cabinet and the student health committee. He was evacuated on April 22. As soon as the university authorities determine where he is, Itano will be sent his diploma—and his medal—by mail. (Douglass, 2007: 46)

Although the number of Asian-American students increased after the war, there were relatively few students of color, particularly African-Americans and Latinos, at the University of California when the affirmative action era began.

Richard Delgado and Jean Stefancic (2000) believe that the Master Plan was a deliberate attempt to keep the university that way by creating a caste-based system. This belief echoes the idea that education reproduces the existing social order, expressed by Touraine (1997), for whom, the American academic system "puts everybody in his place" by making leaders out of students from the "upper strata" and employees out of students "from a lower background," while maintaining the majority of ethnic minorities "in a limited and subalternate vocational and social existence" (109). The community colleges are "a safety valve releasing pressures that might otherwise disrupt the dominant system" (107). According to Touraine (1997), the American academic system, and the Master Plan in particular, took shelter "behind the impervious barrier of professional criteria" (218) in order to rid itself of the problems posed by ethnic groups. Using a "snake" metaphor borrowed from David Riesman, Touraine concludes that the main function of the system is the reinforcement of social hierarchy:

At its head the theme of general education aims to consolidate the ruling elite; at its tail the community colleges must above all release the pressure that could build up against the medium-level institutions and assure, not just the transfer of the best students, but the maintenance of the system as a whole. (Touraine, 1997: 108)

While I do not think that Kerr intended to exclude or marginalize any group, I do believe that his devotion to advancing the core value of excellence made him overlook the importance of diversity.

In 1960, very few academic leaders were thinking about gender and ethnicity. Kerr, who was sincerely interested in equality of opportunity, was probably more sensitive about the plight of marginalized individuals than most of his contemporaries were, but the great university he aspired to create was a culturally white and male institution engaged in a competition for prestige, as reflected in its rankings. Very little value was attached to the cultural contributions of women and people of color during that era. In fact, excellence at that point was construed as the opposite of diversity.

As Deborah L. Rhode (2006) has shown, the pursuit of prestige has had adverse consequences for American universities, because it has made them focus on issues of little or no importance. For example, the adoption of the SAT, which is problematic from multiple points of view, makes sense if we think of it as a means to compare different institutions of higher learning (Douglass, 2007). To this date, SAT scores continue to be a crucial ingredient in rankings. Although they may have limited value as predictors of future academic and professional performance, they are an important weapon in the competition for prestige. Indeed, the University of California adopted the SAT in 1968, when "there was pressure for the university to reduce access in the aftermath of the master plan agreement" (Douglas, 2007: 90). In order to mitigate the impact of this move on diversity, the university increased special admissions from 2 percent to 4 percent at that time. This small concession allowed the university to become more selective and to enhance its competitiveness. Veblen (1918), who saw this obsession with prestige coming, pointed to the various steps universities were taking in order to improve their perceived status. These included such non-academic measures as beautification of campuses to make their buildings and grounds look like palaces and gardens, conveying an impression of opulence and gentility. That is why, as Delgado and Stefancic (2000) indicate, the building of the University of California campuses resulted in gentrification of surrounding areas, as evidenced by the fact that the town of Davis lost most of its people of color when the campus was established. The quest for excellence—identified with prestige—literally drove diversity out.

Kerr's hedgehog vision had a blind spot: he could not see the adverse consequences of his push for competitiveness.

As a result, Kerr had a very hard time understanding the student revolts, which can be interpreted as an early reaction to the push for prestige that underpins the Master Plan. To Kerr's great dismay, the students' revolutionary discourse was taken from his description of the "multiversity." According to Geiger (1993), Kerr was "hoisted on his own petard" (235). In 1964, one year after the publication of *The Uses of the University*, Hal Draper published a widely-read pamphlet, titled *The Mind of Clark Kerr: His View of the University Factory and the New Slavery*, which is a cogent, if inflammatory, critique of the "multiversity." This work, which mentions the plight of Japanese-Americans, as well as that of Latinos, uses the rhetoric of liberation associated with the civil rights movement.

Indeed, the Free Speech Movement's most visible figure, the quintessential hedgehog Mario Savio, made that connection explicitly in his introduction to Draper's 1965 book *Berkeley: The New Student Revolt*, when trying to explain why students revolted at Berkeley before they did so at other universities. Savio said that, just as what oppressed blacks was an exaggerated version of what oppressed the rest of the country, what was wrong with Berkeley was an extreme example of what was wrong at other universities, namely "the factory-like mass miseducation of which Clark Kerr is the leading ideologist" (p. 2). Addressing the students about their role in the "knowledge-factory," Savio told them:

> If this is a firm, and if the board of regents are the board of directors, and if President Kerr in fact is the manager, then I'll tell you something, the faculty are a bunch of employees and we're the raw materials! (Robert Cohen, 2009: 188)

Indeed, in his speech "An End to History," Savio says that Kerr's "multiversity" is "a factory that turns out a certain product needed by industry or government" (Draper, 1965: 181), concluding that

> The most exciting things going on in America today are movements to change America. America is becoming evermore the utopia of sterilized, automated contentment. The "futures" and "careers" for which American students now prepare are for the most part intellectual and moral wastelands. This chrome-plated consumers' paradise would have us grow up to be well-behaved children. But an important minority of men and women coming to the front today have shown that they will die rather than be standardized, replaceable, and irrelevant. (Draper, 1965: 182)

Savio, who made the instructions on computer cards—"do not fold, bend, spindle or mutilate"—the slogan of his generation, told students to "throw their bodies on the gears and the machinery" and bring the institution to a halt (Pelfrey, 2004: 48). While white students rebelled against being standardized by the "multiversity," students of color demanded a place in it. Kerr's hedgehog vision had turned into a nightmare. As student protests grew, Kerr became the focus of great anger on the part of the legislature and the public, which was a major factor in his dismissal.

If Kerr had been a fox, the Berkeley Free Speech Movement might never have happened, for he would not have liberalized and codified the rules regarding free speech. Touraine (1997) notes that Kerr "liberalized political activity on the Berkeley campus to the point of allowing communists to express themselves" (204), but, as Otten (1970) indicates, "ironically it was the 'bureaucratization,' not the substantial liberalization, that caught the eye of the activist students" (160). This follows a well-known pattern discussed by Alexis de Tocqueville (1955 [1856]), who noted that the most dangerous moment for a government is "when it seeks to mend its ways," since a grievance endured when there was no hope for change, appears unbearable "once the possibility of removing it crosses men's minds" (177). The liberalization initiated by Kerr had the effect of encouraging the students to demand more. Otten (1970) explains that the modifications fell behind the students' demands, which "gave rise to the belief that student 'rights' were being whittled away, when in reality they had never existed" (169).

In addition, if Kerr had been a fox, he would not have crafted the Master Plan, nor written his book about the "multiversity," thus depriving the students of a powerful vision to rebel against. In a sense, Ronald Reagan was right: Kerr was instrumental in creating "the mess at Berkeley" (Pelfrey, 2004: 50), not because he failed to control the students, but because, as Robert Cohen (2009) suggests, he provided the ingredients for their very successful revolutionary narrative, which was based on his vivid description of the "multiversity." The trouble with hedgehogs is that they have visions, and visions, besides having blind spots, have lives of their own.

# 11

## Foxes to the Rescue

Kerr's successors tried to guide the university through the rough years that followed his presidency. His immediate successor was Harry Wellman (1967), a respected member of Kerr's senior management team who agreed to serve for one year until a permanent president was chosen. The position went to another member of Kerr's senior management team, his vice president for finance, Charles Johnson Hitch (1968-1975). According to Brian Pusser (2004), the University of California started affirmative action programs at that time "with considerable prodding" from the influential African-American politician Willie Brown (27). Hitch, in his inaugural address on January 1, 1968, called for greater access for minority groups. By the end of his tenure in 1975, the number of students of color had increased dramatically (Johnson, 1996). Douglass (2007) notes the importance of the pressure exerted by another politician, John Vasconcellos, on Hitch and his successor, David S. Saxon (1975-1983), who concentrated on improving academic preparation in the schools through the UC Partnership Program so that more minorities could enter the university.

These efforts met with some resistance, and a white student named Allan Bakke, who had been rejected by the UC Davis Medical School, sued the University of California for setting aside special slots for minority students. In the 1978 *Regents of the University of California v. Bakke* decision, the Supreme Court ruled that, although such special slots, or quotas, were unconstitutional, race and ethnicity could be considered along with other factors in the admissions process. In his majority opinion, Justice Powell mentioned Harvard University, which treated "each applicant as an individual in the admission process" (Douglass, 2007: 122) as the model to follow. This ruling provided support for the diversity efforts of the University of California, which continued to reach out to minorities. However, the University of California did not follow the Harvard model. Instead, it made minor adjustments to its practices, which varied from campus to campus, and continued its outreach efforts. By the end of the 1970s, UC was working with 10,000 students around California, which made its partnership program the largest of its kind in the country (Johnson, 1996).

Both Hitch and Saxon worked hard to preserve academic quality, but they had to deal with difficult political circumstances and bad budgets, so when David P. Gardner (1983-1992) was appointed president in 1983, he decided that the best thing he could do for the university would be to get a large budget increase to compensate for the financial losses of the previous two presidencies. He made friends with important players, including Governor George Deukmejian, who, unlike his predecessors, had made education a top priority. Gardner was able to obtain a spectacular 32 percent budget increase during his first year on the job. Gardner, who "was low-key in manner, precise in speech, analytical in his approach to problems, and impeccably prepared" (Pelfrey, 2004: 63), restored confidence in the university and negotiated a series of strong budgets with which he proceeded to improve the institution, following the hedgehog concept of systemic excellence that had been developed in the Kerr era. As a good fox, he put his talent at the service of a vision articulated by a hedgehog. Indeed, Gardner had a strong personal belief in the idea of systemic excellence, to which he was totally committed, working hard to enhance the quality of the university. During Gardner's tenure, endowments and research funding increased tremendously. This resulted in the greatest building boom in the university's history. Under Gardner's watch, enrollments expanded and the student body became more diverse.

According to Johnson (1996), in eight years, African-American enrollments increased by 38.8 percent, Latinos by 108 percent and Asians by 65 percent. What is more, three of the seven chancellors Gardner appointed came from non-traditional backgrounds: the first two women and the first Asian-American to lead UC campuses. In addition, Gardner convened an all-university faculty conference in 1990 to discuss affirmative action issues. Johnson (1996) states that, although efforts to diversify other areas of the university came slowly, "Gardner's commitment to encompass the changing face of California within the entire UC Community was unqualified and consistent" (18). Johnson (1996) also praises Gardner's leadership in international education, noting that he fostered the expansion of the Education Abroad program to include more countries outside of Europe. In particular, Gardner understood the potential of the Pacific Rim and sought to position the university, the state, and the country as leaders in that part of the world.

What made Gardner so sensitive to diversity issues? His memoirs provide multiple clues. First, he interacted with people of color growing up when he worked thinning sugar beats alongside Mexican and Indian agricultural workers at the family farm in Utah every summer. This experience was amplified during his army years, which he spent in East Asia, doing what he describes as dangerous intelligence work, in close cooperation with Asians. As he states, this experience "upended" many of his "world's realities" (2003: 20). Second, as discussed previously, during his interview for the position of president, he was quizzed about the effect of his Mormon faith on his political views, but that was not the end of the matter. After his appointment as president, but before he started to work, he was approached by Willie Brown's education adviser, Celeste Rose, who asked him if he would be willing to meet with the legislature's minority caucus. Gardner complied, although he sensed that the request flowed from a mistrust of his religious beliefs:

> I accepted but, reading their unexpressed intent, realized that if I were a Catholic, a Protestant, a Jew, or a Muslim they would never have thought it right to inquire into my religious faith; and it was always the same with the press as well: "Gardner, a Mormon," but never "Smith, a Catholic," or "Jones, a Baptist," or whatever. (Gardner, 2003: 153)

Nevertheless, he welcomed the request, as he was eager to "discuss their concerns about minority interests and gender in UC personnel and admission policies and practices before such issues came up in the context of specific and tangible legislative or budgetary differences" (2003: 153). In other words, Gardner's fox instinct told him that this issue could affect his ability to succeed. Brown was a key political figure, and the minority caucus included some fifteen or twenty legislators. In addition, influential California politician John Vasconcellos made his views on the subject of diversity clear early on. These were not people Gardner could afford to alienate. Thus, from the very beginning, Gardner was under pressure to do something about diversity in a way that no other president had been before.

Gardner had to prove himself because he was a Mormon. In addition, being a Mormon probably gave him an appreciation for discrimination, as he experienced some in the course of his career. After he became president, he was criticized for his "Mormon greed," first, because he got a large salary, and then, because he received a good retirement, as he notes bitterly. He also discusses how, in his youth, he was treated with hostility by the Berkeley draft board, which would not promise him a deferment to see him through law school, a development that made him enlist in order to get military service out of the way.

The army, on the other hand, favored him because he was a Mormon, which, he explains, struck him "as being quite odd, indeed astonishing and in each instance quite wrong" because he believed "that persons should be judged as individuals on their own merits and for their own lives and not because of any one or any combination of reasons based on their associations, ethnicity or religion" (2003: 17-18). Gardner adds that his interest in the loyalty oath, the subject of his first book, *The California Oath Controversy*, published in 1967, was connected to his commitment to this principle. Gardner, thus, had experience with the double image of the other—either exceedingly good or exceedingly bad, but never normal—that affects women and minorities of all kinds, and this gave him a glimpse of their troubles.

In addition to having reasons to be more sensitive about diversity issues than his predecessors, Gardner had lived through some of the most difficult moments of the student revolts, which, no doubt, made him understand the depth of feeling surrounding gender and ethnicity. As he notes in his memoirs, he heard radio accounts of Mario Savio and others holding a police car in Sproul Plaza when he was moving from Berkeley, where he had worked at the alumni association, to Santa Barbara, where he had accepted the position of assistant to the chancellor. He did well in this capacity and was promoted to assistant chancellor and then to vice-chancellor-executive assistant, according to him, because increasing levels of student unrest made his services more important. Thus, Gardner's success was tied to the upheavals that cost Kerr his job. According to Gardner, the student revolt of 1964-1965, was a "dry run" for the "real thing," which came when "the antiwar protests at UC gathered force and momentum, as newer minority issues appeared" (2003: 37).

Gardner (2003) explains that the University of California increased student diversity too suddenly and without sufficient preparation. Minority students found themselves alienated in an overwhelmingly white institution. This resulted in unrest, including demonstrations and building takeovers. The university administration found itself sandwiched between the students and the governor, Ronald Reagan, who had run on a platform of stopping campus revolts. For Gardner, both the students and the governor were unreasonable. In fact, he saw the coercive character of the new student activism as a mirror image of the coercive nature of government.

Gardner was involved in helping minority students and faculty members write proposals for a Department of Chicano Studies and a Department of Black Studies, as well as for interdisciplinary research centers in these fields, accomplishments of which he was proud, because "they helped demonstrate to the minority community, on and off campus, that there were alternatives to political action" (2003: 46). Gardner adds that the campus' success with minority students and faculty left "a much reduced field of open issues for the white radicals to protest than would otherwise have been the case" (2003: 47). The goal of his actions seems to have been to smooth things over in a fox-like manner. As for his feelings, he is more negative about white students than about minorities:

> We also made real progress in responding to the concerns of minority students, whose agenda, if not their tactics, at least possessed a strong element of reasonableness, in contrast to the mostly middle- and upper-class white radicals drawn from one faction or another of the Students for a Democratic Society (SDS), whose purposes I saw as principally scapegoating the university for problems they had at home, with the draft, with the Vietnam War, with social or governmental policies, or with other issues that were disturbing or complicating their lives. Whereas the minorities not only had a greater moral base for their demands (aside from the war) but were also more single-minded in seeking their objectives than were the Radical Student Union (a spin-off from the SDS) and other mostly white organizations whose tactics were as random as their issues. (Gardner, 2005: 46)

Although he disapproves of everyone's methods, he finds minority students more reasonable and justified than white students. During these "apprenticeship years," Gardner learned that "the political center of gravity fits between the opposite ends of the political spectrum and how crucial it was, therefore, that the center hold during times of stress" (2003: 64-65).

With this background, it is not difficult to understand Gardner's grasp of the political importance of women and minorities and his efforts to improve their circumstances, not only in the case of undergraduates, but also for graduate students, postdoctoral scholars, faculty members, and administrators. In his memoirs, he gives credit to Eugene Cota-Robles for creating many good programs to enhance diversity at the University of California. Another important figure during this period was the chancellor of the Berkeley campus, Ira Michael Heyman, who took the lead with respect to admissions (Douglass, 2007). In addition to supporting these efforts, Gardner diversified the leadership team. When the famous Latino writer Tomás Rivera, the system's first minority chancellor (Riverside), suffered a fatal heart attack, Gardner proceeded to add women and minorities to the chancellors group. He appointed an Asian male, Chang-Lin Tien, as chancellor at Berkeley and two women, Barbara Uehling and Rosemary Schraer, as chancellors at Santa Barbara and Riverside, respectively. Thus, almost half of the seven chancellors he hired during his tenure as president were women and minorities. He also hired women and minorities in other positions, including Willie Brown's associate Celeste Rose, whom he recruited for his office as a lobbyist for the UC system. Gardner enjoyed a good relationship with Brown, who later supported him very strongly during the controversy regarding his retirement benefits (Pelfrey, 2008a: 5).

I do not think that there is any question but that Gardner made a considerable effort to diversify the UC system at all levels. Anti-affirmative action Regent Ward Connerly understood this very well when he declared that "the Regents fell asleep at the wheel during the Gardner era" (Douglass, 2007: 162). As Gardner notes, he addressed diversity issues in his inaugural address and in many of his speeches and worked on them consistently throughout his tenure, explaining that he was aware of the issues and did the best he could, "which was thought by some to be quite enough, others not enough, and others too much" (Gardner, 2005: 258-259).

Just as Gardner's ability to persuade others to give him money produced a backlash when he used it to secure a good retirement during bad economic times, his desire to increase the number of women and minorities at the university backfired when those who felt excluded by his actions endorsed Proposition 209 shortly after his departure. As Brian Pusser (2004) has pointed out, the Master Plan, by creating intense competition for admissions to the University of California, contributed to the demise of affirmative action when those who felt displaced by women and minorities revolted. For them, Gardner had indeed done too much.

# 12

# Fox Fatigue

Gardner's fox qualities, which he used for the advancement of the university, were not appreciated by the public. In particular, his ability to obtain money caused him and the university a great deal of trouble when he was perceived as using that talent to get himself a good retirement deal. Following the untimely death of his wife, and in the middle of an economic downturn that brought much financial trouble to the university and the state, Gardner announced that he was going to step down from the presidency the following year. As Pelfrey explains:

> To help UC attract and retain skilled administrators despite its budget constraints, the Regents had approved the awarding of deferred compensation and a supplemental retirement annuity to certain UC executives, including the President, as long as they remained with the University for a specific period of time. President Gardner's planned retirement date would have made him ineligible for those benefits, but in recognition of his contributions and the special circumstances of his decision to retire, the Board voted to waive the vesting date and award him both deferred compensation and supplemental retirement funds. (Pelfrey, 2004: 67)

This caused a furor, particularly because it came during a period of cutbacks, when university employees and residents of the state were hurting. According to Pelfrey, months of press attacks greatly damaged the University of California's image:

> For the next several years it seemed as if the University could not escape the head-lines; one media tempest followed another. Most centered on administrative salaries and spending in the Office of the President, but others were sparked by incidents on the campuses—irregularities in fund-raising by campus foundations, disputes at two campuses over the Chancellor's leadership, and even a legislative outcry over the appointment of 1960s activist Angela Davis, now a UC faculty member, to an endowed professorship at Santa Cruz. (Pelfrey, 2004: 68)

This enumeration of troubles is interesting because it shows that public anger was focused on two topics: executive compensation and concessions to women and minorities. These two emotional issues have continued to agitate the public up to the present time.

President Jack W. Peltason (1992-1995), Gardner's successor, faced an enormous budget crisis, which was due, in part, to the decline of California's defense-related industries at the conclusion of the Cold War. During Peltason's three-year tenure, the university's cumulative shortfall was nearly a billion dollars, resulting in such draconian measures as early retirement programs and salary freezes and even cuts for the faculty, reductions in staff positions, and higher fees for students. Peltason increased fund-raising efforts and strengthened ties between the university and industry. Peltason, whom Pelfrey (2008a) describes as "a man of unshakable civility" (8-10), voluntarily forfeited several hundred thousand dollars in compensation benefits, which he asked be used for student scholarships. Before stepping down from the presidency in 1995, he managed to persuade Governor Pete Wilson to agree to a compact that would guarantee a basic level of funding for the university during the next four years. He was less successful in stopping another disaster that affected the university, not coincidentally, during this period of great stress: the attack on affirmative action.

Gardner, who was primarily a fox, had a significant hedgehog side to his personality, which manifested itself in sudden insights. In one of his most important hedgehog moments, he had warned that the 1974 legislature's resolution to establish a goal for the student body to approximate the diversity of the state's population was on a collision course with the University of California's restrictive admission policies, as defined by the Master Plan. This limited the number of students admitted to the top 12.5 percent of the state's high school graduates, selected according to certain academic criteria, such as grades and test scores. Gardner believed that the Master Plan had to be modified to accommodate new demographic realities and was in favor of creating three new campuses, in addition to the nine that were in existence at the time (Douglas, 2007). This vision was not well-received. Money was drying up, and people were not in the mood for visions. Of the three new campuses proposed by Gardner, only one, Merced, came into existence many years after Gardner's departure and after many struggles (Merritt & Lawrence, 2007). What people wanted from Gardner was a fox-like solution, which he provided. Thus, the University of California did not significantly increase its capacity, except for growth on the existing campuses. It also continued using the same academic criteria, composed primarily of a couple of numerical indicators, to determine membership in the top 12.5 percent of the high school class. But since these numerical indicators disfavored members of some minority groups, the university developed supplemental criteria in order to identify promising students from these minority groups. So in effect, the university was using two sets of criteria, a personalized set of criteria for minority groups and a more impersonal and mechanical one for other applicants. Many universities used this kind of dual admissions criteria, which "grafted affirmative action onto a flawed admissions process" (Orfield, 2000: 15). The reason the admissions process was flawed was because it focused only on numerical indicators of limited value rather than on a comprehensive review of students' accomplishments and potential. This was not at all like the Harvard model recommended by Justice Powell. Gardner understood that this admissions policy was a problem when he stated that he could not think of any policy more sensitive, more complicated, and "more important in the long run to the University of California and, in fact, to the relationships among and between the citizens of our state" (Pelfrey, 2004: 74). This was "a prescient remark" (Pelfrey, 2004: 74) because during Peltason's term, in the midst of the severe economic crisis affecting the state and making it lose its optimistic and generous outlook, there was a revolt against affirmative action.

The crisis started when Mr. and Mrs. Jerry Cook complained to a number of regents about the fact that their son James had not been admitted to the UC San Diego medical school, while minority students with lower grades and test scores had been. Although James Cook was admitted to the UC Davis medical school, his parents' complaint resulted in some regents asking the board to eliminate affirmative action. African-American Regent Ward Connerly was very outspoken in his criticism of affirmative action, as was Governor Wilson, who was running for President of the United States and made this issue a key component of his campaign. As Pusser (2004) says, Wilson had discovered that anti-minority feelings could bring him votes when, at the lowest point in his tenure, he won reelection as governor after endorsing Proposition 187, a ballot initiative restricting health and education benefits for undocumented immigrants, which passed but was later blocked by a federal court. This was a clear case of focusing voters' frustration about the economy on minorities. Wilson again used the same tactic with the University of California's admissions controversy—a move that has been described as "a high watermark for political intervention in higher education" (Kennedy, 1997: 14)—and the debate raged all over the country. This controversy coincided with the diversification of the student body in the United States. According to Louis Menand (2010), "in the decade between 1984 and 1994, the total enrollment in American colleges and universities increased by 2 million, but not one of those 2 million new students was a white American-born male" (70). This demographic change had made many people very anxious. That is what Peltason was up against. He tried desperately to buy some time and postpone action until the following year, to no avail. In July of 1995, the regents, through special policies 1 and 2 (SP1 and SP2), voted to abolish consideration of race, gender, and ethnicity in admissions and hiring at the University of California. Soon afterwards, in 1996, the voters passed Proposition 209, which applied the same principles, cleverly phrased as the elimination of "preferences," to all public institutions and government agencies in California. "The University of California—which had been one of the first in the nation to establish affirmative action programs and had argued the *Bakke* case up to the Supreme Court—found itself a leader among American universities in dismantling race-attentive admissions" (Pelfrey, 2004: 76). How did this happen?

The University of California seemed to have become the focus of anger and frustration for many who were suffering around the state. Some were outraged at the corporate lifestyles of its leaders, which they thought came at the expense of students, whose tuition was going up. Others were upset about minority student admissions practices, which they believed came at the expense of white students' access. They blamed their problems downward, on minority students, and upward, on the university leadership. Everyone felt cheated by the University of California, whose leaders appeared to be manipulative and blind. Douglass (2007) notes that "America's public universities were conceived, funded and developed as tools of socio-economic engineering," and the University of California, in particular, in its 1868 state charter, was given the responsibility of "setting the conditions for admission" (6-7). Peltason did not do a good job of explaining the University of California's position, perhaps because he did not have a clear idea about it himself. As Pusser (2004) says, "at a moment when the University of California was called upon to rethink its mission, the nature of its constituency, and the efficacy of its organization in a time of crisis, it turned for the most part to a time-tested strategy of relying on appeals to shared governance, faculty expertise, and a history of success" (83).

According to Connerly, "the picture that emerged was that of an Institution which had *de facto* racial quotas, which refuses to acknowledge the true extent to which race is used in its admission activities, and which is determined to maintain the status quo" (Douglass, 2007: 151). By contrast, Connerly, right or wrong, had an idea that many people could understand. His idea, which had an attractive American ring to it, was that no one should get "preferential treatment." The university's explanations about a convoluted admissions system, distinguishing between people admitted on academic criteria alone and those admitted after consideration of supplemental criteria, did not convince its critics that all applicants got equal consideration. The university not only did not appear to have a compelling hedgehog concept about diversity and inclusiveness, but it also seemed to lack competent fox tactics. Connerly's attacks exposed the weakness of the administration and undermined its credibility.

Part of the problem was that the university was "a house divided" (Pusser, 2004: 218). The faculty was ambivalent about affirmative action, as Martin Trow, a Berkeley professor who opposed affirmative action, showed in a survey he conducted (Douglass, 2007: 160). In any case, neither the faculty nor the regents had a sense of ownership of the university's affirmative action programs or trusted the administration. A contributing factor was that Peltason was not a very good fox, as Karl Pister suggests:

> In a way we have nobody to blame but ourselves, not to say it wouldn't have happened anyway, but we didn't necessarily mount the strongest possible case. It would be interesting to know to what extent a different president might have handled this. I can't see David Gardner allowing that kind of thing to have gone the way it did. Or Dick Atkinson. I think they are very different people from Jack Peltason. Jack was more of a compromiser. (Pusser, 2004: 132)

Gardner and Atkinson were compromisers too, but they were better at it. They knew when to push and fight and when to retreat and regroup. In other words, they were better foxes than Peltason, who came into the job as an interim for one year and ended up having to serve three against his better judgment. He was no match for Connerly, the "rogue regent" who described himself as the "lone ranger" (Douglass, 2007: 170).

Peltason was replaced by Richard C. Atkinson (1995-2003), chancellor of San Diego, who did a good job at fending off attacks on the university, due in part to his political skills and in part to the prosperity of the economy during most of his tenure, which was a period of great growth. As Kerr says, Atkinson, like Gardner and Kerr himself, rode "the rising trends," while Hitch, Saxon, and Peltason rode the "declining trends" (2001b: 414). As chancellor of the San Diego campus, Atkinson had done an extraordinary job of using the campus' expertise to revitalize the local economy, the so-called "Atkinson miracle" (Pelfrey, 2004: 79). He applied the same principles to the UC system as a whole, establishing powerful industry-university cooperative research programs and creating institutes for science and innovation on various campuses with the support of Governor Gray Davis. In addition, he increased student enrollments in science and engineering by 50 percent in just a few years, in order to supply the economy with much-needed experts in these fields. Thus, Atkinson (2007) increased the connections between academia and the corporate world, emphasizing the "rich dividends" that the University of California provided to the citizens of the state (35).

Indeed, in his speeches, time and again, Atkinson talked about the impact of research and development on economic growth, quoting the Council on Competitiveness and the Council of Economic Advisers, which showed that 50 percent of economic growth since World War II had been due to investments in research and development. According to Atkinson (2007), "no state in the country illustrates the connection between knowledge and wealth more vividly than California. Almost all of the industries in which California leads the world—biotechnology, software and computers, telecommunications, multimedia, semiconductors, environmental technologies—were born of university-based research" (41). Atkinson (2007) was not shy about pointing out that "the link between California's success and the success of its universities is clear and direct" (42). During his tenure, the University of California opened a new campus in Merced and established a new center in Washington, DC, as well as facilities in other countries. The university's research performance was recognized by the AAU, which increased the number of UC member campuses by three; the Nobel Prize committee, which granted prizes to eleven UC faculty members; and various national rankings. Atkinson also intensified fund-raising efforts, bringing a great deal more money to the university.

While enhancing the university's academic standing and extramural funding, Atkinson aggressively tried to repair the damage caused by SP1, SP2, and Proposition 209. First, he tried to delay implementation of SP1 and SP2, but, according to Smelser (2010), he was summoned to Sacramento "for a dressing-down by Governor Wilson" and had to write a letter of apology in order to avoid a special meeting of the regents to review his "performance" (149). Pusser (2004) states that, when Atkinson was told that he had to comply with these new rules or else "face dismissal" (199), he quickly retreated. Douglass (2007), however, explains that Atkinson negotiated a compromise to delay eliminating affirmative action for undergraduate admissions for one year, while proceeding to eliminate affirmative action for graduate admissions immediately. Since the only area that was really problematic was undergraduate admissions, in effect he got what he wanted, although the public may have been under the impression that he had caved under pressure. This maneuver was followed by a wide variety of other tactics.

Basically, Atkinson's presidency could be defined as an exploration and testing of the limits. First, he greatly expanded and improved UC's outreach activities, in order to prepare promising underprivileged students for admission to UC, a huge enterprise given the low funding and poor quality of the California public schools that once were the envy of the rest of the country. Among other things, this move sent the message that the University of California welcomed minorities. Atkinson also established a plan to accept the top 4 percent of each high school graduating class. In addition, he drew on his expertise as a psychologist to question the value of some of the standardized tests, which caused a media sensation and forced the ETS to revise them. He also pushed for comprehensive review—the Harvard model. At the end of his tenure, the university was getting ready to switch to a more holistic approach to admissions.

In addition, in 2001, two years before he retired from the presidency, he had the satisfaction of seeing the Board of Regents, including Connerly, rescind SP1 and SP2, although by then this was a symbolic gesture, since Proposition 209 remained in effect. Besides sending a positive message to minorities, this gesture also affirmed the role of the faculty in the admissions process. In a marathon effort to enhance his legacy in this respect before stepping down, Atkinson also revised the University of California's Academic Freedom Policy, strengthening the power of the faculty. Emerging from a controversy about a Berkeley course on Palestinian literature (Post, 2003; Atkinson, 2004), the new policy no longer invokes a principle of neutrality and of letting the facts speak for themselves in which very few people believe today. Instead, it emphasizes the importance of following academic standards to express opinions. Scholars often disagree in their interpretations, and as long as proper research procedures are followed, their opinions should be acceptable. Thus, for example, one could express opinions for or against Palestinian causes, as long as these opinions were based on research that met academic standards. This policy, which has received a great deal of attention, should help the university deal with similar controversies in the future.

After a relatively stable and upbeat presidency, in which he extricated the University of California from the thick of the affirmative action struggles and put it on a path to recovery, Atkinson retired. His profile is that of an energetic and enthusiastic, perhaps even hyperactive, fox, who tried as many tactics as possible to help the institution he represented traverse a politically difficult period while profiting from the economic bonanza of the late 1990s. Atkinson used his fox qualities to protect the University of California's independence and enhance its prosperity, but he was not able to offer a new vision. That vision has remained elusive, as bad economic times and a new wave of attacks on the University of California prevented his successor, Robert C. Dynes (2003-2008), from focusing on developing one.

Like Atkinson, Dynes was chancellor of the San Diego campus, where he was also very involved in enhancing relationships between academia and industry. Indeed, Dynes, a physicist, came from industry, having worked at AT&T Bell Laboratories for many years before joining the San Diego campus. According to Douglass (2007), Dynes did not seem as interested in undergraduate admissions as Atkinson was, among other things, because he was consumed by other problems from the start of his tenure. These included mishaps at the UC-run national laboratories and fighting to retain management over them, in competition with a consortium led by the University of Texas. These problems began in the last year of the Atkinson presidency, when allegations of loss or theft of government property at the Los Alamos National Laboratory resulted in an investigation and the replacement of the director and other administrators. Two investigators fired from Los Alamos, allegedly in retaliation for whistle-blowing, were hired by the Office of the President, which paid them their former salaries retroactive to the dates of their dismissals. After these scandals, the U.S. Energy Secretary decided to open the Los Alamos contract for competition in 2005, rather than giving the University of California an automatic renewal.

Dynes walked into a very difficult situation as president. After one year of disclosures about the problems at the labs, the university's image had been profoundly tarnished. Public perception was that the administration was incompetent and corrupt. As the investigation of Los Alamos continued under his watch, there were further revelations of improprieties involving both security violations and loss or theft of government property. The most disturbing finding was that the improprieties did not seem to be isolated events, but rather part of an arrogant and careless culture. Dynes replaced the recently-hired director with a new one, at an unusually high salary. This did not go unnoticed by the public, which at the time was becoming painfully aware of the increasing gap between rich and poor and was experiencing a growing crisis of confidence in the country's leadership.

People appeared to project their frustrations onto the university and to start to look for questionable practices at UC, which many thought shared the arrogant and careless culture that had been uncovered at the national labs. What they found was a public research university involved in a competition for prestige with the privates and the elite publics, with all that that entailed in terms of good working conditions for faculty members, high salaries and abundant perks for administrators, and consequent circumventing of the rules. In other words, they found a "fox culture" in which leaders worked around the rules in order to be able to keep up with other top research universities. The focus of this "fox culture" was the pursuit of resources to fuel the competition for prestige. For example, due to public pressure, salaries for most high-level administrators at UC are considerably lower than at other elite public universities and much lower than at the privates. One way to deal with this is to offer other perks, such as well-paid positions for partners, generous moving expenses, deferred compensation, or golden parachute provisions. The University of California was doing what it thought necessary to hire experienced leaders who could help it maintain and enhance its academic reputation, which the state expected of it. But the state did not want to know how this was accomplished, so the university did not disclose its methods until it was forced to do so by the media storm that started in Los Alamos and moved to Oakland, Santa Cruz, and Davis—and, to a much lesser degree, the rest of the UC system.

*The San Francisco Chronicle* played a major role in creating this media storm, which focused on the Northern California facilities. It was as a result of this newspaper's inquiries that the Office of the President began an investigation of system Provost M.R.C. Greenwood's role in awarding an administrative position to Linda Goff, a personal friend and business associate whom she had brought from Santa Cruz, as well of Vice President Winston Doby's role in giving a paid internship on the Merced campus to Provost Greenwood's son. Doby was placed on paid investigatory leave and publicly reprimanded, after which he retired. It appears that Greenwood had never asked him to help her son, but Dynes was concerned about the appearance of impropriety, thus his harsh and open rebuke of Doby. As for Goff, it turned out that she did co-own some real estate with Greenwood at the time of her appointment, which did constitute a conflict of interest.

Greenwood was a distinguished scholar and well-known administrator who, among other things, had served as associate director for science under President Clinton, but this episode took place during a period of Republican control of both the federal and California executive branches. Whatever political clout she might have had obviously was not enough, because she was forced to step down abruptly when milder and more discreet measures would have been more appropriate. One might conclude that Dynes was so eager to placate the public that he staged a harsh and public departure for Greenwood, who received a generous severance package, perhaps as compensation for her damaging dismissal. And this was Dynes' biggest mistake, because media disclosure of Greenwood's severance package produced a much greater fury than her original failure to recuse herself from the hiring process resulting in Linda Goff's appointment. This episode opened a series of unusually nasty attacks on the university.

One person who was already under attack when this happened was Denice Denton, who had recently replaced Greenwood as chancellor at Santa Cruz. Denton, who was openly lesbian, was faced with strong criticism from the start due to the generous recruitment package she had received, which, among other perks, included a well-paid position for her partner, Gretchen Kalonji, at the Office of the President, reporting directly to Greenwood. Partner hires are not by any means limited to administrators. The competition for faculty is intense, and such enticements are typical in recruitment. For example, many UC campuses have partner-employment programs in recognition of the fact that many faculty members will not accept job offers unless their spouses or partners are also offered gainful employment on campus or in the area. Thus, hiring partners, once considered nepotism, is now a normal part of business in academia, where "two-body" hires have become routine. The Santa Cruz campus, however, had not been as active as some other UC campuses in this respect. In fact, it appears that the campus had lost some faculty members because of its failure to provide jobs for their partners. Thus, news of Kalonji's position in Greenwood's office was not well-received on a campus that, in addition to lacking a consistent practice of partner hires, was experiencing financial problems. Moreover, some members of the campus community mistrusted Greenwood, whom they perceived as favoring women. The almost simultaneous hiring of her personal friend and business associate, Linda Goff, and Denice Denton's partner, Gretchen Kalonji, for well-paid positions in her office without open searches produced a hostile response. Thus, Denton was hurt by Greenwood's baggage and must have had trouble understanding the reaction to what she probably thought was a generous, but not overly lucrative, recruitment package.

The problem was that Denton's recruitment package made people think about all of the things that were wrong at UC Santa Cruz, and there were many, including a three-year staff salary freeze, which in an area with such a high cost of living meant that the least-paid employees of the campus were stretched to the limit. When Greenwood's generous compensation package was revealed following her resignation in the fall of 2005, the media revisited Denton's recruitment package, including renovations to the chancellor's house. In particular, the media focused on an enclosure that was built on the property for Denton's dogs. Critics pointed out that, while UC was spending money so freely on the renovations to the chancellor's house, it was not offering affordable housing to its faculty, students, or staff. As Paul Fain (2006) says, the dog run in particular made Denton "a punch line and a symbol of excess in the system-wide compensation scandal" (A1) that unfolded that fall. Attacks on Denton became unrelenting after that point. Conservatives were critical of her sexual orientation and progressive ideas and liberals were unhappy about her corporate lifestyle. Her clothes, and even her glasses, were criticized and ridiculed. She was insulted and stalked on a regular basis and she received multiple death threats.

The chancellor's house, which her mother compared to "a tomb" (Fain, 2007: A24), sits alone in the middle of the heavily-wooded campus, and Denton was living there by herself, since her partner was in San Francisco most of the time. In one of the attacks she suffered, someone broke her bedroom window with a parking barricade late at night, and she was afraid for her life. On June 6, 2006, during a campus protest over staff wages and faculty diversity, students surrounded Denton's car, sitting on the trunk and hood and striking it with placards in a very intimidating manner (Fain, 2007). Denton must have felt impotent and bewildered. On June 15, Denton went on medical leave and on June 24 she committed suicide by jumping from the roof of the 400-foot-tall San Francisco building where she shared a rented apartment with her partner. Her mother, who was with her at the time, stated that she was very depressed about her personal and professional life. Indeed, she had failed as chancellor before she could even start.

About the time that the dog run episode hit the press, that is, shortly after the Greenwood compensation scandal, there was another episode involving alleged misuse of university funds. This took place on the Davis campus and involved its former vice chancellor for university relations, Celeste Rose, who is African-American. Rose had served as legislative aid to former California Assembly Speaker Willie Brown, a politician who exerted a great deal of power for a very long time. In her capacity as Brown's aid, she had quizzed David Gardner on diversity issues during his interview for the presidency. Once he got the position, Gardner turned around and hired Rose, who held several positions at the Office of the President between 1983 and 1997. After serving briefly as Executive Director of the National Collegiate Athletic Association's public affairs group, Rose was appointed vice chancellor for university relations at UC Davis in 1998.

This position has two components: university relations proper and fundraising. Rose's background was in university relations, particularly governmental relations. Rose remained in the position until 2005, when she was asked to step down. By then, Willie Brown had been termed out as mayor of San Francisco and had retired from politics. At the same time, the Davis campus was preparing for the upcoming centennial and its biggest campaign ever, which elevated the relative importance of fundraising. On the surface, replacing Rose seemed like business as usual in a fox culture in which administrators are hired and fired largely according to political considerations. However, it appears that she was not given any reason for the decision to let her go. In addition, she was not given enough advance warning of her dismissal to find another position.

Todd Wallack and Tanya Schevitz (2005) reported that Rose was told in February that she had to leave in June. Usually, administrators in such circumstances are given enough time to find a job before news of their stepping down from their current positions becomes known, since people might think that their leaving is performance-related and be reluctant to hire them for other positions. If this account is correct, Rose was denied that opportunity, in addition to not being given any explanation about the decision to replace her. In any event, she hired a lawyer—the prominent UC Davis alumn Melinda Guzmán—and prepared to protect her rights. Anxious to avoid a lawsuit and a scandal involving discrimination, the campus offered her a generous settlement. This settlement came to light in the fall of 2005 when the *San Francisco*

*Chronicle* published an article exposing the deal and pointing out that the regents had not been informed of it, which was a policy violation. The details of the settlement agreement caused a furor.

The media storm of fall 2005 is interesting because it exposed a deep fatigue on the part of the public with the fox culture of the University of California. It was clear that people had very little understanding of, or tolerance for, the current ways of the research university. In addition, it showed that Dynes was simply not as good a fox as some of his predecessors. Finally, it evidenced a considerable degree of racism and sexism. Indeed, of all the administrators of the University of California who could have been criticized for their participation in the fox culture of the institution, the media focused on three females: Greenwood, Denton (who was openly gay), and Rose (who was black). In connection with Greenwood, the media also focused on Doby, a black male. It was not the first time that public anger had been brought to bear on women and minority executives, for, as Pelfrey (2008a) notes, during the economic crisis of the 1990s, one of the issues that elicited most criticism was the granting of a one-year administrative leave to Barbara Uehling when she stepped down from her position as chancellor at Santa Barbara. White male chancellors who received this benefit did not get the same angry reaction. As for Gardner, although a white male, he was a member of a religious minority, which he thinks affected how his compensation agreement was perceived—"Mormon greed." The evidence suggests that he may have been right.

The public seems to react with particular fury when executives from non-traditional backgrounds receive financial benefits enjoyed by other executives at their levels but not by the majority of the population. The same can be said about student admissions. Indeed, during the crisis of the 1990s, public criticism concentrated more on the student admissions process than on executive compensation. The events leading to Proposition 209 coincided with the passage of California's "three strikes and you're out" bill, which increased the prison budget to the detriment of the education budget, according to Arthur M. Cohen (1998: 391). Given the heavily non-white nature of the prison population, this bill can be seen as an example of hostility towards minorities during a time of stress. Proposition 209 can be interpreted as another expression of the same hostility—an attempt to send minorities away from UC and into lesser institutions. By contrast, the feelings of frustration in the middle years of the current decade focused more on executive compensation for women and minorities than on the admissions process. In both cases, however, women and minorities—students or executives—bore the brunt of the attacks. As Christopher Newfield (2008) points out, as the middle class was losing ground and the gap between rich and poor was increasing, women and minorities became targets for popular anger and frustration. Generally considered less deserving, everything they received was seen as excessive.

The impression that readers must have received from the articles and commentaries written during the media storm of fall 2005 was that Greenwood, Rose, and Denton obtained benefits they did not deserve and that they got them because of their status as women and/or minorities. In reality, they all seem to have been mistreated in one way or another. The literature shows that women and minority administrators are more heavily criticized, enjoy shorter tenures, and suffer more abrupt, career-damaging, dismissals than white males. They are almost never given the benefit of the doubt or afforded second opportunities. This certainly appears to have been the case with these three administrators. Greenwood's administrative career was severely damaged by her very public dismissal, and it took years for her to get another administrative position. It is interesting that subsequent investigations of other executives resulted in the secret disciplining of scores of administrators, whose careers Dynes made an effort to protect (Schevitz, 2007). These administrators were treated much more kindly than Greenwood was. Similarly, Rose's administrative career was derailed by the haste with which she was asked to leave. As for Denton, her career as an academic leader was destroyed before it even started. She was not given a first opportunity, let alone a second. As Fain (2006) noted, "experts on university leadership said the stresses on Ms. Denton in her 16 months as chancellor were extreme examples of the anxiety-causing problems that many public-university leaders face" (A1) Denton was an extreme example, indeed, for she was a mobbing victim.

Reporting on a lecture titled "Dysfunctional by Design: Mobbing and Harassment in the Academic Workplace" by Jeanine Stewart, Elizabeth Leigh Farrington (2006) explains that institutions have "hard hierarchies," or power associated with positions, and "soft hierarchies," or power associated with individuals. People at the top of "hard hierarchies" have problems if they cannot get the backing of people at the top of "soft hierarchies." Conflict between hard and soft hierarchies may result in hierarchical dysfunction. In times of transition, when matters are in flux, women and minorities are particularly vulnerable, because they tend to have less inherent power than white males, and people will attack those that they perceive as weak. Women and minorities of high status or aspirations are particularly prone to attacks and can suffer episodes of severe hostility. Women and minorities, who are usually invited to lead during chaotic periods, are often the targets of mobbing, which includes behaviors "such as social isolation, public and private humiliation and ridicule, rumor mongering and threatened violence" (Farrington, 2006: 36). While harassment could consist of a single episode, mobbing involves constant and regular attacks and is far more damaging. Studies show that mobbing can lead to suicide. For example, there is evidence that one in seven suicides in Sweden is related to workplace mobbing (Leymann, 1990, 1996). Mobbing is quite common in academia (Westhues, 2004, 2006). According to Stewart, Denton was a victim of "upward mobbing," in which people of lower status turn on someone of higher rank (Farrington, 2006: 36). Unfortunately, no one seems to have understood what was happening until it was too late.

Denton, who had personal as well as professional difficulties, bailed out by committing suicide. But Greenwood and Rose understood that the only practical thing they could do under the circumstances was to get money to compensate for the loss of future earnings caused by their abrupt dismissals, so they negotiated cash settlements. This was met with anger by the public, which was very troubled by their "golden parachutes." Whether or not people liked the university's recruitment practices, there was some level of understanding about the fact that the market for top-level administrators was competitive. It was much harder for people to understand why the university paid administrators great sums of money after it decided to replace them. This seemed to be the most inexplicable part of the entire pattern of administrative behavior uncovered by the press. It appeared that administrators were either simply helping one another to get lucrative compensation packages both on the way in and on the way out, or else caving in to the threats of women and minorities claiming discrimination. What the public never seems to have realized is that Greenwood and Rose may actually have had a case. In fact, in terms of the exit patterns of administrators, they probably did have a case, because many of their white male colleagues enjoyed less damaging transitions than they did. Indeed, as Sarah Gibbard Cook notes, on average, women presidents stay in office 2.2 fewer years than men do, and they are often "fired overnight " (Wenninger & Conroy, 2007: 148), while male presidents tend to be given advance warning informally, allowing them to look for other administrative positions before it is too late. Cook believes that part of the problem is that decision-makers do not know how to deal with women, so they fail to share this kind of information with them. Minority administrators experience similar treatment. Greenwood and Rose appear to be examples of this pattern of abrupt dismissal. The university was obviously not interested in undertaking an analysis of the exit patterns of its administrators. A settlement was its preferred solution.

This points to an aspect of fox culture that is little understood by the public, that is, the degree to which it is controlled by legal considerations. Lawyers have enormous influence on the decision-making process. For example, rather than deciding personnel cases on the merits, institutions of higher learning often resolve them on the basis of how much legal trouble they expect from unhappy employees. An employee without a lawyer is likely to get worse treatment than one with legal representation, and an employee with a famous lawyer is more likely to get money than one with less formidable legal representation. Attorneys look at the identity of opposing counsel and make their recommendations accordingly. In other words, getting a lawyer and, in particular, the right lawyer, makes an employee much more likely to get a generous cash settlement. The merits of the case may be secondary, or even irrelevant. This is wrong. Fixing this problem, however, will not be easy because making these decisions only on their merits would require consistent compliance with university regulations and a general absence of discrimination.

Administrative transitions are fraught with legal danger, as rules are often broken. For example, in order to remove administrators from certain positions, academic leaders may be required to consult with the Academic Senate, which might want to know why this decision is being made and inquire about the performance of the administrator in question. But it is not uncommon for administrators being removed to have better performance evaluations than those remaining, since replacing administrators is largely a political decision. How could academic leaders justify their choices under those conditions? It is much easier to ask their subordinates to resign and give them some sort of monetary compensation. That is what is usually done. In fact, it is customary to let administrators know quietly of the decision to replace them and give them enough time to find other jobs. Most problems arise when the decision to replace a subordinate is sudden and public and therefore damaging to the career of the departing administrator. Those cases are more likely to result in litigation. I think that the Greenwood and Rose cases were examples of this. Once they found themselves in an impossible situation, they used their administrative acumen to do damage control on their own behalf. As Leonard A. Valverde (2003) points out, women and minority administrators are almost never given the benefit of the doubt or a second chance, since "any blemish mark on their record" (144) will prevent them from ever obtaining another position, which is not the case with white males. Knowing this, Greenwood and Rose fought to protect their rights. Denton is a more complicated case, as I believe that she was a hedgehog who tried to behave like a fox and did not succeed in either respect.

Denton had vision, and it was a vision of diversity and inclusiveness, of empowering the disadvantaged. But she tried to beat the foxes at their own game and negotiated very good conditions for herself and her campus, probably, among other things, because she knew that her administrative success was linked to her ability to get money. Universities, which have become "capital-intensive," as well as "labor-intensive" (Drucker, 1980: 27), need a great deal of funding in order to keep up with their competitors. Thus, administrators are under pressure to bring in dollars. These fundraisers obtain money for themselves, as well as for their institutions. After all, in a culture in which money is so important, compensation defines one's worth. A low-paid president might be perceived as less valuable and therefore command less authority than a well-compensated one. Denton doubtless thought that getting good conditions for herself and her campus would be interpreted as a sign of strength: that she was doing as well as a white male. The problem is that she was not one. Thus, her conditions, particularly the renovation of the chancellor's house, were seen as outrageous and attributed to female capriciousness. Ironically, her requests concerning the chancellor's house were almost certainly more for the campus' benefit than her own, as this facility is used heavily for university functions. It is true that she negotiated accommodations for her pets, which led to the building of the dog run, reportedly a less costly option than upgrading the fence around the entire property (Gumz, 2005). But improvements to the house itself were badly needed, and that is where the bulk of the money went.

Denton may have been advised by UC insiders to request the repairs as part of her recruitment package, as it would have been very difficult to obtain funding for them later. But, of course, there was a reason why past chancellors, who were all from UC and knew the campus well, had let this facility deteriorate. They must have been afraid that the much-needed remodel would generate a negative public reaction, and, if so, they were right. The reaction was quick and brutal and disabled Denton, who after that point had a very difficult time operating. Essentially, her administration had become dysfunctional. Her fox demands regarding funding were in direct conflict with her hedgehog vision of empowering the disadvantaged, whose authenticity was then questioned by her critics. This conflict came to a head on June 6, when she was accosted by protesters, who surrounded her car, sat on it, and accused her of hypocrisy. This episode brought her down literally and metaphorically. One week later, she checked herself into a psychiatric facility and three weeks later she was dead.

Attempting to explain the professional reasons contributing to Denton's suicide, Paul Fain (2007) says that she did "too much, too fast" (A24), and I think that he is right, up to a point. Denton went directly from being dean of engineering at a relatively relaxed institution to being chancellor of a particularly tense campus, without ever having been provost. But there are many cases like this in academia, including the UC system, where these kinds of dean-to-chancellor promotions are not uncommon. A more important reason for her downfall, I believe, is that Denton's administrative style, which apparently had worked well at her previous institutions, was not at all suited to UC Santa Cruz. Denton had what Fain (2007) describes as a "larger-than-life personality" (A24). A vision of diversity and inclusiveness had guided all of her previous actions, leading her to fight many battles on behalf of women and minorities over the years. She had taken very public positions in this respect, including her energetic rebuttal of the famous comments by Lawrence Summers, then president of Harvard, questioning women's ability to engage in science.

Denton had a strong personality, and she had moral authority. She would invoke a vision with passion, and people would follow her, or at least not oppose her. She was accustomed to getting her way in her college, the College of Engineering. The Santa Cruz campus, however, was a far more complex and challenging unit, with many outspoken faculty, students, and staff. It was full of tensions revolving around the differences in compensation between its richest and poorest members, which a rising labor movement was challenging. There was a great deal of resentment against administrators, and all of that resentment became focused on Denton before she even arrived. Even women and minorities were against her.

If Denton had been an ordinary fox, the expectations for improvement would have been lower, but she was a hedgehog and her vision was an egalitarian one. This no doubt contributed to making the campus more aggressive. Many people, including Denton herself, probably, did not understand why she was being criticized by women and minorities, the very groups she had fought so hard, for so many years, to help. But this is actually a common phenomenon. When there is a great deal of repression, things are calmer than when there is hope for change, as Kerr discovered when the students revolted against him after he gave them more freedom. A fox might have kept a tight lid on events, but he was a hedgehog who was faithful to a liberal philosophy. Kerr did not survive. The student revolts were the beginning of the end for him, as we have seen.

Denton faced a more complex situation, in that her newly-acquired fox ways—her success at getting money—undermined her moral authority, and she no longer had a credible vision to call upon. Forcefully invoking a vision had been her hedgehog modus operandi up to that point. She derived all of her strength from her vision. Without it, she was left with no tools to deal with the crisis. The people who would have been her natural power base were critical of her. She had no allies. If she had not tried so hard to be a fox, she might have had many problems, but her moral authority would have remained intact. She might not have survived politically, but at least she could have left administration with honor, a quality that Sharon A. Krause (2002) defines as "the ambitious desire to live up to one's code" (2), which makes it possible for one to "respect oneself even when one is unpopular, or officially unrecognized" (20). Denton could have resigned her chancellor position and lived to fight another day in a different capacity. At the end, it must have been impossible for her to see how she could do either.

# 13

# The Collapse of Fox Culture

The final casualty of the media storm that started in the national labs, raged with the Greenwood, Denton, and Rose cases and continued afterwards was Dynes himself. Although he held on to power for a while longer, he did not survive the events of the fall of 2005 and was not allowed to complete his five-year term. Officially, Dynes retained his title as president, but the UC system-wide provost, Wyatt (Rory) Hume, was appointed as "chief operating officer" for the last year of Dynes' term. I believe that Dynes' problem was that he was neither a good fox nor a good hedgehog. He was neither shrewd enough nor visionary enough, and he rode what Kerr calls "a declining trend," that is, a period of diminished resources. In addition, his tenure coincided with a moment of profound malaise in the country, which affected how the university was perceived and treated. Although he made mistakes, he was also a victim of circumstances beyond his control. He was not the best person for the job, and the job had become impossible.

Dynes was looking for a more democratic vision for the UC system. Even though he was clearly less focused on the admissions debate than Atkinson, he seemed more attuned to women and minorities in other respects. He apparently was involved in improving the status of women and minorities at Bell Laboratories, and his interest in diversity continued when he joined the University of California. Dynes seemed more personally aware than his predecessor of the disadvantages these groups suffered at the faculty, staff, and administrative levels and was more vocal about the need for change. For example, he became involved in such initiatives as the work-life balance project, where he showed more insight into these issues than previous presidents. He also held retreats for upper administration to discuss issues relating to diversity and inclusiveness. He was interested in succession planning and started conversations about this matter with the campuses' top leaders. He was looking for a new vision for the UC system.

Meanwhile, the problems at the labs turned out to be more complicated and more difficult to handle than expected, with a series of mishaps that produced a very negative image of UC. As we have seen, this resulted in a new series of attacks on university administrators, who were presented by the media as both incompetent and greedy. A good fox would have defended the University's practices, as did Gardner, who, according to Louis Freedberg (2006), dismissed criticism of UC compensation practices, calling it "overly simplistic" and "conceptually weak." Gardner's argument was that, unless UC was able to offer faculty and administrators competitive compensation, its world-class status would decline. Gardner got away with this explanation in part because of his skill and in part because of the times. Fox culture was then in full bloom.

Dynes became president in a period of extreme fox fatigue, and he was not a very good fox to begin with. So he conceded that there was a problem. The facts were hard to deny. UC had failed to implement its own policies. In 2004 and 2005, the Office of the President did not submit the annual report on executive compensation to the regents, as it was required to do and had done until that moment. Technically, there were not many other violations of the principles regarding executive compensation that had been approved during the 1990s crisis, as Pelfrey (2008b) has shown. But Dynes stated that he had inherited an office culture of "trying to get away with as much as possible and disclose as little as possible" (Schevitz, 2007). Why did he say that? Was he attempting to deflect the blame onto previous presidents, or was he simply trying to say that the problem was larger than he was?

The salaries the University of California paid to its top executives were not as high as those offered by similar institutions of higher learning. As a result, compensation had to be given through other means, such as increasingly creative perquisites. For example, under President Atkinson, an administrator simultaneously received a temporary housing allowance and two housing-related loans. As the market for academic administrators became more competitive, Dynes found himself offering more and more unusual deals.

The "culture of compensation," as Freedberg (2006) calls it, was bigger than he was and bigger than UC: It was the fox culture of higher education, which reflected the fox culture of the country. The media storm of 2005 took place when the United States was in the midst of a period of extreme fox fatigue, with a disappointed and dispirited public tired of the wars, the dislocations caused by the global economy—including the increasing gap between rich and poor and the lack of basic social services like affordable health care and higher education. Dynes could not change that. Instead, he pushed Greenwood out in a harsh and public manner and did not defend Denton from the uniquely brutal attacks that she was experiencing. He also failed to acknowledge his involvement in the Rose case.

Although he appears to have been sincerely interested in enhancing diversity and inclusiveness in the UC system, Dynes was not sophisticated enough to understand the patterns of behavior surrounding women and minorities. Thus, he was taken by surprise by the unusually nasty attacks he suffered as a result of his connections with Greenwood, Denton, and Rose. He came to experience the fury of which women and minorities are often recipients and which is directed toward white males only when they are perceived as favoring these groups in one way or another. He did not know how to handle the crisis. Instead of resisting the pressure and making rational decisions about Greenwood, Denton, and Rose, he panicked. He tried to distance himself from all three women but could not. In the end, the regents borrowed his technique of making public sacrifices to appease critics, only this time, the sacrificial lamb was Dynes himself. Dynes, who was perceived as beholden to women and minorities, was treated like members of these groups are often treated: he was dismissed abruptly.

Dynes, aware of his political problems, apparently was exploring some job possibilities elsewhere when, in the summer of 2007, he was told to transfer oversight of the day-to-day operations of the university to his provost, Rory Hume, for the duration of his term. What is interesting about this action is that it was so public. If the regents were concerned about Dynes' performance, they could have told him to let Hume have a greater role in decision-making during that last year without announcing this publicly, which would have given Dynes more time to find a new job. But the regents were under pressure to show change, and they decided to do this the same way Dynes had: by the public dismissal of a top administrator. Although Dynes kept his title for the remainder of his term, the damage was done. The regents compensated him for his trouble by giving him a generous faculty salary, plus a one-year administrative leave at the end of his term.

In a statement about his resignation, after reviewing what the university had accomplished under his watch, Dynes expressed dissatisfaction that he had not been able to accomplish more in terms of transforming the university into a more diverse and inclusive institution, stating that this should be an area of "utmost importance" to his successor "and the overall leadership of the University of California" (Hayward, 2007). This shows that what he lamented was not having the opportunity to articulate and implement a new vision of diversity and inclusiveness for the university, that is, not his failure as a fox, but that he had not been a good enough hedgehog.

Following Dynes' August 13, 2007, announcement that he was re-signing from the presidency effective June, 2008, and that he had asked Provost Hume "to act as the University's Chief Operating Officer, in addition to his other duties, effective immediately," the then-chair of the Board of Regents, Richard C. Blum, an investment banker married to U.S. Senator Dianne Feinstein, issued a public letter dated August, 21, 2007. Addressed to the regents and titled "We Need to Be Strategically Dynamic," this letter had a command-and-control tone and seemed to have been written to show that something was being done to address UC's much-publicized problems. The letter began by saying that, over the four years that he had been a member of the Board of Regents, Blum had heard about many problems and seen very few solutions and that it was time to start making improvements. Since these four years coincided exactly with Dynes' tenure as president, this can be seen as a way to blame him for these problems. On the surface, however, Blum attributed the problems to "an overgrown UC administrative infrastructure that substitutes motion for progress." According to Blum, this administra-tive structure, which had not been evaluated in over forty years, was in need of total revamping so that it might become "nimble." After this introduction, Blum proceeded to suggest specific changes in a number of areas, including capital projects, external relations, organizational restructuring and cost savings and operations. He stated that he had asked Hume to work on these projects. The problems that had created the media storm in the fall of 2005 were not highlighted prominently in this document, although Blum did say that there were still "manage-ment problems" in the national laboratories, and he discussed the need to establish long-term compensation strategies in order to avoid "ad hoc, short-term fixes." Nevertheless, the public reacted positively to the critical tone of the letter, which was praised for its candor and seen as a step in the right direction.

Clearly, Blum's letter was both overly critical of UC, which he de-scribed as "dysfunctional," and overly optimistic about how to fix its problems. For example, he referred to the fact that UC's percentage of the state budget had declined from 7.5 percent to 3 percent in the previous twenty years and indicated that this was due to less-than-optimal governmental relations. This suggested that the solution to the problem was better governmental relations. The cited trend, however, is national, and to reverse it would take a great deal more than effective UC advocates in Sacramento.

It is precisely this trend towards de-funding public universities that is at the base of UC's executive compensation practices, which reward those who can bring in dollars. With shrinking levels of support from the state, the university has been forced to look for funds elsewhere, which has changed its culture, creating an increasing gap between rich and poor. That is why student fees are going up, hurting families of modest means. That is why the university has outsourced some functions to private companies, which often pay their employees less. That is why staff salaries are depressed. That is why there is a large academic underclass of lecturers, researchers and other academic employees—what Kerr called the "unfaculty"—which is less well-compensated than the faculty. That is why science faculty members make more money than faculty members in the humanities. And that is also why administrators make more money than faculty members do. Reorganizing the bureaucracy at UC is not going to produce significant improvements, since doing so is based on what Duderstadt and Womack (2003) call "one of the great myths concerning higher education in America," a myth dear to faculty members and regents alike, namely, "that university administrations are bloated and excessive" (135). That is why the touted reorganization involved moving administrators from the Office of the President to the various campuses and letting certain positions go, only to reinstate a good portion of them later, albeit in a reconfigured fashion. Given the numerous mandates the university has to follow, there is a limit to how many positions can truly be eliminated.

Blum surely knew that restructuring the Office of the President was not going to reverse what Sheila Slaughter and Larry L. Leslie (1997) call "academic capitalism." Simply put, higher education is more important to the current post-industrial society than it was to the industrial society that established public universities in this country. While most of the discoveries that made the industrial revolution possible came from outside the university, the information revolution was created primarily by people with advanced degrees, and the current economy depends on college-trained workers, who provide product innovation. So universities, through research and development and teaching and training, are "the font of technoscience for postindustrial economies" (38). What universities produce is very valuable in global markets, thus, the growth of administration, including the creation of centers, which operate as intermediaries between the faculty and the market. At the same time, due to conservative political trends that have resulted in lower taxes and less support for education, public universities have seen their state support reduced, which has forced them to seek funds aggressively from both federal and private sources, including corporate donors.

Organizations tend to take on the characteristics of their resource providers (Slaughter & Leslie, 1997). Thus, the corporatization of the university, whose leaders, required to interact on a daily basis with business executives, come to expect similar high salaries, fancy houses and cars and generous expense accounts. Therefore, compensation for administrators is on the rise. Pay for those faculty members who are heavily invested in research is better than for those who focus more on teaching. The big losers in this transformation are the students, who are neglected by the faculty while being charged higher tuition by the university. On the one hand, the university is receiving less money from the state for teaching, and on the other, it is using much of the money it does take in to support sponsored research in the form of matching funds, equipment, and facilities. Universities spend a great deal more money supporting sponsored research than the grant funds they get to cover direct and indirect costs. The difference is made up with funds coming largely from inexpensive fields, such as those in the humanities and social sciences, which can teach students cheaply and make money that can then be transferred to other parts of the campus. So, contrary to popular myth, the humanities and social sciences are donors, not recipients, of funds in the internal reallocations taking place within universities. In fact, these fields are being effectively cannibalized in order to support the sponsored research race (Newfield, 2008; Cole, 2009; Watson, 2010).

As can be seen, the changes that Kerr noted in *The Uses of the University* have become more pronounced and more pervasive in recent times, as ties between the university and the economy have continued to intensify. Sheila Slaughter and Gary Rhoades (2009) discuss the increasing number of "corporate and university interlocks" (236) that connect institutions of higher learning with the business world through their boards of trustees, recommending that public university trustees "be studied to see if they form networks that are grounded in public good purposes" (255). As they point out, trustees may endorse certain policies and support certain presidents simply because they "enable an academic capitalist knowledge/learning regime" (254) that creates a milieu for the products and services their companies sell. From that point of view, the generous compensation that trustees now give to presidents could be seen as pay for their contributions to the corporate bottom line, rather than recognition of their academic leadership.

Higher education has always been connected to the economy. The importance of money is not new, "What *is* new, and troubling, is the raw power that money directly exerts over so many aspect of higher education" (Kirp, 2003: 3). What used to be considered a necessary evil has become a valued virtue, and universities have adopted corporate ways. Presidents proudly talk about customers and stakeholders, niche marketing and branding. For example, Atkinson declared that "the University of California means business" (Kirp, 2003: 4) and Duderstadt humorously referred to "the University of Michigan, Inc.," comparing it to a Fortune 500 company (Kirp, 2003: 125). This is not a crazy comparison. Universities have indeed become like companies. Big universities have become like big companies, and big companies are in big trouble right now.

Atkinson tried to promote the University of California in this environment. Some of the actions that the institution took during his watch in order to bring in funds elicited great criticism. For example, the agreement between Berkeley's Department of Plant and Microbial Biology and the Swiss pharmaceutical and agrochemical company Novartis was generally seen as having crossed the line. This unusual deal, which gave Berkeley twenty-five million dollars over a period of five years in exchange for certain rights over research findings, made alarm bells ring (Kirp, 2003). Asked about this agreement, Kerr tried to put a positive spin on it by saying that at a place like Berkeley, "the situation is much more likely to go well than it would at lesser places, where faculty aren't as sure as themselves," stating that he was "much more concerned about Novartis II and Novartis III" (Kirp, 2003: 22). This comment, however, showed a considerable amount of anxiety about such agreements. His prediction came to pass, in the sense that Berkeley managed to survive the Novartis deal, but not without significant scars, including bad feelings created by the Ignacio Chapela case.

Chapela, an assistant professor who had published papers critical of genetically-engineered plants and their ability to contaminate native crops, and who had openly opposed the Novartis agreement, was denied tenure by the chancellor upon the recommendation of a university committee that included professors with ties to the company, and against the recommendation of his department and college, which supported his promotion. After many protests involving distinguished academics from around the world, as well as local supporters, Chapela was eventually granted tenure. As Kerr had predicted, Berkeley's libertarian spirit prevailed in the end, but it was not easy.

If companies like Novartis outsource some work to universities, universities, in turn, outsource many of their functions to various vendors. Kirp (2003) points out that, today, outsourcing includes not only auxiliary enterprises, but also teaching, research, and service, as universities employ large numbers of lecturers and researchers and hire administrators from outside. In other countries, universities appoint their academic administrators from within, but in the United States at present, administrators have become members of a managerial class and move from institution to institution with the help of search firms, rather than being faculty members "otherwise engaged for an uncertain period of time" like Kerr (2001b: 34).

The *San Francisco Chronicle* and other such publications, although excessively sensationalistic, are correct in their conclusions that there are connections among the high tuition paid by students, the low pay of some university workers, and the high compensation of others—although the connections are more complicated than the ones they describe. What the press fails to appreciate is that this not a unique problem, affecting an individual university, but an economic system affecting all of public higher education and, in fact, the entire society, as the current national crisis reveals. There is a fundamental lack of solidarity that has made the rich richer and the poor poorer. The university is affected by, and reflects, this lack of solidarity.

Politicians pander to a public that does not want to pay higher taxes, yet demands a plethora of services, including increased crime-suppressing measures. Thus, the number of prisoners has mushroomed, while state support for higher education has shrunk. This has forced public universities to become privatized, with all that that entails in terms of differential compensation for its employees. There is a cause-and-effect relationship between lack of public support for higher education and the tuition hikes that universities are experiencing. To criticize the university for becoming more like a private business is blaming the victim. Using the metaphor of a lady with many suitors, Kerr said that the university had been embraced and led down the garden path: "It has been so attractive and so accommodating; who could resist it and why would it, in turn, want to resist?" (2001a: 92). For Kerr, the better a university was, "the greater its chances of succumbing to the federal embrace" (2001a: 28). Continuing with the courtship metaphor, he quotes the following limerick:

> There was a young lady from Kent
> Who said she knew what it meant
> When men took her to dine,
> Gave her cocktails and wine;
> She knew what it meant, but she went. (Kerr, 2001a: 52)

Kerr says that he was not sure "that universities and their presidents always knew what it meant; but one thing is certain—they went" (2001a: 52).

Private funding is corrupting the university much more than federal funding ever did. The irony is that those who contribute to that corruption with their lack of support complain that the university is not pure. If Kerr had known the poetry of the sixteenth-century Mexican nun Sor Juana Inés de la Cruz, he might have borrowed her verses accusing men of putting women in an impossible situation by criticizing them for not being chaste after working hard to seduce them. Sor Juana tells men that they should either like women the way they make them or make women the way they like them:

> So why are you men all so stunned
> at the thought you're all guilty alike?
> Either like them for what you've made them
> or make of them what you can like. (Trueblood, 1988: 13)

We could say the same thing to the university's critics. To force the university to privatize by drastically reducing public funding, and then to bemoan the high tuition for students, low salaries for workers, and high compensation for executives, which are the direct consequences of privatization, makes no sense. Blum must have known that the university is not to blame for its current predicament, but being afraid that it might lose the little money it was receiving from the state, went along with the myth that these problems are mere managerial deficiencies and spoke about reform to appease critics. I believe that this was the meaning of his letter, which proposed a bureaucratic reorganization. This, of course, could not fix the problems of academic capitalism nor re-fund and re-democratize the university, but it kept the press at bay for a while.

Patrick Callan (2008) notes that, although Americans are more satisfied with higher education than they are with other fields, praising the accessibility of community colleges and the prestige of research universities, there are "signs of a gradual erosion of the public's good will" (A56). Today, college is perceived as more necessary and less available than before, which is making the public very anxious. The number of people who believe the system needs change is growing. In order to keep the public's good will, universities must avoid giving the impression that they are wasting money, for "one could easily imagine a world where people, incensed by their perception of rising tuition and decreasing access, start to focus even more on student-aid scandals, high salaries for coaches, private jets for presidents, and other symbols of profligate spending" (Callan, 2008: A56). Callan advises academic leaders to use public opinion research "to get out in front of the growing demand for accountability" in order "to deflect public unrest." Conventional indices, such as rankings, are not enough. The public wants clear measures of institutional performance and cost-effectiveness. Callan indicates that public universities that have tried this approach have seen an improvement in public confidence and an increase in their budgets. As Martin Trow (1998) has shown, "accountability is an alternative to trust" (16). Indeed, promising reform, as Blum did, is a typical appeasement tactic. Bureaucratic reorganization is harmless. Institutions can always become more efficient, so revising procedures cannot hurt. It might even stimulate the institution to reflection. UC could certainly use some soul-searching.

In 2008, following a national search, Dynes was replaced by Mark Yudof, president of the University of Texas system and an experienced administrator with a focus on accountability. Paradoxically, his own compensation package, valued at $828,000, excluding standard retirement benefits, was almost twice as large as that of his predecessor. This was explained on the basis of talent. In fact, Blum declared that "he's expensive, but he's worth it" (Brown, 2008). To the amazement of many members of the university community, the public accepted this explanation and did not make a big fuss. However, when shortly afterwards, Yudoff appointed two women, Susan Desmond-Hellmann and Linda Katehi, as chancellors of the San Francisco and Davis campuses, respectively, at approximately half his level of compensation, there was a wave of protests reminiscent of the media storm of 2005.

These protests became particularly aggressive towards the new Davis chancellor, Linda Katehi, a distinguished scholar of Greek origin. Before she even arrived, there was an effort to unearth any ties she might have to an admissions scandal at the University of Illinois, where she had been provost. Her critics were grasping at straws, but they went on attacking her in ways reminiscent of the mobbing Denton suffered. The attacks, however, did not reach the same level of intensity or last as long, in large part, probably, because both Yudof and the faculty spoke out strongly on her behalf.

The implication of the attacks Katehi suffered was that she was not worth the money. Indeed, women and minority executives never seem to be perceived as worthy of compensation enjoyed by their peers, but not by common people. We may conclude that Yudof got away with a much bigger package without excessive criticism because, as a white male, he looked the part of the experienced administrator. Indeed, in addition to saying that Yudof was worth the money, Blum compared him to the U.S. presidential candidates, stating that they should feel fortunate that he "only wants to be president of the University of California" (Brown, 2008). This interesting comparison highlights the issue of excessive executive compensation, which many people inside as well as outside of academia have deplored. For example, former Duke President Nannerl O. Keohane (2006) has openly criticized the corporate-level salaries of academic executives, and former Harvard President Derek Bok has bluntly asked the question: "Why should any college president make twice as much as the president of the United States?" (Martin & Samels, 2004: vii). Perhaps Blum was trying to answer this question by implying that Yudof was better than the U.S. presidential candidates. Whatever the purpose of his comment may have been, it is interesting because of the comparison it makes between the leaders of the nation and those of its top institutions of higher learning. These leaders will have to be of like mind if the United States is to recover from its present crisis.

# Part IV

## Looking for the Clark Kerrs of the Future

# 14

# Opportunity for Equality

As we have seen, Kerr made a distinction between "equality of opportunity" and "opportunity for equality." Although in theory everyone can attend a first-rate research university such as the University of California, in practice, many people are forced to go to other kinds of institutions due to increasing cost and a diminishing number of available slots at the most distinguished institutions. As the population continues to grow, and the UC system does not expand, or even shrinks as a result of reduced budgets, these openings will become even scarcer. Like other public universities, what the University of California needs, in order to increase "opportunity for equality," is a commitment to re-fund it with the restoration of state funds lost over recent decades and a budget expansion, which is necessary in order to broaden access. This re-funding process should be accompanied by a commitment to re-democratize the UC system. By this, I mean not only to make it more diverse, but also to reduce the gap between rich and poor by elevating the compensation of employees at the bottom of the scale and reducing the compensation of those at the top. Until now, the University of California has invoked the market to justify the salaries of its high-level administrators, and it was true that if it wanted to recruit the most highly-paid university executives in the country, it needed to meet and exceed the compensation they were receiving elsewhere. But is it necessary or desirable to hire those kinds of executives anymore?

It is interesting to speculate about what would happen if pay for senior managers were kept proportionate to that of other employee groups, instead of being allowed to grow at a much faster pace, as was in fact suggested by the Academic Senate of the University of California a few years ago. This proposal was considered impractical, but was it? We are no longer at the height of fox culture. On the contrary, fox culture has collapsed, and the country is looking for a new hedgehog concept. How will offering enormous compensation packages help us find the Clark Kerrs of the twenty-first century?

Kerr knew that the less financial compensation he received, the more political independence he would have, so he kept his administrative salary relatively low. In addition, he made a point to maintain a faculty lifestyle. He did not buy luxury items with the extra money he received for his administrative work. He wanted to be able to say no. Thus, he never upgraded his lifestyle so that he would not have to lower it when he stepped down from his administrative position. He thought that large salaries made leaders less effective. In academia, as in society as a whole, high compensation creates perverse incentives and is not conducive to the crafting and implementation of a great vision, an inherently dangerous enterprise that might lead to the political demise of its author. If executive compensation were reduced to a level modest enough to attract only people who really cared about the university and its future and were not afraid to lose their administrative positions, we might actually find some Clark Kerrs in our midst.

At present, universities are experiencing what Kerr called "the denigration of leadership" (2001a: 136), which is particularly acute in the case of women and minorities. The collapse of fox culture is bringing down many of the women and minority members of the corporation, who receive the brunt of the discontent against it. A similar discontent with the country's increasingly diverse "power elite" has been noted by the columnist David Brooks (2010), who believes that leaders got more respect in the "days of the WASP ascendancy."

Perhaps one reason why the public has been so negative about the participation of women and minorities in fox culture is that it expected them to have the vision to see its failures and the courage to fight them. Reflecting on African-American leaders, Robert J. Norrell (2009) notes that "they cannot be foxes, or else they are accused of being Uncle Toms or resembling Richard Nixon" (439). The pattern of behavior expressed by this comment can easily be extended to other disadvantaged groups. Discussing the changes the university has experienced under academic capitalism, which coincide with an increase in the number of women and minority administrators, Kirp (2003) observes that, under significant public pressure, universities are becoming more diverse, wondering "into what kind of place" these newcomers are gaining membership (260). As we have seen, woman and minorities are not having an easy ride on the train of academic capitalism. Indeed, many, like Greenwood, Denton, and Rose, are ejected violently. Unlike most of their white male fellow passengers, these administrators were not allowed to stay on board until they could change trains at the next station. Instead, they were kicked off in the middle of the trip.

There is a troublesome paradox affecting women and minorities. On the one hand, they complain that they are being excluded from administrative positions because of their identities. On the other, some people complain that administrative positions seem to be given to women and minorities precisely because of their identities. Both sides speak with great passion. This is probably so because both sides are fundamentally right. Our current system is dysfunctional. It often promotes and demotes women and minorities for the wrong reasons. Let us consider three examples from research universities around the country.

The first case involved a chancellor search. The finalists included a white male and a minority female. The white male, who was a business-as-usual candidate, caused a mildly favorable impression, but the minority female was perceived by most on campus as the stronger candidate. The president, however, gave the job to the white male, with whom he obviously felt more comfortable. This decision dissappointed many people on campus. Aware of these feelings, the new chancellor hurried to appoint a dean of the same gender and ethnicity as the rejected chancellor candidate. The problem was that, in order to do that, he had to by-pass much better qualified candidates for the dean position. The campus was not well-served by either of these appointments. Neither the white male who became chancellor nor the minority female who became dean were the best people for their respective jobs. Situations like this occur all the time in academia. Competent women and minorities are not hired, while non-threatening ones are appointed as tokens (Turner & Myers, 2000; Valverde, 2003; Daryl G. Smith, 2009).

But things are more complicated than that. Many of the women and minorities appointed as tokens turn out to be very competent, which does not prevent them from having problems. Let us examine the second case, which involved a vice chancellor search. Here, the chancellor had an internal candidate whom he favored—an efficient, but not very creative, white male. However, there was a popular minority candidate who had very strong support among all minority groups on campus. Aware that he could not appoint the white male to the position under the circumstances, the chancellor offered the job to a minority candidate of a different ethnicity than the individual these groups had supported. The successful candidate, who turned out to be a good administrator, never had the backing of the chancellor, who evidently was not happy about having been forced to hire this person. After becoming aware of the circumstances leading to the appointment, and in view of the chancellor's continued lack of support, the new vice chancellor accepted an offer elsewhere as soon as the opportunity arose. Here, the minority candidate was competent but was not chosen for the right reasons, which made for a short and difficult tenure.

Some women and minority administrators are not privy to the politics resulting in their appointments, which can place them in awkward situations. The third case is an example of this. Tired of a lack of representation at the highest levels of the administration, members of a minority group pressured the president to appoint one of their own as chancellor. They nominated many well-qualified candidates from around the country in the hope that one of them would be picked. Determined not to appoint any of the nominated candidates, the president hired another member of the same ethnic group. But the individual he chose had a very low identification with that ethnic group. Immediately upon arrival, the new chancellor offended members of the campus community with naïve remarks that revealed a lack of appreciation for the challenges facing this and other minority groups. In the end, everyone was unhappy. Whites were unhappy because they felt that they had to cave in to the demands of the minority group. The minority group was unhappy because it did not get the kind of person it wanted. And the new chancellor was unhappy because of the general lack of support this situation had created.

All of these candidates were pawns in the game of fox culture, which is a game of avoidance. First of all, women and minorites are not usually hired unless there is some sort of pressure—whether general, a desire for greater diversity at the institution overall which affects all searches, or particular, a desire for greater diversity in specific positions which affects only a small number of searches. Second, women and minorities are often hired for the wrong reasons. When forced to hire from female and minority ranks, the establishment looks for those who least threaten the status quo, in other words, those who most ressemble the compliant white males of fox culture. Sometimes, there are surprises. People who appear to be compliant turn out not to be, in which case they may be replaced sooner than they otherwise would have been. Whether or not they are compliant, women and minorities tend to have short political lives. Even when they are liked by those who have power over them, they may simply be perceived as redundant once other women and minorities are hired for other positions. There is a women and minorities slot mentality. Women and minorities know it and get nervous when they see one of their own recruited for another position, as that might result in their dismissal. Like temporary guests in an academic house they do not own and which has limited guest capacity, women and minorities often regard the arrival of new temporary guests with apprehension. Sometimes they do not support women and minority candidates because they fear the impact of their presence on their own precarious situation (Wenniger & Conroy, 2001).

These games make it very difficult for women and minorities to achieve anything. Their access to power is too accidental. They cannot build administrative careers, because the foundation is shaky, subject to forces beyond their control and often beyond their understanding. There is a place for them in the system but this is a marginal women and minorities slot. They are not on equal footing with the white males who are hired for regular positions. Many women and minority applicants lose administrative positions to white males with lesser qualifications. The explanations given often include the fact that, even though they were very well-qualified, the institution in question was looking for an administrator with more experience. An examination of the résumés of the successful white male candidates, however, often reveals that they do not have more experience than the unsuccessful women and minority candidates. They obviously are simply perceived as having more experience because of who they are.

Women, in particular, complain about not being trusted with budgets. Valian (2000) points out that people judge women according to "gender schemas" rather than according to reality (7). In addition, "men receive a greater reward for their performance than do women, independent of all other factors" (19). In the case of assessing budgetary experience, this means that men's performance tends to be overrated, while women's is not only underrated, but in fact perceived as absent, due to the negative gender schema concerning females and numbers.

Minorities complain about preconceptions regarding their ability to raise money. Chang-Lin Tien (1998), who had to fight this particular perception, also notes that, while having a German or French accent is acceptable and perhaps even prestigious, having a Spanish or Chinese one is "considered an indication of a lack of schooling" (34). Indeed, when he became chancellor at Berkeley, he was advised by some alumns and others to get a coach in order to eliminate his Chinese accent, which he refused to do. Henry Trueba (1999), who reviews some of the indignities minorities suffer in academia, also mentions having experienced discrimination on account of his Spanish accent, which was mentioned publicly—described as a "Mexican accent" (75)—by an administrator as a reason to deny him a position.

Both women and minorities complain about being ignored at meetings. The pattern is well-known. A woman and/or a member of a minority group makes a remark, which is ignored. A few minutes later, a white male makes the same suggestion, which is then eagerly received and followed by the group, perhaps even with praise for the white male's offering such good advice (Pasque, 2010). The problem with this pattern is that the contributions of women and minorities remain invisible. This affects the job interview process directly. When women and minority candidates discuss their accomplishments, their comments do not reach the audience the way white males' observations do. People, in effect, hear different things, and what they hear is that white males have accomplished more. Women and minority administrators need to worry about being ignored, because it leads directly to being undervalued and skipped over (Valian, 2000; Valverde, 2003).

While being rejected for positions for which they are well-qualified, women and minority candidates may suddenly be contacted by a university that is looking for diversity and which appears, out of the blue, often in a hurry, to offer them a position. Clearly, the problem is that they are not being seriously considered for regular positions, only for women and minority slots. The search firms' explanations are not difficult to decode. "This institution is looking for someone with a great deal of experience" means "it is looking for a white male." "This institution would be a very good match for you" means "it is looking for diversity." Bridges, Eckel, Córdova, and White (2008) note that, even when women and minorities "find themselves in the right stepping stone positions," they frequently do not have the opportunity to move up. Instead, "people almost stumble into positions" (7). This is probably due to women and minorities not being considered for regular positions but only for women and minority slots. Instead of a level playing field, what these candidates find is a small playpen, where women and minorities are allowed to take turns. They only get an offer when there is an opening in the playpen.

The English word "career" comes from the French word "carriere," which means "road," "race-course for wagons" ("carrus" is Latin for "wagon"). While white males participate in an open race-course on a level playing field, women and minorities often find themselves running in circles inside the small playpens in which they are placed. Even when they get the same positions as men, those positions do not mean the same thing. What for white males is a stepping stone, for women and minorities is often a dead end. This is why women and minorities have less positional power than white males do. They do not really have careers in the literal sense of the word because they are not running alongside the white males on a level course. In fact, they are not on the playing field at all. In Kerr's terminology, they might appear to have "equality of opportunity," but they do not have "opportunity for equality." Rather, they stumble into positions only when there is an opening in the play pen. Besides being profoundly frustrating for the individuals involved, this system is a tremendous waste of talent. The problems caused by this dysfunctional system are clear: not enough women and minorities, not in the right places, not for the right reasons, not for the right lengths of time and not with the right treatment. As a result, many of them have a hard time for, as Daryl G. Smith (2009) points out, leaders who are tokens "may find it difficult to succeed" (70).

According to Daryl G. Smith (1995), there are four dimensions of diversity that coincide with phases of its evolution: representation of previously-excluded groups, inclusive climate, inclusive curriculum, and institutional transformation. She adds that, without sufficient diversity of representation, an institution cannot engage the other three dimensions. Yet universities continue to ignore the existence of a glass ceiling caused by "the subtle and not so subtle forms of bias that are introduced at every level" (239). Thus, while the student body may be quite diverse, the lack of significant diversity among faculty members, administrators, and trustees places institutional decision-making at risk, due to a lack of multiple perspectives. This is certainly the case with the University of California, whose faculty members continue to be largely male and overwhelmingly white. Kerr noted this as a problem in his 1980 version of *The Uses of the University* (chapter 5, 2001):

> Progress in participation of minorities and women at the faculty level again has been slow, but faster for women than for minorities. The as-yet-smaller sizes of pools of trained people is one reason, but another is that federal programs got off to a late start, after the massive new hirings of the 1960's were past. Still another reason is the difficulty governmental agencies have in challenging the autonomy of universities and their meritocratic standards—and of course prejudice on campus plays a role. (Kerr, 2001a: 131)

Since that time, the percentages of women and minority faculty members have not improved as much as they should have. Both women and minorities remain underrepresented with respect to their presence in the population. In fact, they are even underrepresented in proportion to their presence in the pool of trained people. It would take strong leadership on the part of the administration to change this trend. The problem is that the administration itself continues to be heavily white and male, particularly when it comes to the kinds of academic leadership positions that could make a difference in this area.

According to Belle Rose Ragins (1995), there are three structural indicators of unequal power relations among diverse groups in organizations. The first and most obvious is rank: women and minorities hold lower positions than white males do. The second is tracking: when women and minorities are given high-level positions, these tend to be in relatively unimportant areas. The last is positional power, which varies according to the identity of the incumbent. Thus, women and minorities have less authority than do white males who occupy the same positions. This lack of power is the result of an accumulation of "micro-inequities," including "exclusion from informal peer support, networking and mentoring; restricted information and a lack of feedback from supervisors and coworkers; inadequate or inaccurate performance appraisals by supervisors or work groups; and inequitable delegation of tasks" (94). Basically, power-holders have a limited perspective, which causes a perceptual distortion of women and minorities, whose actions are misread and whose work is underappreciated. As a result, women and minorities are undermined and sabotaged, and their careers tend to plateau prematurely. In the eyes of the decision-makers, women and minorities do not appear as competent as white males, simply because they do not look or act like white males. Consequently, very few women and minorities reach the top echelons of academic administration.

Women and minorities who are members of executive teams tend to have positions in non-academic areas, while key academic administrators such as provosts, vice chancellors for research, vice provosts, deans, and graduate deans are usually white males. Moreover, the few women and minorities who occupy such key academic positions seem to have low positional power, as suggested by their apparent shorter tenure—the revolving door syndrome. This, coupled with their chronically small numbers, is an impediment to their having a real impact on an institution. Like other research universities around the country, the University of California has never had a critical mass of women and minorities in key academic leadership positions.

Needless to say, the system also excludes many white males who do not follow the tenets of fox culture. Kerr conceded to the foxes in 2001, because he knew that if he had applied for his old job as president of the University of California at that moment, he would not have gotten it. People like him did not become presidents anymore. This must change. The university needs to articulate and implement a new hedgehog concept, and the only way to do this is by "interrupting the usual and challenging myths" (Daryl G. Smith, 2009: 176). This process must start at the top.

According to Kerr, "management is the principal determinant of the productivity of labor" (1960: 137). This is why the "most success-ful new policies in higher education have come from the top" (2001a: 136). Kerr warned about a growing division between duty and survival in university presidents:

> Presidential duty calls for matching, over the foreseeable future, expenditures with resources, while preserving access for students, quality in teaching and research, and institutional autonomy from excessive state interference; for concentration on the long run and overall welfare of the institution. Presidential survival depends, on the contrary, on not calling undue attention to longer-run difficult prospects, on making adjustments year by year, on choosing adjustments that lead to the least powerful immediate protests (as by cutting plant maintenance and the purchase of books), on encouraging early retirements on favorable terms, on postponing new appointments, and on not making adjustments that can be pushed up the line to trustees—or out to external authorities, or down to the provosts and deans, or that can be saved for the attention of successors. Survival depends heavily on not disturbing any current faculty members. (Kerr, 2001a: 181-182)

And, of course, when the annual executive compensation of academic leaders is several times the salary of a full professor, the former have very strong incentives not to engage in behavior that might upset the status quo. Kerr adds that different university presidents are devoted to duty and survival in unequal proportions, "because the latter at least survive," pointing out that the contributions of the former "will appear the greater ten or twenty years later" (2001a: 182). In troublesome times, when duty is more important than ever, the tendency is toward survival. Discussing what he calls "the politics of caution," Kerr states that "no presidential 'giants' have as yet emerged to take leadership; indeed, it is problematical how many will" (2001a: 184). Kerr believed that in the future, as the university continues to decentralize, there should be more emphasis on team leadership, which must be pluralistic and at the same time coherent: the president should be able "to build and maintain the team of his or her choice" (2001a: 191). Ideally, the president should also be able to serve for a long time in order to coordinate efforts and bring projects to fruition "so that there is less disparity between their horizons and those of their institutions" (2001a: 192).

Martin Trow (1981) stresses the importance of having strong presidents, attributing the success of the American research university partly to the amount of discretion its leaders have enjoyed. It is important to preserve that discretion. Kerr and Gade (1981) quote the president of a research university who said that if an occasional administrator abuses discretion, "it makes more sense to replace the administrator than to remove the discretion" (147). According to Shapiro (2005), "the age of globalization might be the moment in human history when rights, interests, and utilitarian calculations converge to yield a clearer moral landscape for us all" (113), and academic administrators must exert moral leadership by explaining what universities do and whose interests they serve. Indeed, the need for vision is greater than ever, for, as Richard Tarnas says, "as a civilization and as a species we have come to the moment of truth, with the future of the human spirit, and the future of the planet, hanging in the balance. If ever boldness, depth, and clarity of vision were called for, from many, it is now" (413). In other words, this is a time for hedgehogs.

This is not to say that we do not need foxes. Foxes are always valuable. Any administrative team should have a good number of them, perhaps even a majority. Universities need executive teams whose members "have complementary frame orientations" (Bensimon, 1989: 121). The problem is that we need hedgehogs in key positions and have almost none at all at a time when the university, like the country, needs direction. We need a more balanced administration, populated by a new generation of hedgehogs and foxes who reflect, understand, and appreciate the diversity of the population they serve. As Kerr (2001a) points out, leadership does matter. This is particularly true at the "multiversity," which derives its unity "not from its function but from its administration" (Touraine, 1997: 256). The University of California's hedgehog concept needs to be revised to include a new balance between merit and worth, but no revision is possible without a change at the top, for as Kerr saw very clearly, reform in academia is seldom a bottom-up process:

> Virtually all successful major reforms or revolutions in the academic world have come into being and probably will continue to come into being through leadership from the top—or from the outside—through the instrumentality of an Eliot or a Napoleon. (Kerr, 2001a: 99)

As president of Harvard University at a crucial stage in its development, Eliot was able to shape that institution into the elite university it became by acting from the top. Napoleon, as ruler of France, had the opportunity to shape the country's higher education system by applying pressure from outside. In the United States, changes involving a greater emphasis on diversity historically have come from the top (the federal government) and from outside (the civil rights movement). At present, external forces are more local than national: under pressure from the business sector, states are asking their top public universities to open their doors to an increasingly diverse population.

As the first decade of the twenty-first century draws to a close, it is becoming clear that some of the most important problems facing the world in this new era will be related to the color line or, rather, to the multiple color lines separating marginal groups from dominant ones in various countries around the globe. Most new entrants to the workforce in the United States will be women, minorities, and immigrants. Research shows that unmanaged diversity often results in problems, for, although it increases creativity, it decreases cohesion. Diversity is a practical, as well as a moral, imperative, but it needs to be taken seriously and managed carefully (Cox, Jr. & Finley, 1995; Thomas, 1995; Ely & Thomas, 2001; Page, 2007).

Interactions among people from different cultures are increasing abroad and at home, most particularly in California, which must once again address the balance between selectivity and access as its population fully engages the knowledge-based, global economy, so we must ask ourselves again what the university is for: What are the uses of the university? Kerr answered this question in the final paragraph of the 1963 version *The Uses of the University*:

> It seems appropriate to conclude with Alfred North Whitehead's prophetic words in 1916 on the place of intellect: "In the conditions of modern life, the rule is absolute: the race which does not value trained intelligence is doomed. Not all your heroism, not all your social charm, not all your wit, not all your victories on land or sea, can move back the finger of fate. Today we maintain ourselves. Tomorrow science will have moved forward yet one more step, and there will be no appeal from the judgment which will be pronounced on the uneducated."
>
> These are the uses of the University. (Kerr, 2001a: 95)

His answer is still valid. As Du Bois (1903b) warned, if we do not lift marginalized peoples up, they will pull us down. Without trained intelligence and trained leadership, we are indeed doomed, so one of the most important uses of the university today must be the preparation of diverse elites for a diverse society. This cannot be done if the academic house is not itself diverse and democratic—a house co-owned by all its residents rather than a single-owner house with a small number of temporary guests. We must urgently increase "opportunity for equality" in order to raise the "multiversity" to "the height of the times."

# 15

# Leadership Renewal

In the fall of 2006, President Robert Dynes and the then-chair of the Board of Regents, Gerald Parsky, established a Study Group on University Diversity to collect information and make recommendations for improvements in each of four areas handled by four distinct work teams: undergraduate student diversity; graduate and professional student diversity, including postdoctoral scholars; faculty diversity; and campus climate. In its Overview Report to the Regents, the Study Group, which was co-chaired by Regent Parsky and then-Provost and Executive Vice President Hume, made three core recommendations: to affirm the fundamental importance of diversity, to declare the need for change, and to emphasize the value of clear and consistent data.

After reviewing the history of the University of California, which was created as a pluralistic and inclusive institution offering opportunity to all students in the state, the report recommended the adoption as regents policy of a diversity statement, which was later approved by the academic senate and endorsed by the president. That statement declares that "the State of California has a compelling interest in making sure that people from all backgrounds perceive that access to the University is possible for talented students, staff, and faculty from all groups," adding that the knowledge that the university serves all parts of the community equitably "helps sustain the social fabric of the state." After explicitly renewing the University of California's commitment to the realization of its historic promise to identify and cultivate talent throughout the state, the statement ends by specifically acknowledging "the acute need to remove barriers to the recruitment, retention, and advancement of talented students, faculty, and staff from historically excluded populations who are currently underrepresented" (Overview Report: E-1).

With respect to the need for change, the report states that, although there are areas of success, the University of California has not kept up with the pace of demographic change in the state. The numbers of women and minorities among faculty and students, both graduate and undergraduate, have not improved since the 1980s, that is, since the David Gardner presidency. In addition, their distribution is uneven throughout the university, with very low or no representation in some areas, which affects campus climate. The Study Group notes that "change is urgently needed to bring UC to the level of diversity it needs to fulfill its mission and to create campus climates that support that diversity" (Overview Report: 6).

Finally, the report stresses the value of clear and consistent data, which is necessary to "shine a light" on the university's successes and failures in supporting diversity. In particular, the report calls for holding university leaders accountable for progress by requiring that the president make an annual report to the regents on the status of diversity at the university. The president should "(1) identify trends, including areas of progress or concern; (2) allow for meaningful comparisons among campuses and, where appropriate, among academic fields; and (3) include appropriate contextual data that illuminate University performance." In addition, "the report should address climate issues every year" (Overview Report: 7).

The rest of the Overview Report is devoted to summarizing the findings of the work teams about undergraduate, graduate, professional and postdoctoral students, faculty, and campus climate. The Overview Report explains that staff members are not covered by its recommendations, because the university's newly-created standing committee, known as the Staff Diversity Council, is dealing with those issues. Indeed, an update on that council's activities is included in the Overview Report as an attachment (D-1). The amount and quality of the work that council achieved is impressive. Its five subcommittees dealt with data collection and reporting, evaluation and assessment of initiatives; recruitment, retention, and promotion issues; talent management and succession planning issues; and work climate matters. This council is expected to meet with the president and to report to the regents annually on its progress.

What first comes to mind when reading the Regents' Overview Report and the Staff Diversity Council Update is that neither of them mentions the university's executives. The groups targeted for change are graduate and undergraduate students, faculty, and staff. No reflection is offered on the composition of the senior management teams on the various campuses and at the Office of the President. The president, chancellors, and other executives are supposed to oversee the proposed push for diversification, but they themselves are not, apparently, subject to scrutiny. Their existence as a group is not even acknowledged. Yet, from the point of view of implementation of the regents' recommendations, they are the most crucial group of people at the university. The chances for success of the push for diversification proposed by the regents will depend on the interest and energy with which the president, chancellors, vice chancellors, provosts, vice provosts, deans, and other high-level administrators assume their responsibilities in this respect and on their credibility. The president cannot very well ask the chancellors to enhance diversity on their campuses if he does not first put together a diverse group of vice presidents and chancellors. The chancellors, in turn, cannot easily ask their campuses to diversify their student bodies, faculty, and staff, if they do not first diversify their vice chancellors, provosts, vice provosts, deans, etc. As currently constituted, the leadership of the university, and of each of its campuses, lacks the moral authority necessary to ask the members of the university community to effect change.

A cursory examination of the senior management teams of the various UC campuses and the Office of the President reveals that they lack diversity. In fact, not only do they not reflect the gender and ethnic composition of the state's population or of their student bodies, but in many cases, they are not even meeting their own, modest, affirmative action goals. Contrary to what many people believe, Proposition 209 did not cancel the University of California's affirmative action obligations as a federal contractor, including a commitment "to apply every good faith effort to achieve prompt and full utilization of minorities and women in all segments of its workforce where deficiencies exist," as the university's affirmative action statement notes, explaining that "these efforts conform to all current legal and regulatory requirements, and are consistent with University standards of quality and excellence" (University of California Office of the President Affirmative Action Plan, 2008-2009: iii). In order to comply with federal regulations, written affirmative action plans are prepared by each campus and by the Office of the President every year. Deficiencies are expected to be identified and corrected. This requires extensive record-keeping systems. Thus, the annual affirmative action plans are a good source of information about the diversity of the workforce, including that of executives. Unfortunately, these plans do not necessarily all follow the same format. For example, important high-level academic administrative positions, such as deans, are not always listed as members of the senior management team. This makes it difficult to compare the various campuses and the Office of the President in terms of progress in diversifying their respective leadership teams. Whatever format these plans follow, however, they show that there is insufficient diversity among executives and that this problem is not being remedied in a timely fashion.

The UC affirmative action plans show "underutilization" of women and minorities year after year. "Underutilization" exists when the percentage of women and minorities in a job category ("representation" or "incumbency") is smaller than the percentage of their presence in the workforce ("availability"). Availability analyses are conducted separately for women and for each of several minority groups. In the case of executives, the pool of potential candidates includes people from other institutions as well as individuals from within an institution who have the qualifications to aspire to positions at that level. For example, for a chancellor position, the pool would include individuals with experience at the chancellor, provost, or equivalent levels, while for a provost position, the pool would consist of people with provost, dean, or equivalent experience. In both cases, potential candidates would come from similar institutions, that is, major research universities, as well as from the University of California itself.

The UC system's various senior management teams are not as diverse as they could be if they were not underutilizing women and minorities. In order for the campuses to meet their affirmative action goals, they would have to add women and minorities to their senior management teams, but this is not happening. The figures remain roughly the same year after year, which means that no real progress is being made. High-level administrators often blame the pipeline when the issue of under-representation of women and minorities among their ranks is raised. As we have seen, however, the university's own affirmative action plans show that these groups are underutilized, and those plans are quite conservative in their estimates, since they are based on national statistics and do not take into consideration factors, such as the desirability of the institution, that might make external candidates want to take jobs there in preference to other universities or the presence at the institution of talented women and minorities who could be mentored and encouraged to become candidates for various positions. The fact that there is confirmed underutilization of women and minorities validates the sense of invisibility that many members of these groups often express. Contrary to the popular myth that women and minorities have a wealth of opportunities for promotion, when regular positions open up, no one seems to remember that these individuals exist, are qualified, and are available (Daryl G. Smith, 2009). They only seem to be tapped when the system feels the need to fill some women and minority slots.

Similar situations have been observed at other institution of higher learning throughout the country. Women and minorities are underutilized at all levels, from presidential posts to faculty positions (American Council on Education 2007). Women are underrepresented as department chairs in relation to their numbers in the faculty, and they are underrepresented among the faculty in relation to their numbers among Ph.D.s (Mason & Goulden, 2002; Niemeier & González, 2004; White, 2005). Therefore, we cannot blame all problems on the pipeline, as Donna Shalala (Wenniger, 2007) warned, noting that there were departments at her institution, the University of Miami, which had never even interviewed a female candidate for a faculty position. The situation with minorities is not very different (Turner & Myers, 2000; Moody, 2004; Daryl G. Smith, 2009). As Daryl G. Smith (1995) has demonstrated, claims that there is a pipeline problem and that there is a bidding war for a small number of minority faculty members are greatly exaggerated. Even the most elite minority Ph.D.s do not often get multiple offers, and some do not get any offers at all. Contrary to popular myth, minority faculty members are underutilized. A highly-accomplished young Chicana summarized her feelings, and those of many members of minority groups, as follows:

> I would say that I find it a little surprising that I do not regularly get phone calls with regards to recruitment. We are so few, it's amazing that most universities will say, "We can't find anybody," yet persons like myself are not recruited. I think I should be getting phone calls, and I don't get phone calls. (Daryl G. Smith, 1995: 70)

Minority faculty members who are in traditional fields are particularly underutilized, while those with expertise in ethnic issues do better (Daryl G. Smith, 1995). When it comes to traditional fields, women and minorities apparently are not perceived as sufficiently competent. The same thing happens with administrative positions. The more important and central an administrative position is, the more likely that it will be given to a white male.

For Patricia Digh (Burnim, 2007), who believes that universities do not need small adjustments but rather systemic transformation, the composition of the administration "is the story that you are telling and what people are hearing. Change does not happen until an organization and its leaders change their story" (B51). The story the University of California is telling, and what many people are hearing, is that this is an institution that does not reflect the present, let alone the future, of the state. The University of California is not alone in that. On the contrary, it mirrors the situation at all American research universities. This state of affairs is simply more dramatic and obvious at UC because of the demographic composition of the state, which makes the lack of diversity at the top particularly startling. It is time to acknowledge that "the march of diversification in universities is becoming and will become an established historical fact" (Smelser, 2010: 123). "The question is not whether we want diversity or whether we should accommodate diversity, for diversity is clearly our present and our future." The question is: "How we can build diversity into the center of higher education?" (Daryl G. Smith, 2009: 3). The issues of diversity must be confronted "not just because they are important to a special group, but because they are vital to all institutions and the nation" (Daryl G. Smith, 1989: 73).

David Damrosch (1995) believes that pressure to change the university will originate with women and minorities. This is why I do not think that a call for diversity is a special plea for women and minorities, but simply a call for systemic transformation, as these groups are destined to be catalysts for change. I would add to these groups the many white males who are unhappy with fox culture and are eager to help articulate and implement a new hedgehog concept for the university.

During the course of the twentieth century, the University of California became an academic superpower with an annual budget bigger than those of many states. "No university or university system has such a major share of research dollars coming from the federal government, and private giving to UC exceeds that of any non-profit institution except the Salvation Army" (Pelfrey, 2004: 92). This enormous academic enterprise is led by executives whose business acumen must be high if they are to succeed at advancing the institution in the current world. Yet business acumen alone is not enough. Universities should do more than follow the market. They should lead. The only way to change the level of consciousness of the University of California is to energize its leadership. In the words of Jim Collins (2005), the University of California has to start by getting "the right people on the bus" (41-64) before it can confront "the brutal facts" (65-89) and develop a new "hedgehog concept" (95-96). This will require "level 5 leadership" (17-40), that is, leaders who combine personal humility with "ferocious resolve." What we need now is a diverse team of leaders with that level of determination and foresight. These leaders must be able to develop and implement a new hedgehog concept that embraces diversity and inclusiveness and is responsive to current societal needs.

Kerr and Gardner were the right kinds of leaders for the times in which they lived, but each era creates its own challenges. At present, we need leaders who can bring other perspectives to higher education. Identifying and developing a broad pool of talent should be a top priority at this time for the University of California. As Collins (2001, 2009) emphasizes, truly successful institutions choose their leaders from within their ranks. Indeed, this was the case with Kerr and Gardner.

Both presidents were given opportunities for leadership very early in their lives, as they explain in their memoirs. Kerr was made chancellor of the Berkeley campus without ever having served as dean or provost. He had distinguished himself as a member of the academic senate during the loyalty oath controversy and, on the basis of that promise, he was appointed chancellor. Gardner's rise was even more spectacular, because he was not even a faculty member when he started out. He was a young staff member on the Berkeley campus, the director of the newly-created alumni foundation, when he was told that, if he ever wanted to become chancellor, he should get a Ph.D. and a faculty position first, which he did. This led to his appointment as vice president for extension of the UC system and later as president of the University of Utah. Senior administrators saw leadership potential in both young men and gave them opportunities to develop it, which was the right thing to do. These were not the only administrators who benefited from informal succession planning. For example, Sproul and Wheeler also were promoted very early on promise, more than on accomplishments. Sproul and Gardner were non-academic administrators, while Wheeler and Kerr were faculty members with no significant administrative experience. All were quite young. Except for Wheeler, all were internal candidates.

Institutions of higher learning need to develop more talent this way. They should engage in succession planning by identifying talented academics—both hedgehogs and foxes—and giving them a chance to develop and lead. They must look for men and women, gay and straight, white and minority, native and foreign-born, in short, for all kinds of people, because they need them all. They also must seek out a balance of scientists and non-scientists, as it is important for leaders to bring multiple perspectives to the table. Robert M. Berdahl (Lawrence, 2006), former chancellor of the Berkeley campus, noted that during his tenure, he was the only non-scientist among his fellow chancellors in the UC system. Lack of intellectual diversity cannot be beneficial for an institution as complex as the university is today. The more complex the university becomes, the more diverse its leaders must be. Only a diverse group of hedgehogs will know how to connect the pieces into a powerful vision, a new hedgehog concept, and only a diverse group of foxes will have enough shrewdness to identify and seize important opportunities in the service of that new hedgehog concept.

Higher education in the United States still has much to contribute to the world. One area where this country is well ahead of all others is inclusiveness. With all of the problems that it faces in this area—and as we have seen, it faces many—the United States still has more experience and expertise dealing with diverse populations than any other country in the world (Daryl G. Smith, 2009). The extensive bibliography on this topic produced in the United States shows that this country has been unusually self-reflective. As other nations engage the knowledge-based, global economy and experience an increase in interactions among people from different backgrounds, they will need a model for inclusiveness, and this country can offer such a model. So this is an area where the United States has a competitive advantage. Within the United States, the University of California, with its multicultural and international orientation, is ideally situated to lead in this area, as Slosson saw so clearly one hundred years ago. It is now time to realize that vision.

# 16

# Succession Planning

According to a report issued by the American Council on Education (2007), the numbers of women and minorities in presidential positions at colleges and universities have not increased significantly since 1998, and these groups are underrepresented as presidents in relation to their numbers as senior administrators. This report, which highlights the fact that almost half of all college presidents are age sixty-one or older, a situation that offers opportunities for renewal, recommends considering more women and minorities with non-traditional backgrounds for presidencies, as well as promoting more women and minorities to chief academic officer positions—the most traditional preparation for the presidency. Women of color, in particular, are extremely underrepresented at this level (3 percent versus 6 percent for men of color, already a very low figure), reflecting what we know about their status, which is worse than that of minority males and white females (Moody, 2004; Turner & Myers, 2000). At doctorate-granting institutions, the situation is even more critical than in academia at large. In fact, some minority groups are almost or totally absent. For example, not a single Hispanic served as chief academic officer at any of the institutions responding to the survey.

In order to address these deficiencies, Jacqueline E. King and Gigi G. Gómez (2008) recommend that institutions of higher learning identify, mentor, and promote diverse pools of internal candidates through succession planning. This is a practice very popular in the business sector, where it has received much attention in the past few decades, but most particularly during the last few years. In part, this may be due to the impending retirement of the baby boomers, which will create many voids in a wide variety of organizations. Recent disasters, such as September

11 and Hurricane Katrina, have also exposed managerial weaknesses in this respect (Atwood, 2007). Today, the business sector is focusing on succession planning more than ever before, which has led to the publication of numerous books and articles on this subject.

All studies stress that succession planning is not the same as replacement hiring. Succession planning provides an organization with a surplus of talent by helping members realize their potential, which should not be confused with performance. A person performing satisfactorily at one level might not do well at the next, and vice versa (Ong, 1989). People who do well at certain tasks, such as open-ended debates or general planning exercises, are not necessarily good potential leaders, although they are often identified as such (Cohen & March, 1974). In other words, sounding good is not enough. Potential should not be determined casually.

The most important ingredient for a successful succession plan is probably the attitude of the leadership. Few people can develop their potential without organizational support, and that begins at the top. Highly successful organizations have a critical mass of passionate advocates who understand that succession planning is the key to sustainability. Some organizations do succession planning within units, while others take a more global approach, looking for potential across units, but all successful enterprises are engaged in some sort of talent management, whether they do it openly or in secret. Such concerns realize that people come before jobs and strategies, not the other way around (Ong, 1989). Action does not necessarily follow goals, for "human choice behavior is at least as much a process for discovering goals as for acting on them" (Cohen & March, 1974: 220). So it is important to have creative human beings engaged in this dual process of discovery and action.

According to Mark R. Sobol, Phil Harkins, and Terry Conley (2007), the single most important accomplishment by the legendary chairman and CEO Jack Welch at General Electric was building an integrated system of succession planning, since the ability to make wise decisions regarding people is the most crucial source of competitive advantage. Indeed, when many asked why Japanese companies were so successful, Peter F. Drucker (1980) observed that "Japanese top management may spend more time thinking about management succession than on anything else" (229). What Welch did was to follow the Japanese model of succession planning.

Successful organizations engage in a considerable amount of teaching, mentoring, and coaching to identify, develop, and utilize existing talent, including the talent of women and minorities. This should be true of universities as well, but, thus far, it has not been. There are valuable nation-wide mentoring programs, such as the American Council on Education Leadership Program and the Harvard Institute for Educational Management, but there is very little training of executives at the institutional level.

Although academia is becoming more like business in many respects—not all of them positive—it has not borrowed one of the best attributes of business culture: its tradition of hiring chief executive officers from within (Blumenstyk, 2005). The best companies groom talented employees for positions of leadership. Indeed, Jim Collins (2001) has shown that the most outstanding businesses have had an insider at the helm. Collins (2009) also notes that most of the fallen companies he has studied had outside chief executive officers, stating that "leaders who fail the process of succession set their enterprises on a path to decline" (60). Although some universities, such as Emory University and the University of Pennsylvania, are beginning to establish training programs for academic leaders (Selingo, 2009; Santovec, 2010), most have never considered such a course of action. They should do so, because there are fewer and fewer external candidates of superior quality, and they tend to stay for shorter and shorter periods of time (Mead-Fox, 2010).

According to Blumenstyk (2005), the 2005 Chronicle of Higher Education Survey of Presidents, which looks at the leaders of four-year colleges, masters and doctoral/research universities, shows that only 19 percent of respondents were internal candidates. The vast majority of presidents came from other institutions. One reason is that the public sector considers many factors other than performance in choosing and keeping executives, with politics occupying a prominent role. William J. Rothwell (2005) notes that, in the public sector, the fortunes of executives are usually tied to a particular administration. A change of administration generally results in the replacement of many or all members of the executive team. As for university presidents, their fates depend on the changing moods of their campuses, their trustees, and the public. Presidential searches are highly political. First, because of shared governance, faculty members can essentially veto candidates, and internal candidates always have some baggage. Second, external candidates bring prestige to the institution, which can increase its status by hiring administrators from more important universities. Finally, external candidates may be more able to effect change, which is a valid reason to hire them.

External hires are appropriate and desirable under certain circumstances. Indeed, for middle management positions, external hires can be particularly important. At the dean level, for example, external hires can be very helpful in two respects. First, they can bring new ideas to all of the departments in the college and, second, they can expand the pool of potential presidential candidates. The experience of serving as dean gives the external administrator an opportunity to become acculturated and prepare for higher-level service. It is easier to move as a dean than as a provost, chancellor or president, positions so far removed from the everyday affairs of an institution that their incumbents have a hard time understanding local issues if they do not have previous knowledge of them. Perhaps that is why most respondents to the Chronicle survey did not feel "very well prepared" for their first presidency. Indeed, the survey found that "insider presidents" served longer, which allowed them to have more of an impact on their institutions (Blumenstyk, 2005).

Some people are beginning to question the conventional wisdom about the importance of national searches (Barden, 2010). James J. Duderstadt (2007) thinks that governing boards should demand that their institutions engage in succession planning, and Rita Bornstein (2005) and Tim Mann (2010) believe that more of an effort should be made to prepare potential candidates for presidencies through talent development programs and that new presidents should be mentored, as well. One institution that has been doing this is the University of Notre Dame, where administrators are carefully groomed for the presidency (Malloy, 2006). For example, five years before Father Theodore Hesburgh stepped down from the presidency, a number of younger colleagues were invited to take major leadership positions with the understanding that one of them would eventually be selected as his successor. In the end, the candidates had to go through a full interview process and be fully vetted before a decision was made. Without that period of training, however, it would have been difficult to find an appropriate replacement. As a Catholic institution with religious leadership, Notre Dame draws its leaders from a very limited pool.

The Notre Dame case is interesting, not only for that university's success in recruiting good presidents but also for its development of high-level administrators. Those candidates who were groomed for the presidency but not appointed to it became very effective vice-presidents, which might not have happened if they had not been selected from the faculty for presidential grooming to begin with. The example of Notre Dame is intriguing, because it shows that when an institution of higher learning goes looking for talent in the raw, it finds it, which means that much talent is wasted because it is never sought out.

Most research universities do not engage in the kind of search Notre Dame conducts, which is similar to what frequently happens in the business world. But research universities need to plan for the future as much as, or more than, corporations, for without planning, what we get is a decision-making process based on informal judgments. These are problematic, because they result in such negative outcomes as:

> recency bias (performance or potential is assessed with a heavier-than-desirable emphasis on recent and singular successes or failures); pigeonholing or stereotyping (supervisors develop impressions of individuals that are difficult to change); the halo or horn effect (supervisors are overly influenced in their judgments of individuals by singular events); the Pygmalion effect (supervisors see what they expect to see); and discrimination (treating people differently solely as a function of sex, race, age, or other factors unrelated to job performance). (Rothwell, 2005: 72)

These informal judgments result in "homosocial reproduction" (Rothwell, 2005: 19), as they tend to lead to the selection of administrators who are clones of the powerholders.

Some of the best American research universities have had mostly "insider presidents," which may account, to some extent, for their success. According to Duderstadt (2007), elite research universities, including the Ivy League, Stanford, and the University of California, have had more insider presidents than other institutions of higher learning, in part, because they have a stronger "sense of institutional self-confidence" (91). So having "insider presidents" is both a cause and an effect of high academic quality. Almost all of these "insider presidents," however, have been white males. Whatever grooming of potential candidates may have taken place has not been formal and has obviously not been extended to women and minorities, who continue to be at the margins of power. This is not because these elite universities do not hire administrators internally. On the contrary, not only have many of their presidents come from within, but numerous high-level administrators have also. One would think that this ability to identify and promote leaders from within would offer a great opportunity for elite universities to develop their own women and minority administrators. Yet the women and minorities in their midst remain largely invisible, their administrative talent untapped, their leadership potential unrealized. Why?

Women and minorities have trouble being perceived as leadership material, even when they have the most traditional administrative credentials and, most particularly, when they do not (Valian, 2000; Valverde,

2003). The traditional career path is to become a department chair and then dean, provost and president. But the percentage of women and minority deans is quite small. This is because women and minorities have trouble becoming department chairs, a selection controlled by the academic guild, which continues to be largely white and male (Niemeier & González, 2004). This means that decision-makers must insure both that women and minorities have access to traditional academic leadership positions and that those who have shown leadership ability in less traditional positions are considered for higher-level administrative posts. The president has an important role to play in this respect. Erroll B. Davis (2008) believes that trustees must choose presidents "who understand how to instill leadership throughout the institution" (A64). These presidents must create systems that identify and develop leadership much earlier and much better than is presently the case. They must constantly be on the look-out for potential leaders of all backgrounds.

"The president must walk the walk and make sure that the cabinet and senior leadership are diverse. What one does speaks a lot louder than what one says" (Burnim, 2007: B49). It is not enough for presidents to have open searches. Presidents have an obligation to take personal action to expand the number of people who are in a position to aspire to the top spots. This can be done by identifying, mentoring, and promoting talented women and minorities, as well as white males, in other words, by engaging in succession planning so that some day these people can aspire to the presidency. "The public-sector executive must begin to consider the end right at the beginning" (Rothwell, 2005: 344).

"While presidents, ultimately, come and go, *how* they come and go has a profound effect on the institution and largely determines the difference between extended periods of failure and success" (Martin, Samels, & Associates, 2004: 20). Perhaps because academic culture is built on the tenure system, leaders in academia seem to have a hard time facing and accepting their impending loss of power, a step necessary to plan for their own succession. As a result, transitions are not as smooth as they could be. In many cases, there is a mix of "unplanned continuity" and "discontinuity:" "Discontinuity with the achievements of a leader's immediate predecessor and continuity (or regression to) the more mediocre state of affairs preceding that predecessor" (Hargreaves & Fink, 2006: 70-71). In other words, innovative leaders are pulled out before their innovations take root, and their less creative successors abandon their projects and return to the status quo. In order to break this pattern, leaders should remain for longer periods of time.

In addition, it is important to spread power about. Sustainable leadership is "emergent distributed leadership" (Hargreaves & Fink, 2006: 122) or broad bottom-up participation. Sustainability, thus, demands diversity. Paradoxically, the women, minorities and other non-traditional leaders who can most contribute to institutional diversity have shown the least degree of personal sustainability. The system has a tendency to reject them and return to traditional leaders, who prolong the status quo with their longer political lives. It behooves us to break this vicious circle and to appoint and retain non-traditional leaders until they have had a chance to make their mark. As Cohen and March (1974) note, power is prone to tautology: a person who gets things done has power and a person who has power gets things done. Women and minorities, who are perceived as having less power than white males—and in politics, perception is reality—may simply not be able to get as many things done, unless a special effort is made to empower them through a succession planning exercise that allows them to move from the political outskirts of an institution towards its center of gravity.

One problem is that, unlike business, where there is a simple and clear bottom line, namely profit, higher education focuses on excellence, a concept that is open to interpretation. Bill Readings (1996) thinks that excellence is the currency of the transnational university, which he describes as a bureaucratic corporation, as opposed to the nation-state university, which was centered on the concept of culture. Whereas culture is concrete and specific (a body of knowledge that citizens must share in order to operate in the nation-state) excellence is abstract and vague (the best of everything whatever that happens to be). Unfortunately, women and minorities are not considered excellent by nature. No matter how distinguished, they are seldom perceived as "the best." They generally are not seen as bringing the same kind of prestige to an institution as white males bring. As Judith Glazer-Raymo (1999) states, at the top of the administrative hierarchy "promotions are more likely to be based on trust than on performance" (154). And women and minorities are simply not trusted the way white males are.

Academia is not an easy place to assess administrative performance. Academic administrators can take any number of paths. There are many options, and it is hard to establish a cause-and-effect relationship between academic policy and prestige enhancement (Cohen & March, 1974). There is a considerable time-lag, and oftentimes the results of a given academic policy are not felt until years later when it is not entirely clear that the change that has taken place is attributable to the policy. People

are obsessed about assessment precisely because it is notoriously difficult to assess progress in academia. In the absence of a clear bottom
line, administrators' success is often a matter of perception, and women
and minorities are not perceived as high achievers. The state of the
economy also affects the perception of success to a great degree. During good times, academic administrators tend to be seen as doing well,
but during bad times, they are often considered failures. Universities
are subject to social forces in a way that companies are not. There are
faculty, students, parents, trustees, donors, politicians, and journalists
to please. Academic administrators are often hired to appease one or
more of these constituencies rather than to improve the elusive bottom
line. Indeed, some people would say that the university, understood as
the faculty, takes care of itself, and the administration takes care of the
public. In the words of A. Bartlett Giamatti (1990), faculty members are
the "permanent officers" of the university (43), while administrators are
only temporary ones. Administrators come and go, but faculty members
stay. While the administration is subject to external pressures, the faculty
is quite self-sufficient and keeps the institution going at all times.

Rothwell (2005) makes a distinction between technical and managerial staff and advocates succession planning for both groups, as well as
dual-career ladders allowing people to move back and forth between
technical and managerial jobs. In a business setting, technical staff
would include such employees as engineers, lawyers, and scientists,
that is, workers with expertise in certain areas. In an academic environment, the technical staff is the faculty, which has academic expertise.
But, as Amanda H. Goodall (2009) points out, all faculty members also
are, to some degree, managers, in the sense that they are responsible
for budgets and personnel, including students, staff, and other faculty
members. As directors of academic programs, principal investigators
on grants, and committee members or chairs, professors are engaged in
numerous managerial activities. Indeed, one could make a distinction
between two kinds of academic administrators: deans and above, who
are professional administrators, and department chairs and below, who
could be characterized as casual administrators. This is the difference
between the corporation and the guild, in Kerr's terminology. The casual
managers and permanent officers of the guild keep the university running.
The professional managers and temporary officers of the corporation act
as intermediaries between the university and the public.

In addition to casual and professional administrators, universities
have a core of "nonpositional leaders" (Astin & Leland, 1991: 6), that is,

people who exert "leadership from the margin" (Contreras, 1998: 150). These kinds of leaders do not have power, but they do have influence. Typically, nonpositional leaders have a base of supporters and a limited set of issues to address. Women and minority leaders often are nonpositional, due largely to their being excluded from positions of power. Nonpositional leaders, who usually are strong advocates for the causes they defend, are sometimes perceived as troublemakers, which precludes them from being considered for administrative jobs. The opposite should be the case. A good succession planning strategy will seek to identify nonpositional leaders with a view to their possible transformation into positional leaders. This is particularly important, as many nonpositional leaders might be hedgehogs whose views have been in conflict with the tenets of fox culture. Looking for administrative talent in this group would be a worthwhile endeavor.

Developing leadership is a communal task, and it requires a significant collective effort to nurture a good administrator, whether casual or professional. Some casual administrators become professional administrators when they transition from department chair (the highest post within the guild) to college dean (the lowest post in the corporation). There is a sharp difference between these two positions. Chairs represent the faculty to the administration, while deans represent the administration to the faculty. That is the fault line between the guild and the corporation. Many tensions that develop at that level can be interpreted as clashes between the two cultures. Yet deans are usually chosen from among department chairs and other faculty leaders—a process faculty members jokingly call going over to the dark side. There is an implicit understanding that becoming a dean is crossing a border into a different, and less benign, territory. Indeed, that is where the career ladder changes. Once a faculty member becomes a dean, other professional administrative positions, such as provost and president, open up. So the selection of deans is very important. And since deans tend to be chosen from among those faculty members who have served as department chairs, the selection of these casual administrators should not be casual at all.

Any succession planning effort worth its salt should pay a great deal of attention to the selection of department chairs. Yet, although these crucial academic leadership positions provide the best experience for higher administration, incumbents are not usually chosen according to administrative talent, but rather on the basis of seniority (Hearn, 2006). The position of department chair tends to rotate among those senior members of a department who least challenge the status quo. In this context, search committees "operate with a de facto blackball system" (Hearn, 2006: 169). They eliminate unwanted candidates, leaving only those whom their colleagues find the least offensive. These are not necessarily the best leaders. In addition, since they know that their jobs are temporary, they often are not inclined to effect changes that might upset their colleagues, who can make their lives unpleasant after the end of their tenure as department chairs.

For Hearn (2006), teaching involves leadership, and leadership involves teaching, so there should be a way to prepare faculty members to become academic administrators. Many candidates for high-level administrative positions are functionally qualified, but lack leadership abilities. Perhaps this is because so little effort is spent developing the pool. Academics often become administrators for the wrong reasons, so the administrative track includes a fair number of people who are not very inspiring, while many interesting individuals are excluded from it.

Rather than seeing department chair positions as rotating jobs that any senior faculty member who can get along with his or her colleagues can fill, we should regard them as a prime source of academic leaders and make an effort to groom faculty members for these positions. Identification and mentoring of creative and energetic faculty with leadership qualities, including women and minorities, should be conducted on a regular basis. Although not all faculty members schooled for these positions would get them, the university would always benefit from having a pool of faculty members well-trained in management, particularly since all faculty members are casual administrators of one kind or another. Young faculty members today often express a desire for managerial training, as they find themselves having to deal with budget and personnel issues in labs and other settings. Perhaps all new faculty members should receive some such training, which would also serve the purpose of identifying early on those who could eventually become professional administrators. In this way, everyone would receive some benefit, and fewer people would feel excluded from the decision-making process. This would be particularly important for women and minority faculty members, who tend to be less satisfied with the profession than are white males (Finkelstein, Seal, & Schuster, 1998).

If picking true leaders to serve as department chairs is important, the selection of strong deans is crucial. At American universities, deans have a great deal more power than at institutions of higher learning in other parts of the world (Rhodes, 2001). Indeed, in the United States, deans control budgets, and the budget is the policy. Deans also have a great deal to say about the selection of department chairs and faculty members. In addition, they provide general direction for their colleges, which they represent to external constituencies. Working with department chairs, deans run the university on a daily basis. A good dean can inspire a college, while a bad dean can demoralize one. It is, thus, particularly important that deans be visionary. While positions such as department chair, director of an institute or associate dean are the best preparation to become dean, nonpositional leaders, that is, people who have shown leadership qualities without holding administrative posts, should be considered for the job as well, provided that they have the personal skills necessary to operate in an executive capacity.

Deans are natural candidates for provost and president positions and should be mentored so that they are able to aspire to these positions in due time. Deans have three career options: up, out, or back. Deans can be promoted to higher-level positions, can move laterally to similar positions, or can return to the faculty, that is, leave the corporation to go back to the guild. Due to "recency bias," there is a tendency to hire provosts and presidents from the group of current deans. This excludes a great deal of talent, as there are many former deans who are highly qualified but are excluded simply because they have left the corporation and have returned to the guild. Since such moves are seldom voluntary, it is assumed that there must be something wrong with them, without taking into consideration the highly-political nature of academic administration, where leaders are let go for all kinds of non-competence-related reasons. Since not everyone is able and/or willing to relocate in order to continue in administration, many deans decide to go back to the faculty rather than to move. Some are eager to renew themselves intellectually, finding inspiration in teaching and scholarship. Excluding this important group from the pool of potential provosts and presidents is short-sighted.

Succession planning must involve seeking out former deans and persuading them to consider undertaking other administrative positions. The same should be done with former provosts, chancellors, and presidents. The best talent may be found among those who are not currently involved in administration but have the insight afforded not only by their previous experience but also by the time they have had to reflect on it. In parliamentary systems, politicians alternate periods of service with periods of rest. One of the most famous examples of this is Sir Winston Churchill, who, after his so-called "wilderness years," returned to government to do the best job of his life as leader of the United Kingdom during World War II. It was precisely the time that he had to read, write, and think in the intervening years that made it possible for him to refine his vision and become one of the most inspiring politicians in modern history. Academics who follow the pattern of Plato's ideal leader, the "philosopher king," who combines action and reflection, should be considered prime candidates for higher-level positions. However, many former presidents, provosts, and deans of great knowledge and wisdom are not being tapped for administrative positions, while less competent, original, and courageous current administrators are getting jobs simply because they are still inside the administrative machine. This amazing shortcoming of the current system, which discards those who, for whatever reasons, leave the corporation to return to the guild, needs to be addressed. The connection between the guild and the corporation must be a two-way street. As Rothwell (2005) suggests, people should have dual-career ladders and be able to move back and forth between technical and managerial jobs, that is, between the guild and the corporation. A productive succession planning process must enhance the circulation of talent.

In addition to being an important source of talent to draw upon when looking for academic leaders, former administrators are a natural pool of mentors for current administrators, as well as for the younger generations (Bridges, Eckel, Córdova, & White, 2008). In fact, former administrators, particularly former presidents, should be tapped for a variety of positions, including membership on boards of regents, as Duderstadt and Womack (2003) have suggested. One of the most important contributions former administrators can make is to provide a sense of history. Oftentimes, administrators face the challenges they meet without any knowledge of how similar situations were handled in the past at their universities and at other institutions of higher learning around the country. As a result, they waste a great deal of time and make mistakes that could have been avoided with a minimum of information and advice. Even problems labeled as "surprises" are not really that surprising, as they are types of events that recur over time and, therefore, it is possible to prepare for them (Smelser, 2010). Former administrators can provide an historical perspective so that current administrators do not find themselves having to reinvent the wheel and so that the younger generations begin to acquire an understanding of how things work. Virtually all campuses have numerous former administrators on their faculties or as emeriti/ae. Yet academics do not usually seek the advice or help of former presidents, chancellors, provosts, or deans, which is a great waste of knowledge and wisdom. Such members of the campus community should be engaged in advising current administrators as well as in training future leaders.

Women and minority mentors should particularly be tapped, for, as Nannerl O. Keohane (2007) notes, young people from these groups are in great need of "precursors and companions" (78).

At the same time, we must keep in mind that one of the main purposes of mentoring is to confer what Ragins (1995) has termed "reflected power" (109), so mentors should be influential. For example, people who have white male mentors often do better than those who are mentored by women and minorities, precisely because the former have more power than the latter. Current administrators, who generally have more power than former administrators, should put their influence to good use and become involved in mentoring, as well. Ideally, academics should have a variety of mentors who can provide the advice, encouragement and power they need to make it to the next level, so that more of them are in a position to become presidents some day.

Bringing diversity to the college presidency has never been addressed with sustained energy (Bridges, Eckel, Córdova, & White, 2008). There is a tendency to have token candidates and to view diversity as a one-time commitment: once some women and minority administrators have been hired, no more are sought. Yet the challenges facing society are too complex to be addressed by a limited group of leaders. We need all the talent we can get and cannot afford to miss underappreciated ability. So we must address the problems affecting women and minority administrators head on. We know that they are underestimated and over-scrutinized and enjoy shorter tenures than white males do (Wenniger & Conroy, 2001). This can be very discouraging to them, as Leonard A. Valderde (2003) notes:

> The feeling of being treated unfairly emerges while in service, but it is accentuated after leaving. The feeling of unjust treatment is highlighted when one views the treatment of the successor, especially if the successor is a white male. It is easy to observe the dual standards being applied (forgiveness to the incumbent, lesser expectations, overlooked omissions, etc.). (Valverde, 2003: 152)

We also know that women and minorities are not given enough feedback about their performance and do not have enough sponsors who can vouch for them (Ragins, 1995). We must develop systems to deal with all of these problems and do a better job at retaining women and minority leaders.

A particularly difficult issue to address is the fact that women and minority leaders oftentimes do not conform to expectations, because they do not act and look like white males. A great deal of education will be necessary to make people understand that inclusion "is not so much about treating everyone the same as it is about preventing their differences from being an unfair hindrance" (Bridges, Eckel, Córdova, & White, 2008: 5). Accordingly, institutions of higher education need to become more sophisticated so that they can recognize good leaders when they see them, including not only women and minorities but also white males who do not conform to the tenets of fox culture. This will require courage, imagination, and training. It is easy to find leaders in the usual places. To find leaders in places where they are likely to be overlooked by the casual observer can only be done through a deliberate, thoughtful, and sustained process of succession planning.

# Conclusion:
# The Roads Ahead

In order to overcome the excesses of fox culture and revitalize themselves and the rest of society, universities need to develop a new vision, which they can do only by recruiting hedgehogs to lead them. This is a moment for hedgehogs. That does not mean that universities do not need foxes, only that they do not need as many foxes as they presently have and, most particularly, that they must break away from fox culture. They need more hedgehogs, and they need foxes who put their shrewdness at the service of a new hedgehog concept articulated by those hedgehogs. Given the current diversity of the state and the country, the hedgehogs and foxes of the future should include a considerable number of women and minorities. Thus, universities should engage in succession planning in order to identify, mentor, and promote a new generation of diverse leaders who can craft and implement a new vision. This book calls for updating the University of California's hedgehog concept, taking into account the changes that Kerr overlooked. This will require a process of leadership renewal.

However, it is important to realize that, to a large degree, the fortunes of a public university like UC are in the hands of external constituencies—the federal and state governments, foundations, corporations, individual donors and members of the public. Although leadership matters, the margin for leadership is very restricted. In addition to the right kind of academic leaders, therefore, we need the right kind of political and economic circumstances in the state, the country, and the world. All the stars must be aligned in order for a new vision to emerge, be carried out and succeed. For this reason, the book concludes with a brief review of the current circumstances of public higher education in California and the rest of the country, including recommendations for national, state, and university leaders.

As I was writing this book, I saw the economy of the country and the state become progressively worse and eventually collapse, bringing down with it the University of California, which lost a huge part of its public funding in a very short period of time. This sudden and acute crisis resulted in deep reductions in programs, fewer students, higher fees, layoffs for many employees, and furloughs for the others. This is the largest crisis the university has faced since its inception, and it is the final act in the collapse of fox culture. What is at stake now is much more than money, it is the vision—the hedgehog concept of systemic excellence, the idea that all qualified Californians can aspire to enter a first-rate research university. There are talks of dismantling the UC system. Although perhaps this will not happen officially, it is already taking place de facto due to the lack of funding. We are no longer honoring the California Master Plan for Higher Education's promise to educate the top 12.5 percent of high schools students in the state. California State University is also having problems meeting its commitment to take the top 33.3 percent, and the community colleges no longer are able to accommodate all students who wish to attend. And this is happening when the state must start to prepare for considerable increased demand for public higher education. According to the California Postsecondary Education Commission (Carla Rivera, 2010), the state must serve 16 percent more students in 2019 than in 2008. So the state is losing talent when it most needs it. These losses must be stopped and reversed.

There is a push to bring in more out-of-state students, who pay much higher fees than in-state students. Although bringing out-of-state students is desirable, it should not be done at the expense of displacing California students, as Atkinson (2009) warns. Out-of-state students, including international students, should be welcomed because they enlarge the talent pool and make for a more stimulating academic environment (Douglas & Edelstein, 2009), not because they expand revenues with their non-resident tuition payments. In order to increase the number of international students and participate in the global competition for talent, while simultaneously looking after the education of resident students, whose numbers should also increase, I believe that the Master Plan should be revised upward. In the knowledge age, more than 12.5 percent of the state's high school class should be able to attend a top public research university of international renown like UC, which should also enroll significant numbers of non-resident students. An increase from 12.5 percent to 15 percent, suggested by various groups in the last few years, seems in order. We must preserve and enhance access and quality at the same time. We cannot give up either. This is easier said than done, but it must be accomplished, if California is to have any hope of recovery.

The problems of California are not unique. On the contrary, they are emblematic of what is happening in the United States as a whole. The economic crisis that afflicts the country is forcing American public universities to change. After losing public support steadily over the last few decades, they now have reached a crossroads. The two paths before them are: (1) to preserve quality at the expense of access (privatization) or (2) to preserve access at the expense of quality (massification). Privatization leads to social poverty. Massification leads to intellectual poverty. Neither road can lead the country to recovery.

There is despair in the air, but I believe that there is something that we can do. We can choose another road: a thorny and uphill road, the most difficult road, but the only one that can take us to a better future. We can actually re-fund and re-democratize high education, if our leadership adheres to the following recommendations.

## At the National Level

Realize that, as Irwin Feller (2009) says, actions—or the lack thereof—have consequences. Newfield (2008) notes that "there has never been a middle class in history that was not created by public infrastructure" (272). According to Goldin and Katz (2008), at present, the United States, which enjoyed great economic equality and a large middle class during the first three quarters of the twentieth century, is the "country with the most unequal income and wage distribution of any high-income nation" (45). This can be tied directly to the fact that it has fallen behind other industrialized countries in terms of educating its citizens. Tuition at public universities is now more than 10 percent of median family income, as opposed to 4 percent during the post-World War II period through the 1970s, when universities began to lose public funding and tuition started to rise. Research shows that states with high tuition at their public universities have lower overall college-going rates than states where public universities have more affordable tuition. The middle class is collapsing, because the country has allowed its public infrastructure to decline, including its public research universities, which are rapidly becoming privatized and out of reach for large segments of the population. There will be no recovery for the middle class until that infrastructure is rebuilt. It is possible to have high-quality private universities, but high quality private universities cannot create economic opportunity. If public research universities lose their role as an engine of middle class creation and become enclaves for the elite, the country will lose all hope of ever rebuilding its former prosperity.

The nation's leaders must do whatever is required to revitalize public higher education. A national master plan for higher education needs to be drawn up in order to win what Goldin and Katz (2008) have called the race between education and technology and to rebuild and expand the middle class. This is too important to be left to the whims of the voters of individual states. Federal funds and federal oversight will be needed to overcome this crisis.

Robert J. Birgeneau and Frank D. Yeary (2009) have recently proposed the creation of a hybrid model of public research universities to be funded jointly by the states and the federal government through an initiative similar to the Morrill Act. A parallel proposal has been advanced by Paul N. Courant and James J. Duderstadt (2010), who favor the idea of creating federal block grants for institutions of higher learning, in addition to the federal grants that are currently given to individual students and to faculty members. These proposals should be taken very seriously. As state after state withdraws support from its public universities, the federal government must decide whether to let them wither (and with them the country) or to take action. Perhaps the moment has come to realize George Washington's dream and to create a network of national universities to give the country the push it needs to catch up and move ahead. We need immediate and sustained action. As Robert Zemsky (2009) has suggested, we do not need another national commission, but "a multiyear process" (A24). Higher education cannot be treated in an ad hoc manner. Nor can addressing its problems be postponed. The gravity of the situation cannot be overstated. We need bold action, and we need it now.

## At the State Level

Recognize that getting out of the present impasse will require courage. Higher education cannot be funded with dwindling discretionary funds. It has to be a top priority. California, in particular, has become ungovernable due to its ill-conceived initiative system, which has created a state constitutional requirement for a two-thirds supermajority vote of the legislature to raise taxes. As a practical matter, this means that revenue can never be raised in the state, no matter how badly it is needed. In addition, the majority of the state budget is committed to a series of fixed uses and is unavailable for discretionary spending, such as higher education. Other initiatives, like "three-strikes" sentencing, have caused California's prison population to expand dramatically, at a huge cost to the state. California must stop spending money on projects that get quick votes, such as building new prisons, and start investing in things that result in lasting advantages, like re-building higher education. The state must protect and enhance the California Master Plan for Higher Education, which is one of its greatest achievements. To do otherwise is simply suicidal. In particular, the state needs to support the University of California, which until now has been considered the best public university in the world. California is known and admired around the globe because of this outstanding institution, which has been a model for others. To let it go now would be a mindless waste of resources and the surest path to irreversible decline.

## At the University Level

Wake up and act. Although it is true that the university has been a victim of circumstances and that many have tended to blame the victim here, the university is not totally powerless. It always has had a double function. On the one hand, it reflects society; on the other, it changes it. With an increasing gap between rich and poor, American research universities recently have reflected what was happening in society without making much of an effort to change it. The time has come for them to take leadership and assert themselves as a true "uplifting principle." As Gray (2009b) suggests, universities, which are "over-burdened by an excess of ambitions," need to "return to basics" (16). Universities should be "what other institutions are not primarily commissioned to be," that is, "the homes of intellectual development and cultivation" (Gray, 2009c: 22). This transformation needs to start at the top. Page Smith (1990), who thought that money was killing the spirit of the university, stressed that Dante reserved the hottest place in hell "for those who, in a time of moral crisis, maintain their own neutrality" (160).

Enough is enough. What started as a legitimate competition for executive talent has turned into a game of musical chairs, in which executives move from institution to institution in pursuit of ever-increasing compensation, a system that is fostered by the search firms, which make a great deal of money with this game. In 2006, approximately half of all university and college presidents hired in the Unites States reported being recruited with the assistance of a search firm, while in 1985, the figure was one in six (Weisbrod, Ballou, & Asch, 2008). Rather than looking for actual accomplishments, search committees seem to be seeking prestige, as defined by market desirability. It is a vicious circle: the more money an executive makes, the more desirable he or she becomes, without any apparent consideration of actual performance. In fact, some executives now are moving so often that they simply do not have time to accomplish anything anywhere. But even if they stayed in one place long enough to effect meaningful change, they would not feel at liberty to do so, because that might upset the individuals to whom they report and endanger their positions and their enormous salaries. Afraid of having to go back to the faculty and losing their perks and, even more so, of not being able to land an even better-paid job at another institution, presidents have great incentives to avoid any decisions that might derail their administrative careers. The moment they get a position, they begin to plan on how to obtain the next one. There seems to be an increasing consensus that the presidential position is becoming "a stopping point on a one-way track (university administration) with no exit to a faculty track" (Weisbrod, Ballou, & Asch, 2008: 272). This system is not conducive to the articulation of large visions.

As Duderstadt (2000) notes, "while some itinerant presidents can occasionally accomplish a good deal in the short time they remain at a particular institution, more frequently they simply take the easy course, appeasing trustees, faculty, and alumni, and avoiding anything that might rock the boat" (254). Executives who are making several times the salaries they could command as full professors and who want to keep that level of compensation, whether at their present institutions or at other universities where they might move in the near future, simply do not have the freedom to rock the boat, as Kerr knew very well, which is why he refused to let his salary rise excessively. This problem is so serious that Robert Birnbaum (1992) has suggested that presidents be allowed to keep their salaries when they step down. This would be particularly doable if executive compensation were more modest, which could be accomplished by connecting it to faculty compensation at some sort of reasonable ratio, as Constantine Curris (2009) has suggested. We need to start closing "the gap between leaders and followers" (Nelson, 2009: 188)

Hiring executives from within would help reduce costs and increase creativity. At present, General Motors is trying to go back to basics by hiring homegrown talent—this is how businesses became great in the first place (Vlasic, 2009). Universities, which suffer from the same ailments that plague big businesses, would be well-advised to take similar measures. What we do by offering huge salaries and perks is to create a system of perverse incentives that insures that we will not get independent leaders and, in the few cases in which we do, those huge salaries and perks will destroy their credibility and render them powerless.

However difficult it might appear to be, we must go back to basics in the area of executive compensation. And the reason we need to do this is not because the public is angry with us, but rather because this is the best way, perhaps the only way, to get visionary leaders who can break away from fox culture and articulate a new hedgehog concept for the university. As we have seen before, foxes, in fact, do their best work when there is a hedgehog concept to follow. The best example of this is Gardner, who succeeded brilliantly, largely because he put his considerable shrewdness at the service of the great vision articulated by Kerr. Another fox who did a superb job in the service of a hedgehog concept enunciated by a previous president was Sproul, who carried out Wheeler's agenda with great success. But foxes cannot articulate a new hedgehog concept. Only hedgehogs can do that. The University of California has had hedgehogs at all of the key moments in its development: the three founding presidents (Durant, Gilman, and LeConte), the builder of the Berkeley campus (Wheeler) and the builder of the UC system (Kerr). I believe that the university is at a point in which a new vision is again needed to move the university to a new level. As Kerr stated, "there is no single presidential 'type'" (1986: xviii) because "there is no such thing as an all-purpose talent" (1984: 17-18). Yet the university continues to tap foxes for practically all key leadership positions. Kerr could not be selected as president of the University of California today. We must create a situation in which people like Kerr can reach the top again.

Wheeler (1926), who was a hedgehog, warned of the dangers of developing "a separate administrative caste" (133). Wheeler also was very much in favor of public higher education, which he considered essential for the well-being of the country. For him, American society "would never settle down into stratification by caste" (226) as long as there was public education. Furthermore, a state university not only serves the state but "represents the state" (147). This is why it is important for its top-level administrators to act as servants of the state, rather than as corporate executives.

Academic leaders, and here I include the faculty, who are the "permanent officers" of the university, together with administrators, regents, and all those who care about the American public research university, must step up to the plate of change. We cannot ask national and state leaders to re-fund the university if we are not willing to re-democratize it and create a new vision of fairness. This is the third road, the road of innovation, the road that requires that we do different things, like establishing a reasonable connection between executive and faculty compensation and making the path between the corporation and the guild a two-way street in order to promote the circulation of talent.

I suspect that Kerr conceded to the foxes because he believed that the country's decline was inevitable. If he had thought that the country had any hope of recovery, he would not have given up on the hedgehogs. In the prologue to the 2001 edition of *The Uses of the University*, he made this very clear when he confessed that what he saw ahead was a road "filled with potholes, surrounded by bandits, and leading to no clear ultimate destination" (2001a: vii). I would like to believe that there are other roads and that one of them leads to a better-educated, more prosperous, and more inclusive society. Writing this book was an attempt to find that road.

# Epilogue

*My long two-pointed ladder's sticking through a tree*
*Toward heaven still,*
*And there's a barrel that I didn't fill*
*Beside it, and there may be two or three*
*Apples I didn't pick upon some bough.*
*But I am done with apple picking now.*
>—Robert Frost, "After Apple-Picking,"
>*The Poetry of Robert Frost*, 68.

This personal reflection on American higher education does not fall far from Kerr's thinking. In part, this is because even when he did not see things clearly he intuited them, so his work provides the clues necessary to explore the things that he missed. But the main reason my study is so focused on his work is because of the natural affinity with his thinking that drew me to him in the first place. The apple does not fall far from the tree.

Kerr might have liked this agricultural metaphor, for, having been raised on a farm, he loved trees, most particularly apple trees. As E. Alden Dunham (University of California, Berkley, 2004*)* wrote, as a teenager, Kerr "could identify 50 varieties of apple trees in the dead of winter!" (8). His love for this fruit was so famous that Pennsylvania State University dedicated its living apple museum—the only one in the country—to him. As an apple connoisseur, Kerr was very particular about the apples he ate, favoring certain varieties over others and going to great lengths to obtain them. In remembrance of his passion for this fruit, beautiful baskets of his favorite apples were prominently displayed during his memorial service in Berkeley on February 20, 2004. As apples are symbols of knowledge and immortality, this was an appropriate decor to celebrate the life of a man who did so much to advance education.

Coming from apple country myself—I was born and raised in Asturias, the Pennsylvania of Spain, mines, steel mills, and all—I share Kerr's love for apples down to the last detail: Cortland apples are my favorite, as they were his. Thus, it seems appropriate to close my personal reflection by saying that its purpose was simply to look for the two or three apples upon the bough Kerr didn't pick. Now, it is up to the younger generation to take the barrel that Kerr did not fill to other trees, where there are fresh apples ready to be picked.

# References

Allmendinger, David F. (1974). *Paupers and Scholars*. New York: St. Martin's Press.

Altbach, Philip G. (2007). "Empires of Knowledge and Development." *World Class Worldwide: Transforming Research Universities in Asia and Latin America*. Ed. Philip G. Altbach, & Jorge Balán. Baltimore, MD: The Johns Hopkins University Press, 1-28.

American Council on Education. (2007). *The American College President*. Washington, DC: American Council on Education, Center for Policy Analysis.

Ashby, Eric. (1962). "The Administrator: Bottleneck or Pump?" *Daedalus*, 91, 2: 264-278.

Association of Governing Boards of Universities and Colleges. (1984). *Presidents Make a Difference: Strengthening Leadership in Colleges and Universities*. Washington, DC: Commission on Strengthening Presidential Leadership, Association of Governing Boards of Universities and Colleges.

Astin, Helen S., & Carole Leland. (1991). *Women of Influence, Women of Vision: A Cross-Generational Study of Leaders and Social Change*. San Francisco: Jossey-Bass Publishers.

Atkinson, Richard A. (2004). "Academic Freedom and the Research University." *Proceedings of the American Philosophical Society*, 148, 2: 195-204.

Atkinson, Richard A. (2007). *The Pursuit of Knowledge: Speeches and Papers of Richard C. Atkinson*. Ed. Patricia A. Pelfrey. Los Angeles & London: University of California Press.

Atkinson, Richard A. (2009). "Defining the University of California of the Future." *Research and Occasional Papers Series*, Center for Studies in Higher Education, University of California, Berkeley, 11.09.

Atwood, Christee Gabour. (2007). *Succession Planning Basics*. Alexandria, VA: ASTD Press.

Axtell, James. (1976). *The School upon a Hill: Education and Society in Colonial New England*. New Haven, CT: Yale University Press.

Babbitt, Irving. (1986). *Literature and the American College: Essays in Defense of the Humanities*. Washington, DC: National Humanities Institute.

Barden, Dennis M. (2010). "Where Will You Find Your Future Leaders? The Time Has Come for Colleges and Universities to Get Serious about Succession Planning." *The Chronicle of Higher Education*, 56, 17: D20-D21.

Barnett, Thomas P.M. (2007). "Barnett: Enough of the Hedgehog." *Knowsnews.com*, January 6. http://www.knoxnews.com/news/2007/jan/06/barnett-enough-of-the-hedgehog/?print=1.

Barzun, Jacques. (1959). *The House of Intellect*. New York: Harper & Brothers.

Bass, Bernard M. (1985). *Leadership and Performance beyond Expectations*. New York: Free Press.

Bawa, Kamaljit, Ganesan Balachander, & Peter Raven. (2008). "A Case for New Institutions." *Science*, 319, 5860: 136.

Bendiner, Robert. (1962). "The Non-Teachers." *Horizon*, 5, 1: 14-19.

Benjamin, Harold R.W. (1965). *Higher Education in the American Republics*. New York: McGraw-Hill Book Company.

Bennis, Warren G., & Burt Nanus. (1985). *Leaders: The Strategies for Taking Charge*. New York: Harper & Row.

Bensimon, Estela M. (1989). "The Meaning of 'Good Presidential Leadership': A Frame Analysis." *The Review of Higher Education*, 12, 2: 107-123.

Berlin, Isaiah. (1953). *The Hedgehog and the Fox*. New York: Simon & Schuster.

Beschloss, Michael R. (1980). *Kennedy and Roosevelt: The Uneasy Alliance*. New York & London: W.W. Norton & Company.

Birgeneau, Robert J., & Frank D. Yeary. (2009). "Rescuing Our Public Universities." *The Washington Post*, September 27.

Birnbaum, Robert. (1988). *How Colleges Work: The Cybernetics of Academic Organization and Leadership*. San Francisco: Jossey-Bass Publishers.

Birnbaum, Robert. (1992). *How Academic Leadership Works*. San Francisco: Jossey-Bass Publishers.

Blum, Richard C. (2007). *We Need to be Strategically Dynamic*. August 13. http://www.universityofcalifornia.edu/future/blumpaper0807.pdf

Blumenstyk, Goldie. (2005). "Outside Chance for Insiders." *The Chronicle of Higher Education*, 52, 11: A28-A29.

Bok, Derek. (2006). *Our Underachieving Colleges: A Candid Look at How Much Students Learn and Why They Should be Learning More*. Princeton, NJ: Princeton University Press.

Bolman, Lee G., & Terrence E. Deal. (1984). *Modern Approaches to Understanding and Managing Organizations*. San Francisco: Jossey-Bass Publishers.

Bornstein, Rita. (2005). "The Nature and Nurture of Presidents." *The Chronicle of Higher Education*, 52, 11: B10-B11.

Bowen, Howard R. (1982). *The State of the Nation and the Agenda for Higher Education*. San Francisco: Jossey-Bass Publishers.

Bowen, William G., & Derek Bok. (1998). *The Shape of the River: Long-term Consequences of Considering Race in College and University Admissions*. Princeton, NJ: Princeton University Press.

Boyd, Brian. (2009). *On the Origins of Stories: Evolution, Cognition, and Fiction*. Cambridge, Massachusets, & London, England: The Belknap Press of Harvard University Press.

Boyer, Ernest, & Fred M. Hechinger. (1981). *Higher Learning in the Nation's Service*. Washington, DC: Carnegie Foundation for the Advancement of Teaching.

Boyer, Ernest. (1990). *Scholarship Reconsidered: Priorities of the Professoriate*. San Francisco: The Carnegie Foundation for the Advancement of Teaching & Jossey-Bass Publishers.

Breneman, David. (2008). "Elite Colleges Must Stop Spurning Critiques of Higher Education." *The Chronicle of Higher Education*, 54, 23: A40.

Bridges, Brian K., Peter D. Eckel, Diana I. Córdova, & Byron P. White. (2008). *Broadening the Leadership Spectrum: Advancing Diversity in the American College Presidency*. Washington DC: American Council on Education.

Brint, Steven. (2007). "Can Public Research Universities Compete?" *Future of the American Public Research University*. Ed. Roger L. Geiger, Carol L. Colbeck, & Roger L. Williams. Rotterdam & Taipei: Sense Publishers, 91-118.

Brooks, David. (2010). "The Power Elite." *The New York Times*, February 19.

Brown, J.M. (2008). "Mark Yudof Named New Head of UC System." *Santa Cruz Sentinel*, March 28.

Bundy, McGeorge. (1963). "Of Winds and Windmills: Free Universities and Public Policy." *Higher Education and the Federal Government*. Ed. Charles G. Dobbins. Washington, DC: American Council on Education.

Burnim, Mickey L., Patricia Digh, & Laura Skandera Trombley. (2007). "What Can Be Done to Diversify Executive Suites?" *The Chronicle of Higher Education*, 54, 5: B48-B53.

Burns, James McGregor. (1956). *Roosevelt: The Lion and the Fox*. New York: Harcourt, Brace & World, Inc.

Burns, James McGregor. (1978). *Leadership*. New York: Harper & Row.

Burns, James McGregor. (2003). *Transforming Leadership: A New Pursuit of Happiness*. New York: Atlantic Monthy Press.

Bush, Vannevar. (1945). *Science-The Endless Frontier: A Report to the President on a Program for Postwar Scientific Research*. Washington, DC: United States Government Printing Office.

Callan, Patrick, & John Immerwahr. (2008). "What Colleges Must Do to Keep the Public's Good Will." *The Chronicle of Higher Education*, 54, 18: A56.

Carnegie Council on Policy Studies in Higher Education. (1980). *Three Thousand Futures: The Next Twenty Years for Higher Education*. San Francisco: Jossey Bass Publishers.

Castañeda, Carlos E. (1938). "The Beginnings of University Life in America." *Preliminary Studies of the Texas Catholic Historical Society*, 3, 4.

Castells, Manuel. (2009). *Communication Power*. Oxford: Oxford University Press.

Clark, Burton R. (1995). *Places of Inquiry: Research and Advanced Education in Modern Universities*. Berkeley, Los Angeles, & London: University of California Press.

Clark, Stephen. (2009). "Obama's Tardiness Sets Him Apart from Bush." *FoxNews.com*, February 6. www.foxnews.com/politics/first100days/2009/02/05

Clifford, Geraldine J. (1995). *"Equally in View": The University of California, Its Women, and the Schools*. Berkeley, CA: Center for Studies in Higher Education & Institute of Governmental Studies, University of California, Berkeley, Chapters in the History of the University of California, 4.

Cohen, Arthur M. (1998). *The Shaping of American Higher Education: Emergence and Growth of the Contemporary System*. San Francisco: Jossey-Bass Publishers.

Cohen, Michael D., & James G. March. (1974). *Leadership and Ambiguity: The American College President. A General Report Prepared for The Carnegie Commission on Higher Education*. New York: McGraw-Hill Book Company.

Cohen, Robert. (2009). *Freedom's Orator: Mario Savio and the Radical Legacy of the 1960s*. Oxford & New York: Oxford University Press.

Cole, Jonathan R. (2009). *The Great American University: Its Rise to Preeminence, Its Indispensable National Role, Why It Must Be Protected*. New York: PublicAffairs.

Collins, Jim. (2001). *Good to Great: Why Some Companies Make the Leap...and Others Don't*. New York: HarperBusiness.

Collins, Jim, & Jerry I. Porras. (2004 [1994]). *Built to Last: Successful Habits of Visionary Companies*. New York: HarperBusiness.

Collins, Jim. (2005). *Good to Great and the Social Sectors: Why Business Thinking is not the Answer: A Monograph to Accompany Good to Great: Why Some Companies Make the Leap...and Others Don't*. Boulder, CO: Jim Collins.

Collins, Jim. (2009). *How the Mightly Fall: And Why Some Companies Never Give In*. New York: HarperCollins.

Contreras, A. Reynaldo. (1998). "Leading from the Margins of the Ivory Tower." *The Multicultural Campus: Strategies for Transforming Higher Education*. Ed. Leonard A. Valverde, & Louis A. Castenell, Jr. Walnut Creek, CA, London, & New Delhi: Altamira Press, 136-161.

Cordasco, Francesco. (1960). *Daniel Coit Gilman and the Protean Ph.D.: The Shaping of American Graduate Education*. Leiden: E.J. Brill.

Courant, Paul N., & James J. Duderstadt. (2010). "Needed: A National Strategy to Preserve Public Research Universities." *The Chronicle of Higher Education*, 56, 17: A36.

Cowley, William H., & Don Williams. (1991). *International and Historical Roots of American Higher Education*. New York: Garland Publishing Inc.

Cox, Taylor H., Jr., & Joycelyn A. Finley. (1995). "An Analysis of Work Specialization and Organization Level as Dimensions of Workforce Diversity." *Diversity in Organizations: New Perspective for a Changing Workplace*. Ed. Martin M. Chemers, Stuart Oskamp, & Mark A. Costanzo. Thousand Oaks, CA, London, & New Delhi: Sage Publications, 62-88.

Curris, Constantine. (2009). "How to Stop the Arms Race in Presidential Pay." *The Chronicle of Higher Education*, 56, 16: A22-A23.

Damrosch, David. (1995). *We Scholars: Changing the Culture of the University*. Cambridge, MA, & London: Harvard University Press.

Davis, Erroll B. (2008). "Colleges Need to Offer Clear Paths to Leadership." *The Chronicle of Higher Education*, 54, 45: A64.

Delgado, Richard, & Jean Stefancic. (2000). "California's Racial History and Constitutional Rationales for Race-Conscious Decision Making in Higher Education." *UCLA Law Review*, 47, 6: 1521-1614.

Diamond, Jared M. (1997). *Guns, Germs and Steel: The Fates of Human Societies*. New York: W.W. Norton & Co.

Diamond, Nancy. (2006). "'Time, Place and Character': The American College and University Presidency in the Late Twentieth Century." *Perspectives on the History of Higher Education*, 25: 157-181.

Dobbins, Charles G., Ed. (1963). *Higher Education and the Federal Government*. Washington, DC: American Council on Education.

Dodds, Harold W. (1962). *The Academic President-Educator or Caretaker?* New York: McGraw-Hill.

Douglass, John Aubrey. (2000). *The California Idea and American Higher Education: 1850 to the Master Plan*. Stanford, CA: Stanford University Press.

Douglass, John Aubrey. (2002). "From Multi- to Meta-University: Organizational and Political Change at the University of California in the 20th Century and Beyond." *Research and Occasional Papers Series*, Center for Studies in Higher Education, University of California, Berkeley, 4.02.

Douglass, John Aubrey. (2006). "The Waning of America's Higher Education Advantage: International Competitors Are No Longer Number Two and Have Big Plans in the Global Economy." *Research and Occasional Papers Series*, Center for Studies in Higher Education, University of California, Berkeley, 9.06.

Douglass, John Aubrey. (2007). *The Conditions of Admission: Access, Equity, and the Social Contract of Public Universities*. Stanford, CA: Stanford University Press.

Douglass, John Aubrey. (2009a). "Treading Water: What Happened to America's Higher Education Advantage?" *Globalization's Muse: Universities and Higher Education Systems in a Changing World*. Ed. John A. Douglass, C. Judson King, & Irwin Feller. Berkeley, CA: Berkeley Public Policy Press, Institute of Governmental Studies, University of California, Berkeley, 165-186.

Douglass, John Aubrey, & Richard Edelstein. (2009b). "The Global Competition for Talent: The Rapidly Changing Market for International Students and the Need for a Strategic Approach in the US." *Research and Occasional Papers Series*, Center for Studies in Higher Education, University of California, Berkeley, 8.09.

Draper, Hal. (1964). *The Mind of Clark Kerr: His View of the University Factory and the New Slavery*. Berkeley, CA: Independent Socialist Club.

Draper, Hal. (1965). *Berkeley: The New Student Revolt*. New York: Grove Press, Inc.

Drew, David E. (2005). "Three Flaws in the Education System and How to Fix Them." *The Claremont Newsletter*, 2, 1: 1-4.

Drucker, Peter F. (1980). *Managing in Turbulent Times*. New York: Harper & Row, Publishers.

Du Bois, W.E.B. (1903a). *The Souls of Black Folk: Essays and Sketches*. Chicago: A.C. McClurg & Company.

Du Bois, W.E.B. (1903b). "The Talented Tenth." *The Negro Problem: A Series of Articles by Representative Negroes of To-day*. New York: J. Pott & Company, 30-75.

Duderstadt, James J. (2000). *A University for the 21st Century*. Ann Arbor, MI: The University of Michigan Press.

Duderstadt, James J., Daniel E. Atkins, & Douglas Van Houweling. (2002). *Higher Education in the Digital Age: Technology Issues and Strategies for American Colleges and Universities*. Westport, CT: American Council on Education & Praeger.

Duderstadt, James J., & Farris W. Womack. (2003). *The Future of the Public University in America: Beyond the Crossroads*. Baltimore, MD: The Johns Hopkins University Press.

Duderstadt, James J. (2007). *The View from the Helm: Leading the American University During an Era of Change*. Ann Arbor, MI: The University of Michigan Press.

Dzuback, Mary Ann. (1991). *Robert M. Hutchins: Portrait of an Educator*. Chicago: The University of Chicago Press.

Ely, Robin J., & David A. Thomas. (2001). "Cultural Diversity at Work: The Effects of Diversity Perspectives on Work Group Processes and Outcomes." *Administrative Science Quarterly*, 46, 2: 229-273.

Fain, Paul. (2006). "In Apparent Suicide, Chancellor Dies in a Fall." *The Chronicle of Higher Education*, 52, 44: A1.

Fain, Paul. (2007). "Too Much, Too Fast." *The Chronicle of Higher Education*, 53, 20: A24.

Farrell, Elizabeth F. (2007). "Is Bigger Any Better?" *The Chronicle of Higher Education*, 54, 13: A23-A24.

Farrington, Elizabeth Leigh. (2006). "Hierarchical Dysfunction and Mobbing in the Academy." *Women in Higher Education*, 15, 10: 35-36.

Feller, Irwin. (2007). "Who Races with Whom; Who is Likely to Win (or Survive); Why." *Future of the American Public Research University*. Ed. Roger L. Geiger, Carol L. Colbeck, & Roger L. Williams. Rotterdam & Taipei: Sense Publishers, 72-90.

Feller, Irwin. (2009). "Size, Share, and Structure: The Changing Role of America's Public Research Universities." *Globalization's Muse: Universities and Higher Education Systems in a Changing World*. Ed. John A. Douglass, C. Judson King, & Irwin Feller. Berkeley, CA: Berkeley Public Policy Press, Institute of Governmental Studies, University of California, Berkeley, 67-80.

Fernández-Armesto, Felipe. (2003). *The Americas: A Hemispheric History*. New York: The Modern Library.

Ferrier, William W. (1930). *Origin and Development of the University of California*. Berkeley, CA: The Sather Gate Book Shop.

Fichte, Johann Gottlieb. (1968 [1808]). *Addresses to the German Nation*. New York: Harper & Row.

Finkelstein, Martin J., Robert K. Seal, & Jack H. Schuster. (1998*). The New Academic Generation: A Profession in Transformation*. Baltimore: The Johns Hopkins University Press.

Fischer, Karin. (2008). "Despite Doubts, 3 Prominent Universities Sign Deals with a Saudi University." *The Chronicle of Higher Education*, 54, 27: A22-A23.

Fish, Stanley. (2007). "Bound for Academic Glory?" *The New York Times*, December 23.

Fisher, James L. (1984). *Power of the Presidency*. London: American Council on Education & Macmillan Publishing Company.

Flexner, Abraham. (1910). *Medical Education in the United States and Canada*. New York: Carnegie Foundation for the Advancement of Teaching.

Flexner, Abraham. (1946). *Daniel Coit Gilman: Creator of the American Type of University*. New York: Harcourt, Brace & Company.

Flexner, Abraham. (1994 [1930]). *Universities: American, English, German*. New Brunswick, NJ, & London: Transaction Publishers, with a new introduction by Clark Kerr.

Freedberg, Louis. (2006). "UC's Culture of Compensation." *San Francisco Chronicle*, February 27.

Friedman, Thomas L. (2009). "More Poetry, Please." *The New York Times*, October 31.

Frost, Robert. (1969). *The Poetry of Robert Frost: The Collected Poems, Complete and Unabridged*. Ed. Edward Connery Lathem. New York: Holt, Rinehart & Winston.

Gaines, Danielle. (2009). "UC San Diego Profs Come Up with Budget Fixer: Close UC Merced." *Merced Sun-Star*, July 9.

Galbraith, John Kenneth. (1990). *A Tenured Professor: A Novel*. Boston: Houghton Mifflin.

Gándara, Patricia. (1995). *Over the Ivy Walls: The Educational Mobility of Low-Income Chicanos*. Albany, NY: State University of New York Press.

Gardner, David P. (1967). *The California Oath Controversy*. Berkeley & Los Angeles: University of California Press.

Gardner, David P. (2005). *Earning my Degree: Memoirs of an American University President*. Berkeley, Los Angeles, & London: University of California Press.

Gardner, Howard. (1995). *Leading Minds: An Anatomy of Leadership*. New York: Basic Books.

Gardner, John W. (1990). *On Leadership*. New York: The Free Press.

Geiger, Roger L. (1986). *To Advance Knowledge: The Growth of American Research Universities, 1900-1940*. New York & Oxford: Oxford University Press.

Geiger, Roger L. (1993). *Research and Relevant Knowledge: American Research Universities Since World War II*. New York & Oxford: Oxford University Press.

Geiger, Roger L. (2004). *Knowledge & Money: Research Universities and the Paradox of the Marketplace*. Stanford, CA: Stanford University Press.

Geiger, Roger L. (2007). "Expert and Elite: The Incongruous Missions of Public Research Universities." *Future of the American Public Research University*. Ed. Roger L. Geiger, Carol L. Colbeck, & Roger L. Williams. Rotterdam & Taipei: Sense Publishers, 15-33.

Giamatti, A. Bartlett. (1990). *A Free and Ordered Space: The Real World of the University*. New York & London: W.W. Norton & Company.

Glazer-Raymo, Judith. (1999). *Shattering the Myths: Women in Academia*. Baltimore & London: The Johns Hopkins University Press.

Goldin, Claudia, & Lawrence F. Katz. (2008). *The Race Between Education and Technology*. Cambridge, MA, & London: The Belknap Press of Harvard University Press.

Góngora, Mario. (1979). "Origin and Philosophy of the Spanish American University." *The Latin American University*. Ed. Joseph Maier, & Richard W. Weatherhead. Albuquerque, NM: University of New Mexico Press, 17-64.

González, Cristina. (2001). "Undergraduate Research, Graduate Mentoring, and the University's Mission." *Science*, 293, 5335: 1624-1626.

González, Cristina. (2002). "Graduate Education in Germany and the United States: From Isolation to Cooperation." *Academic Leader*, 18, 4: 5 & 8.

González, Cristina. (2007). "Hedgehogs, Foxes, Leadership Renewal and Succession Planning." *Research and Occasional Papers Series*, Center for Studies in Higher Education, University of California, Berkeley, 17.07.

González, Kenneth P., & Raymond V. Padilla. (2008). *Doing the Public Good: Latina/o Scholars Engage Civic Participation.* Sterling, VA: Stylus.

Goodall, Amanda H. (2009). *Socrates in the Boardroom: Why Research Universities Should be Led by Top Scholars.* Princeton, NJ: Princeton University Press.

Gould, Stephen Jay. (2003). *The Hedgehog, the Fox, and the Magister's Pox: Mending the Gap Between Science and the Humanities.* New York: Harmony Books.

Graham, Hugh D., & Nancy Diamond. (1996). *The Rise of American Research Universities: Elites and Challengers in the Postwar Era.* Baltimore, MD: Johns Hopkins University Press.

Gray, Hanna Holborn. (1983). *The Higher Learning and the New Consumerism.* Washington, DC: American Enterprise Institute for Public Policy Research.

Gray, Hanna Holborn. (1998). "On the History of Giants." *Universities and Their Leadership.* Ed. William G. Bowen, & Harold T. Shapiro. Princeton, NJ: Princeton University Press.

Gray, Hanna Holborn. (2004). "The Challenge of Leadership and Governance in the University." *Knowledge Matters: Essays in Honour of Bernard J. Shapiro.* Ed. Paul Axelrod. Montreal & Kingston, London, Ithaca: McGill-Queen's University Press, 93-100.

Gray, Hanna Holborn. (2009a). "The Uses of the University Revisited." *Clark Kerr Lectures on the Role of Higher Education in Society*, 1. University of California, Berkeley, November 16.

Gray, Hanna Holborn. (2009b). "Uses (and Misuses) of the University Today." *Clark Kerr Lectures on the Role of Higher Education in Society*, 2. University of California, Berkeley, November 18.

Gray, Hanna Holborn. (2009c). "Searching for Utopia." *Clark Kerr Lectures on the Role of Higher Education in Society*, 3. University of California, Davis, November 20.

Gumz, Jondi. (2005). "Critics Question Expense of UCSC Chancellor's Dog Run." *Santa Cruz Sentinel*, December 9.

Hargreaves, Andy, & Dean Fink. (2006). *Sustainable Leadership.* San Francisco: Jossey-Bass Publishers.

Harris, Michael R. (1970). *Five Counterrevolutionists in Higher Education: Irving Babbit, Albert Jay Nock, Abraham Flexner, Robert Maynard Hutchins, Alexander Meiklejohn.* Corvallis, OR: Oregon State University Press.

Hayward, Brad. (2007). "UC President Dynes to Step Down." *UCnews*, University of California Office of the President, August 13.

Hearn, Thomas K., Jr. (2006). "Leadership and Teaching in the American University." *University Presidents as Moral Leaders.* Ed. David G. Brown. Westport, CT: American Council on Education & Praeger Series on Higher Education, 159-176.

Herbst, Jurgen. (1982). *From Crisis to Crisis: American College Government, 1636-1819.* Cambridge, MA: Harvard University Press.

Huffington, Arianna. (2004). "Ronald Reagan, Hedgehogs and the November Election." *Arianna Online*, June 8. http://ariannaonline.huffingtonpost.com/columns/printer_friendly.php?id=715

Huffington, Arianna. (2008). "Microtrends vs. Macrotrends: Why Obama is Winning." *The Huffington Post*, February 28. http://www.huffingtonpost.com/arianna- huffington/microtrends-vs-macrotrend_b_88962.html

Hutchins, Robert Maynard. (1956). *Freedom, Education and the Fund: Essays and Addresses, 1946-1956*. New York: Meridian Books.

Hutchins, Robert Maynard. (1952 [1936]). *The Higher Learning in America*. New Haven, CT: Yale University Press.

Jaspers, Karl. (1959 [1946]). *The Idea of the University*. Boston: Beacon Press.

Jaspers, Karl. (2000 [1947]). *The Question of German Guilt*. New York: Fordham University Press.

Johnson, Dean C. (1996). *The University of California: History and Achievements*. Berkeley, CA: Regents of the University of California.

Justus, Joyce Bennett, Sandria B. Freitag, & L. Leanne Parker, Eds. (1987). *The University of California in the Twenty-First Century: Successful Approaches to Faculty Diversity*. Berkeley: University of California.

Kelly, Jessica. (2007). "Harvard Aid Plan Offers Tuition Discounts: One of the Nation's Elite Universities Eases Financial Burden on Middle-Class Families." *CNNMoney. Com*, December 27. http://money.cnn.com/2007/12/26/pf/college/harvard/index.htm

Kennedy, Donald. (1997). *Academic Duty*. Cambridge, MA: Harvard University Press.

Keohane, Nannerl O. (2006). *Higher Ground: Ethics and Leadership in the Modern University*. Durham & London: Duke University Press.

Keohane, Nannerl O. (2007). "Crossing the Bridge: Reflections on Women and Leadership." *Women and Leadership: The State of Play and Strategies for Change*. Ed. Barbara Kellerman, & Deborah L. Rhode. San Francisco: Jossey-Bass Publishers.

Kerr, Clark, John T. Dunlop, Frederick H. Harvison, & Charles A. Myers. (1960). *Industrialism and Industrial Man: The Problems of Labor and Management in Economic Growth*. Cambridge, MA: Harvard University Press.

Kerr, Clark, & Marian L. Gade. (1981). "Current and Emerging Issues Facing American Higher Education." *Higher Education in American Society*. Ed. Philip G. Altbach, & Robert O. Berdahl. Buffalo, NY: Prometeus Books, 129-149.

Kerr, Clark, & Marian L. Gade. (1986). *The Many Lives of Academic Presidents: Time, Place & Character*. Washington, DC: Association of Governing Boards of Universities and Colleges.

Kerr, Clark, & Marian L. Gade. (1989). *The Guardians: Boards of Trustees of American Colleges and Universities, What They Do and How Well They Do It*. Washington, DC: Association of Governing Boards of Universities & Colleges.

Kerr, Clark, Marian L. Gade, & Maureen Kawaoka. (1994a). *Troubled Times for American Higher Education: The 1990's and Beyond*. Albany, NY: State University of New York Press.

Kerr, Clark, Marian L. Gade, & Maureen Kawaoka. (1994b). *Higher Education Cannot Escape History: Issues for the Twenty-First Century*. Albany, NY: State University of New York Press.

Kerr, Clark. (2001a [1963]). *The Uses of the University*. Cambridge, MA, & London: Harvard University Press.

Kerr, Clark. (2001b). *The Gold and the Blue: A Personal Memoir of the University of California (1949-1967), Volume 1: Academic Triumphs*. Berkeley, Los Angeles, & London: University of California Press.

Kerr, Clark. (2002). "Shock Wave II: An Introduction to the Twenty-First Century." *The Future of the City of Intellect: The Changing American University*. Ed. Steven Brint. Stanford, CA: Stanford University Press.

Kerr, Clark. (2003). *The Gold and the Blue: A Personal Memoir of the University of California (1949-1967), Volume 2: Political Turmoil.* Berkeley, Los Angeles, & London: University of California Press.

King, C. Judson. (2006). "An Analysis of Alternatives for Gaining Capacity so as to Maintain Access to the University of California." *Research and Occasional Papers Series,* Center for Studies in Higher Education, University of California, Berkeley, 5.06.

King, C. Judson. (2009). "University Roles in Technological Innovation in California." *Globalization's Muse: Universities and Higher Education Systems in a Changing World.* Ed. John A. Douglass, C. Judson King, & Irwin Feller. Berkeley, California: Berkeley Public Policy Press, Institute of Governmental Studies, University of California, Berkeley, 279-298.

King, Jacqueline E., & Gigi G. Gómez. (2008). *On the Pathway to the Presidency: Characteristics of Higher Education's Senior Leadership.* Washington, DC: American Council on Education.

Kirp, David L. (2003). *Shakespeare, Einstein, and the Bottom Line: The Marketing of Higher Education.* Cambridge, MA: Harvard University Press.

Krause, Sharon R. (2002). *Liberalism with Honor.* Cambridge, MA, & London: Harvard University Press.

Lakoff, George. (2009). "The Obama Code." *FiveThirtyEight.Com,* February 24. www.fivethirtyeight.com/2009/02/

Lanning, John Tate. (1940). *Academic Culture in the Spanish Colonies.* Port Washington, NY: Kennikat Press.

Lanning, John Tate, & Rafael Heliodoro Valle, Eds. (1946). *Reales Cédulas de la Real y Pontificia Universidad de México de 1551 a 1816.* México, DF: UNAM, Imprenta Universitaria.

Lawrence, Francis L. (2006). *Views from the Presidency: Leadership in Higher Education.* New Brunswick, NJ: Transaction Publishers.

Leonhardt, David. (2010). "In Health Care Bill, Obama Attacks Wealth Inequality." *The New York Times,* March 23.

Levine, Arthur. (1987). "Clark Kerr: The Masterbuilder at 75." *Change,* 19, 2: 12-35.

Levine, Arthur. (1997). "Higher Education's New Status as a Mature Industry." *The Chronicle of Higher Education,* 43, 21: A1 & A19-A22.

Lewin, Tamar. (2008). "Universities Rush to Set Up Outposts Abroad." *The New York Times,* February 10.

Lewis, Harry L. (2006). *Excellence without a Soul: How a Great University Forgot Education.* New York: Public Affairs.

Leymann, Heinz. (1990). "Mobbing and Psychological Terror at Workplaces." *Violence and Victims,* 5, 2: 119-126.

Leymann, Heinz. (1996). "The Content and Development of Mobbing at Work." *European Journal of Work and Organizational Psychology,* 5, 2: 165-184.

Longfellow, Henry Wadsworth. (1893). *The Complete Poetical Works of Longfellow.* Cambridge, MA: Houghton Mifflin Company.

Lucas, Christopher J. (1994). *American Higher Education: A History.* New York: St. Martin's Griffin.

Lucas, Christopher J. (1996). *Crisis in the Academy: Rethinking Higher Education in America.* New York: St. Martin's Press.

MacDonald, Victoria-María. (2004). *Latino Education in the United States: A Narrated History from 1513-2000.* New York: Palgrave Macmillan.

Machiavelli, Niccolò. (1995). *The Prince.* London: Penguin Books.

Machlup, Fritz. (1962). *The Production and Distribution of Knowledge in the United States.* Princeton, NJ: Princeton University Press.

Madariaga, Salvador de. (1928a). "Americans Are Boys: A Spaniard Looks at Our Civilization." *Harper's Magazine*, 157, 937-942: 239-245.

Madariaga, Salvador de. (1928b). *Aims and Methods of a Chair of Spanish Studies: An Inaugural Lecture Delivered Before the University of Oxford on 15 May 1928*. Oxford: Clarendon Press, 1928.

Malloy, Edward S. (2006). "Succeeding a Legend at the University of Notre Dame." *University Presidents as Moral Leaders*. Ed. David G. Brown. Westport, CT: American Council on Education & Praeger Series on Higher Education, 87-101.

Mann, Tim. (2010). "Attrition Among Chief Academic Officers Threatens Strategic Plans." *The Chronicle of Higher Education*, 56, 39: A80.

Marginson, Simon. (2010). "The Rise of the Global University: 5 New Tensions." *The Chronicle of Higher Education*, 56, 37: A76.

Marías, Julián. (1972 [1956]). *America in the Fifties and Sixties: Julián Marías on the United States*. University Park, PA & London: The Pennsylvania State University Press.

Marsden, George M. (1994). *The Soul of the American University: From Protestant Establishment to Established Non-belief*. New York: Oxford University Press.

Martin, James, & James E. Samels & Associates, Eds. (2004). *Presidential Transition in Higher Education: Managing Leadership Change*. Baltimore, MD: The Johns Hopkins University Press.

Mason, Mary Ann, & Marc Goulden. (2002). "Do Babies Matter: The Effect of Family Formation on the Lifelong Careers of Academic Men and Women." *Academe*, 88, 6: 21-27.

May, Henry F. (1993). *Three Faces of Berkeley: Competing Ideologies in the Wheeler Era, 1899-1919*. Berkeley, CA: Center for Studies in Higher Education & Institute of Governmental Affairs, Chapters in the History of the University of California, 1.

Mead-Fox, David. (2009). "Tackling Higher Education's Leadership Scarcity." *University World News*, 0072, April 19. http://www.universityworldnews.com/article.php?story=20090416193526437

Mead-Fox, David. (2010). "It's Getting Harder to Find Superior Leaders: To Compete for the Best Talent, Colleges Must Rethink how they Recruit Executives Externally and Internally." *The Chronicle of Higher Education*, 56, 17: D25-D26.

Menand, Louis. (2010). *The Marketplace of Ideas*. New York & London: W.W. Norton & Company.

Méndez Arceo, Sergio. (1952). *La Real y Pontificia Universidad de México: Antecedentes, tramitación y despacho de las reales cédulas de erección*. México, DF: UNAM, Consejo de Humanidades, Ediciones del IV Centenario de la Universidad de México.

Merritt, Karen, & Jane Fiori Lawrence, Eds. (2007). *From Rangeland to Research University: the Birth of the University of California, Merced*. San Francisco: Jossey-Bass.

Millett, John D. (1962). *The Academic Community: An Essay on Organization*. New York: McGraw-Hill.

Mills, Andrew. (2008). "Emirates Look to the West for Prestige." *The Chronicle of Higher Education*, 55, 5: A1-A23.

Mills, Nicolaus. (2010). "Obama Should Take a Cue from FDR: Go to the people (before the midterm elections)." *The Chronicle of Higher Education*, 56, 27: B11-B12.

Moberly, Sir Walter. (1949). *The Crisis in the University*. London: SCM Press Ltd.

Moody, Ann. (2004). *Faculty Diversity: Problems and Solutions*. New York & London: Routledge Falmer.

Morrill, James L. (1960). *The Ongoing State University*. Minneapolis, MN: University of Minnesota Press.

Münsterberg, Hugo. (1913). *American Patriotism and Other Social Studies*. New York: Moffat, Yard & CO.

Murphy, Franklin D. (1976*). My UCLA Chancellorship: An Utterly Candid View*. Interviewed by James V. Mink. Los Angeles: University of California Oral History Program.

Nelson, Stephen J. (2009). *Leaders in the Crossroads: Success and Failure in the College Presidency*. Lanham, New York, Toronto, & Plymouth, UK: Rowman & Littlefield Education.

Nerad, Maresi. (1999). *The Academic Kitchen: A Social History of Gender Stratification at the University of California, Berkeley*. Albany, NY: State University of New York Press.

Nerad, Maresi, & Mimi Heggelund, Eds. (2008). *Toward a Global PhD? Forces and Forms in Doctoral Education Worldwide*. Seattle, WA: University of Washington Press.

Nevins, Allan. (1962). *The State Universities and Democracy*. Urbana, IL: University of Illinois Press.

Newfield, Christopher. (2008). *Unmaking the Public University: The Forty-Year Assault on the Middle Class*. Cambridge, MA, & London: Harvard University Press.

Newman, John Henry. (1996 [1891]). *The Idea of the University*. Ed. Frank M. Turner. New Haven: Yale University Press.

Niemeier, Debbie, & Cristina González. (2004). "Breaking Into the Guildmasters Club:What We Know About Women Science and Engineering Department Chairs at AAU Universities." *National Women's Studies Association Journal*, 16, 1: 157-171.

Nisbet, Robert. (1992). *Teachers and Scholars: A Memoir of Berkeley in Depression and War*. New Brunswick, NJ: Transaction Publishers.

Norrell, Robert J. (2009). *Up from History: The Life of Booker T. Washington*. Cambridge, MA, & London: The Belknap Press of Harvard University Press.

Oakley, Ed, & Doug Krug. (1991). *Enlightened Leadership: Getting to the Heart of Change*. New York: Simon & Schuster.

Ong, Sze Ann. (1989). *Succession Planning-Concepts, Issues and Implementation*. Master of Business Administration Thesis, University of California, Berkeley.

Orfield, Gary. (2000). "Campus Resegregation and its Alternatives." *Chilling Admissions: The Affirmative Action Crisis and the Search for Alternatives*. Ed. Gary Orfield, & Edward Miller. Cambridge, MA: Harvard Education Publishing Group, The Civil Rights Project, Harvard University.

Organization for Educational Co-operation and Development (OECD). (1990). *Reviews of National Policies for Education: Higher Education in California*. Paris: Organization for Educational Co-operation and Development (OECD).

Ortega y Gasset, José. (1993 [1930]). *The Revolt of the Masses*. New York: W.W. Norton.

Ortega y Gasset, José. (1997 [1930]). *Mission of the University*. New Brunswick, NJ, & London: Transaction Publishers, with a new introduction by Clark Kerr.

Otten, A. Michael. (1970). *University Authority and the Student: The Berkeley Experience*. Berkeley, Los Angeles, & London: University of California Press.

Padilla, Arthur. (2005). *Portraits in Leadership: Six Extraordinary University Presidents*. Westport, CT: ACE & Praeger Series on Higher Education.

Page, Scott A. (2007). *The Difference: How the Power of Diversity Creates Better Groups, Firms, Schools and Societies*. Princeton, NJ: Princeton University Press.

Partin, Agnes Edwards. (2006). *Student Life at the University of California, Berkeley, During and After World War I: The Letters of Agnes Edwards Partin, 1917-1921.* Ed. Grace E. Moremen. Lewiston, New York: The Edwin Mellen Press.

Pasque, Penny A. (2010). *American Higher Education, Leadership, and Policy: Critical Issues and the Public Good.* New York: Palgrave Macmillan, 19-73.

Pedersen, Olaf. (1997). *The First Universities: Studium Generale and the Origins of University Education in Europe.* Cambridge: Cambridge University Press.

Peers, Edgar Allison "Bruce Truscot." (1943). *Red Brick University.* London: Faber & Faber.

Pelfrey, Patricia A. (2004). *A Brief History of the University of California.* Berkeley, California: University of California.

Pelfrey, Patricia A. (2008a). "Origins of the Principles for Review of Executive Compensation 1992-93." *Research and Occasional Paper Series,* Center for Studies in Higher Education, University of California, Berkeley, 6.08.

Pelfrey, Patricia A. (2008b). "Executive Compensation at the University of California." *Research and Occasional Paper Series,* Center for Studies in Higher Education, University of California, Berkeley, 7.08.

Pettitt, George A. (1946). *Primitive Education in North America.* Berkeley & Los Angeles: University of California Press, University of California Publications in American Archaeology and Ethnology, 43, 1.

Pettitt, George A. (1966). *Twenty-eight Years in the Life of a University President.* Berkeley, CA: University of California.

Pfister, Joel. (2009). *The Yale Indian: The Education of Henry Roe Cloud.* Durham, NC & London: Duke University Press.

Post, Robert C. (2003). "Academic Freedom and the 'Intifada Curriculum.'" *Academe,* 89, 3: 16-20.

Pusser, Brian. (2004). *Burning Down the House: Politics, Governance, and Affirmative Action at the University of California.* Albany, NY: State University of New York Press.

Ragins, Belle Rose. (1995). "Diversity, Power, and Mentorship in Organizations: A Cultural, Structural, and Behavioral Perspective." *Diversity in Organizations: New Perspective for a Changing Workplace.* Ed. Martin M. Chemers, Stuart Oskamp, & Mark A. Costanzo. Thousand Oaks, CA, London, & New Delhi: Sage Publications, 91-132.

Ramón y Cajal, Santiago. (2000 [1898]). *Advice for a Young Investigator.* Cambridge, MA, & London: A Bradford Book, The MIT Press.

Rashdall, Hastings. (1936). *The Universities of Europe in the Middle Ages.* Oxford: Clarendon Press, 3 volumes.

Readings, Bill. (1996). *The University in Ruins.* Cambridge, MA: Harvard University Press.

Reuben, Julie A. (1996). *The Making of the Modern University: Intellectual Transformation and the Marginalization of Morality.* Chicago: University of Chicago Press.

Rhode, Deborah L. (2006). *In Pursuit of Knowledge: Scholars, Status, and Academic Culture.* Stanford, CA: Stanford Law and Politics.

Rhodes, Frank H.T. (2001). *The Creation of the Future: The Role of the American University.* Ithaca, NY: Cornell University Press.

Rivera, Carla. (2010). "16% Rise in Undergrads on California's State Campuses Predicted." *Los Angeles Times,* March 11.

Roberts, John, Águeda M. Rodríguez Cruz, & Jurgen Herbts. (1996). "Exporting Models." *A History of the University in Europe.* Volume 2. Ed. Walter Rüegg. Cambridge: Cambridge University Press, 256-282.

Rosovsky, Henry. (1990). *The University: An Owner's Manual.* New York & London: W.W. Norton & Company.

Rothblatt, Sheldon, Ed. (1992). *The OECD, The Master Plan and the California Dream: A Berkeley Conversation.* Berkeley: Center for Studies in Higher Education.

Rothblatt, Sheldon. (1993). "The Limbs of Osiris: Liberal Education in the English-Speaking World." *The European and American University since 1800.* Ed. Sheldon Rothblatt, & Björn Wittrock. Cambridge: Cambridge University Press, 19-73.

Rothblatt, Sheldon. (1997). *The Modern University and its Discontents: The Fate of Newman's Legacies in Britain and America.* Cambridge: Cambridge University Press.

Rothblatt, Sheldon. (2007). *Education's Abiding Moral Dilemma: Merit and Worth in The Cross-Atlantic Democracies, 1800-2006.* Oxford: Symposium Books, Oxford Studies in Comparative Education, 16, 2.

Rothwell, William J. (2005). *Effective Succession Planning: Ensuring Leadership Continuity and Building Talent from Within.* New York: American Management Corporation.

Rudolph, Frederick. (1962). *The American College and University: A History.* New York: Alfred A. Knopf.

Rüegg, Walter. (1992). "The Rise of Humanism." *A History of the University in Europe.* Volume 1. Ed. Walter Rüegg. Cambridge: Cambridge University Press, 442-468.

Sample, Steven B. (2002). *The Contrarian's Guide to Leadership.* San Francisco, California: Jossey-Bass Publishers.

Sánchez, George I. (1970). *The Development of Higher Education in Mexico.* Westport, CT: Greenwood Press.

Santovec, Mary Lou. (2010). "Succession Planning Gives Women a Shot at Leadership." *Women in Higher Education*, 19.

Schevitz, Tanya. (2007). "Regents Excuse UC President in Salary Scandal." *San Francisco Chronicle*, May 18.

Schumpeter, Joseph Alois. (1949). *The Theory of Economic Development: An Inquiry into Profits, Capital, Credits, Interest, and the Business Cycle.* Cambridge, MA: Harvard University Press.

Scott, David K., & Susan M. Awbrey. (1993). *Transforming Scholarship. Change*, 25, 4: 38-43.

Selingo, Jeffrey. (2008). "Americans Split on Government Control of Tuition." *The Chronicle of Higher Education*, 54, 30: A1 & A21-22.

Selingo, Jeffrey. (2009). "Emory U. Trains Its Own Leaders." *The Chronicle of Higher Education*, 55, 41: B3-B4.

Shapiro, Harold T. (2005). *A Larger Sense of Purpose: Higher Education and Society.* Princeton & Oxford: Princeton University Press.

Shils, Edward, & John Roberts. (2004). "The Diffusion of European Models Outside Europe." *A History of the University in Europe.* Volume 3. Ed. Walter Rüegg. Cambridge: Cambridge University Press, 163-230.

Sinclair, Upton. (1906). *The Jungle.* New York: Doubleday, Page & Co.

Sinclair, Upton. (1923). *The Goose-Step: A Study of American Education.* Pasadena, CA: Upton Sinclair.

Slaughter, Sheila, & Larry L. Leslie. (1997). *Academic Capitalism: Politics, Policies, and the Entrepreneurial University.* Baltimore, MD & London: The Johns Hopkins University Press.

Slaughter, Sheila, & Gary Rhoades. (2004). *Academic Capitalism and the New Economy: Markets, State, and Higher Education.* Baltimore & London: The Johns Hopkins University Press.

Slosson, Edwin E. (1977 [1910]). *Great American Universities*. New York: Arno Press.

Smelser, Neil J. (2005). "Coolness in Controversy: The Story of California President Emeritus David Gardner." *California Monthly*, 116, 1: 28-29.

Smelser, Neil J. (2010). *Reflections on the University of California: From the Free Speech Movement to the Global University*. Berkeley, Los Angeles, & London: University of California Press.

Smith, Adam. (1914 [1776]). *An Inquiry into the Nature and Causes of the Wealth of Nations*. Volume 1. London & New York: J.M. Dent & Sons & E.P. Dutton & Co., Everyman's Library, 412.

Smith, Daryl G. (1989). *The Challenge of Diversity: Involvement or Alienation in the Academy?* Washington, DC: ASHE-ERIC Higher Education Report, 5.

Smith, Daryl G. (1995). "Organizational Implications of Diversity in Higher Education." *Diversity in Organizations: New Perspective for a Changing Workplace*. Ed. Martin M. Chemers, Stuart Oskamp, & Mark A. Costanzo. Thousand Oaks, CA, London, & New Delhi: Sage Publications, 220-244.

Smith, Daryl G. (1996). *Achieving Faculty Diversity: Debunking the Myths*. Washington, DC: Association of American Colleges and Universities.

Smith, Daryl G. (2009*). Diversity's Promise for Higher Education: Making It Work*. Baltimore, MD: The Johns Hopkins University Press.

Smith, Page. (1990). *Killing the Spirit: Higher Education in America*. New York: Viking.

Sobol, Mark R., Phil Harkins, & Terry Conley, Eds. (2007). *Linkage Inc.'s Best Practices for Succession Planning*. San Francisco: John Wiley & Sons, Inc.

Stadtman, Verne A. (1970). *The University of California, 1868-1968*. New York: Mc-Graw-Hill Book Company.

Steger, Hanns-Albert. (1979). "The European Background." *The Latin American University*. Ed. Joseph Maier, & Richard W. Weatherhead. Albuquerque, NM: University of New Mexico Press, 87-122.

Stuart, Mary Clark. (1980). *Clark Kerr: Biography of an Action Intellectual*. Ann Arbor, MI: Doctoral Dissertation, the University of Michigan.

Tarnas, Richard. (1991). *The Passion of the Western Mind: Understanding the Ideas That Have Shaped Our World View*. New York: Ballantine Books.

Taylor, Angus E. (1998). *The Academic Senate of the University of California: Its Role in the Shared Governance and Operation of the University of California*. Berkeley, CA: Institute of Governmental Studies Press.

Tetlock, Philip E. (2005). *Expert Political Judgment: How Good is it? How Can We Know?* Princeton, NJ: Princeton University Press.

Thelin, John R. (2004). *A History of American Higher Education*. Baltimore, MD & London: The John Hopkins University Press.

Thomas, R. Roosevelt, Jr. (1995). "A Diversity Framework." *Diversity in Organizations:New Perspective for a Changing Workplace*. Ed. Martin M. Chemers, Stuart Oskamp, & Mark A. Costanzo. Thousand Oaks, CA, London, & New Delhi: Sage-Publications, 245-263.

Tien, Chang-Lin. (1998). "Challenges and Opportunities for Leaders of Color." *The Multicultural Campus: Strategies for Transforming Higher Education*. Ed. Leonard A. Valverde, & Louis A. Castenell, Jr. Walnut Creek, CA, London, & New Delhi: Altamira Press, 32-49.

Tocqueville, Alexis de. (1955 [1856]). *The Old Régime and the French Revolution*. Garden City, NY: Doubleday Anchor Books.

Touraine, Alain. (1997). *The Academic System in American Society*. New Brunswick, NJ, & London: Transaction Publishers, with a new introduction by Clark Kerr.

Trow, Martin. (1970). "Reflections on the Transition from Elite to Mass to Universal Higher Education." *Daedalus*, 99, 1: 1-42.

Trow, Martin. (1981). "Comparative Reflections on Leadership in Higher Education." *Higher Education in American Society*. Ed. Philip G. Altbach, & Robert O. Berdahl. Buffalo, NY: Prometeus Books, 277-296.

Trow, Martin. (1998). "On the Accountability of Higher Education in the United States." *Universities and Their Leadership*. Ed. William G. Bowen, & Harold T. Shapiro. Princeton, NJ: Princeton University Press, 15-61.

Trow, Martin. (2003). "In Praise of Weakness: Chartering, the University of the United States, and Dartmouth College." *Research and Occasional Papers Series*, Center for Studies in Higher Education, University of California, Berkeley, 2.03.

Trueba, Enrique T. (1999). *Latinos Unidos: From Cultural Diversity to the Politics of Solidarity*. Lanham, Boulder, New York, & Oxford: Rowman & Littlefield Publishers, Inc.

Trueblood, Alan S., Ed. (1988) *A Sor Juana Anthology*. With a foreword by Octavio Paz. Cambridge, MA, & London: Harvard University Press. London: Harvard University Press.

Turner, Caroline Sotello Viernes, & Samuel L. Myers, Jr. (2000). *Faculty of Color in Academe: Bittersweet Success*. Boston, MA: Allyn and Bacon.

University of California, Berkeley. (2004). *Remembering Clark Kerr: 1911-2003*. Program of February 20 Memorial Service.

*University of California-Diversity Statement*. (2006). http://www.universityofcalifornia. edu/regents/regmeet/sept07/re111attach.pdf

*University of California Office of the President Affirmative Action Plan*. (2008-2009). http://hrop.ucop.edu/documents/aap_vol_1_08_09.pdf

*University of California-Study Group on University Diversity, Overview Report to the Regents*. (2007). http://www.universityofcalifornia.edu/news/2007/diversityreport0907.pdf

Valian, Virginia. (2000). *Why So Slow? The Advancement of Women*. Cambridge, MA, & London: The MIT Press.

Valverde, Leonard A. (2003). *Leaders of Color in Higher Education: Unrecognized Triumphs in Harsh Institutions*. Walnut Creek, CA, Lanham, New York, Toronto, & Oxford: Altamira Press.

Van Doren, Charles. (1991). *A History of Knowledge: Past, Present, and Future*. New York: Ballantine Books.

Veblen, Thorstein. (1918). *The Higher Learning in America*. New York: B.W. Huebsch.

Veblen, Thorstein. (1899). *The Theory of the Leisure Class*. New York: Macmillan.

Véliz, Claudio. (1994). *The New World of the Gothic Fox: Culture and Economy in English and Spanish America*. Berkeley, Los Angeles, & London: University of California Press.

Vest, Charles M. (2007). *The American Research University from World War II to World Wide Web: Governments, the Private Sector, and the Emerging Meta-University*. Berkeley, Los Angeles, & London: University of California Press & Center for Studies in Higher Education, University of California, Berkeley.

Veysey, Lawrence R. (1965). *The Emergence of the American University*. Chicago & London: The University of Chicago Press.

Vlasic, Bill. (2009). "In the Changeover at G.M., a New Hands-On Attitude." *The New York Times*, December 15.

Wallack, Todd, & Tanya Schevitz. (2005). "UC Davis Cuts Deal to Avoid Bias Suit: Ex-Vice Chancellor Gets $205,000 job—Regents Didn't Know." *San Francisco Chronicle*, December 19.

Washington, Booker T. (1903). "Industrial Education for the Negro." *The Negro Problem:A Series of Articles by Representative Negroes of To-day*. New York: J. Pott & Company, 7-29.

Washington, Booker T. (1951 [1901]). *Up from Slavery: An Autobiography.* Garden City, NY: Doubleday & Company, Inc.

Watson, Robert N. (2010). "The Humanities Really Do Produce a Profit." *The Chronicle of Higher Education*, 56, 28: A36-A37.

Weisbrod, Burton A., Jeffrey P. Ballou, & Evelyn D. Asch. (2008). *Mission and Money: Understanding the University*. Cambridge: Cambridge University Press.

Wenniger, Mary Dee, & Mary Helen Conroy, Eds. (2001). *Gender Equity or Bust! On the Road to Campus Leadership with Women in Higher Education*. San Francisco: Jossey-Bass Publishers.

Wenniger, Mary Dee. (2007). "Symposium Offers Lessons from Life of Denice Denton." *Women in Higher Education*, 16, 9: 1-2.

Westhues, Kenneth, Ed. (2004). *Workplace Mobbing in Academe: Reports from Twenty Universities*. Lewiston, New York: Edwin Mellen Press.

Westhues, Kenneth, Ed. (2006). *The Remedy and Prevention of Mobbing in Higher Education: Two Case Studies*. Lewiston, New York: Edwin Mellen Press.

Wheeler, Benjamin Ide. (1926). *The Abundant Life*. Berkeley, CA: University of California Press.

White, Judith S. (2005). "Pipeline to Pathways: New Directions for Improving the Status of Women on Campus." *Liberal Education*, 91, 1: 22-27.

Wittrock, Björn. (1993). "The Modern University: The Three Transformations." *The European and American University since 1800*. Ed. Sheldon Rothblatt, & Björn Wittrock. Cambridge: Cambridge University Press.

Wolff, Robert Paul. (1997). *The Ideal of the University*. New Brunswick, NJ, & London: Transaction Publishers.

Wright, Bobby. (1991). "The 'Untameable Savage Spirit': American Indians in Colonial Colleges." *The Review of Higher Education*, 14, 4: 429-452.

Wriston, Henry M. (1959). *Academic Procession: Reflections of a College President*. New York: Columbia University Press.

Yollin, Patricia. (2008). "New UC President to Earn $591,000, Plus Perks." *The San Francisco Chronicle*, March 28.

Young. Charles E. (2003). "Clark Kerr: A Quiet Force." *The Chronicle of Higher Education*, 50, 17: B10-B11.

Yudof, Mark G. (2008). "Are University Systems a Good Idea?" *The Chronicle of Higher Education*, 54, 23: A37.

Zaleznik, Abraham. (2008). *Hedgehogs and Foxes: Character, Leadership, and Command in Organizations*. New York: Palgrave Macmillan.

Zemsky, Robert. (2009). "Will Higher Education Ever Change as It Should?" *The Chronicle of Higher Education*, 55, 43: A24-A25.

# Index